THE BEST JOB IN POLITICS

Exploring How Governors Succeed
As Policy Leaders

Alan Rosenthal

Los Angeles | London | New Delhi
Singapore | Washington DC

Los Angeles | London | New Delhi
Singapore | Washington DC

For information:

CQ Press
An Imprint of SAGE Publications, Inc.
2455 Teller Road
Thousand Oaks, California 91320
E-mail: order@sagepub.com

SAGE Publications Ltd.
1 Oliver's Yard
55 City Road
London, EC1Y 1SP
United Kingdom

SAGE Publications India Pvt. Ltd.
B 1/I 1 Mohan Cooperative Industrial Area
Mathura Road, New Delhi 110 044
India

SAGE Publications Asia-Pacific Pte. Ltd.
33 Pekin Street #02-01
Far East Square
Singapore 048763

Copyright © 2013 by CQ Press, an Imprint of SAGE Publications, Inc. CQ Press is a registered trademark of Congressional Quarterly Inc.

All rights reserved. No part of this book may be reproduced or utilized in any form or by any means, electronic or mechanical, including photocopying, recording, or by any information storage and retrieval system, without permission in writing from the publisher.

Printed in the United States of America

Library of Congress Cataloging-in-Publication Data

Rosenthal, Alan

The best job in politics: exploring how governors succeed as policy leaders/Alan Rosenthal.

p. cm.
Includes bibliographical references.

ISBN 978-1-4522-3999-6 (alk. paper)

1. Governors—United States. 2. Governors—United States—Powers and duties. 3. Governors—United States—History—20th century. 4. Governors—United States—History—21st century. 5. Political leadership—United States—States. I. Title.

JK2447.R67 2012
352.23′2130973—dc23   2011051917

This book is printed on acid-free paper.

Acquisitions Editor: Charisse Kiino
Production Editor: Elizabeth Kline
Copy Editor: Amy Marks
Typesetter: C&M Digitals (P) Ltd
Proofreader: Lawrence Baker
Indexer: Jean Casalegno
Cover Designer: Paula Goldstein,
          Blue Bungalow Design
Marketing Manager: Jonathan Mason

12 13 14 15 16 10 9 8 7 6 5 4 3 2 1

About the Author

Alan Rosenthal is professor of public policy and political science at the Eagleton Institute of Politics at Rutgers University.

He has addressed and/or consulted with legislatures in more than two-thirds of the states and has worked with the National Conference of State Legislatures (NCSL), the Council of State Governments (CSG), the State Legislative Leaders Foundation (SLLF), and the National Governors Association on various activities and projects. In 2006, he was given an award for lifetime achievement from NCSL and SSLF.

In his home state, New Jersey, he chaired the Ad Hoc Commission on Legislative Ethics and Campaign Finance, which in 1990 was appointed by the Speaker of the Assembly and the President of the Senate. In 1992 and 2001 he was selected to chair the New Jersey Congressional Redistricting Commission. In 2011 he was chosen by the Chief Justice of the New Jersey Supreme Court to serve as the eleventh ("tiebreaker") member of the State Legislative Apportionment Commission. In 1993 he received the Governor's award for Public Service in New Jersey. He currently chairs the Joint Legislative Committee on Ethical Standards, a committee of the New Jersey Legislature.

He has written extensively on state legislatures and state politics. His books include: *The Third House: Lobbyists and Lobbying in the States* (Revised ed., 2001); *Drawing the Line: Legislative Ethics in the States* (1996); *The Decline of Representative Democracy* (1998); *Republic on Trial,* with Burdette Loomis, John Hibbing, and Karl Kurtz (2003); *Heavy Lifting: The Job of the American Legislature* (2004); and *Engines of Democracy: Politics and Policymaking in State Legislatures* (2009). In recognition of the contribution his published work and career has made to "the art of government through the application of social science research," he was given a lifetime-achievement award by the American Political Science Association.

Contents

Preface

I have spent practically my entire career observing state legislatures—writing about them, consulting with them, and teaching students and legislators themselves about these remarkable institutions. One of the major functions of the legislature, in my judgment, is balancing the power of the executive. Although I had touched on the subject of why legislatures find this function difficult to perform, I thought it worthwhile to explore the subject further and from the perspective of the governor rather than that of the legislature. Thus, this book is about governors and, in particular, about governors exercising policy leadership in their states. In the research and writing of this book, I have come to appreciate the institutional challenges that the legislature faces in trying to be a coequal branch and balance the governor.

My friends who serve in and work for legislatures tease me for having deserted them and gone over to what they call "the dark side." Governors and their policy leadership may indeed be the dark side, but not in the *Star Wars* sense my friends had in mind. Whereas many of my colleagues in political science have shed bright analytical light on legislatures, only a hardy few of them have taken on the study of governors, who have been left pretty much in the dark. We may know about individual governors in our own states, but we know relatively little about the species. Governors rarely receive any attention outside of their own states and beyond their terms of office unless they run for president or are accused of misbehavior in office. Yet, state by state, governors have the most significant, as well as the best, job in politics. They are the driving force behind the major public policies that are enacted by their legislatures. This is not to downplay the importance of legislatures, courts, political parties, and interest groups, all of whom play a vital part in the policy processes. It is, however, to acknowledge the central role of the executive.

This book, then, is intended to offer students of state politics and policymaking, as well as legislators and other participants in lawmaking, a better idea of how and how well policy leadership by governors works. It covers what I refer to as the contemporary generation of governors—those who have served in the fifty states over the past thirty years. It is written from the perspective of governors, including those I interviewed, those I surveyed, and those whose memoirs and biographies I read. I admit to more than my fair share of hubris in attempting to understand and generalize about how and why governors succeed as policy leaders.

As with my work on legislatures, I bring to this study of governors a great respect for state political institutions and the people who make representative democracy work. I am especially indebted to those former governors who responded to the questions I asked on a mail survey or in face-to-face or telephone interviews. I am also grateful to the National Governors Association for its assistance in soliciting cooperation from several hundred former governors throughout the states. Ray Scheppach, who was NGA's executive director at the time I undertook this study, Barry Van Lare, a former deputy director, and Nikki Guilford, who is director of the NGA's Office of Management Consulting and Training, were enormously helpful.

At Rutgers, Marc Weiner and Orin Puniello of the Survey Research Center at the Bloustein School provided invaluable assistance. They collected and analyzed data and gave me counsel and encouragement (something they repeated when we teamed up later on as "the eleventh member" of the New Jersey State Redistricting Commission). At the Eagleton Institute of Politics, which for many years has indulged my legislative proclivities, a newly created Center on the American Governor undertook oral histories of New Jersey's governors, beginning with Brendan Byrne and Tom Kean. The archived interviews provided useful grist for my gubernatorial mill and the attention the Institute lavished on governors furnished the ideal atmosphere in which to think and write about them.

Where I really needed help was in getting things organized and done. Gloria Minor played a major role day-to-day keeping me on as clear a track as possible. The most challenging job of all was the manuscript's journey from draft to draft, improving the text and reducing errors along the way. As with so much else, my wife, Lynda, looked out for me here. I truly appreciate the work she did translating my handwriting into words, from the original draft through several revisions.

Janet Donovan, University of Colorado at Boulder; Four political scientists—Daniel Palazzolo, University of Richmond; Sarah Poggione, Ohio University; and Stephen Stambough, California State University, Fullerton—reviewed the manuscript for CQ Press. I've followed many of their suggestions, and I want to thank them. This is my seventh book with CQ Press, with whom I have (I think) developed a pleasant and productive relationship. I appreciate the efforts of Brenda Carter, Charisse Kiino, and the people who have had a hand in copyediting, producing, promoting, and marketing my books for almost twenty-five years. Even more, I appreciate the efforts of those who have read them.

Frankly, I do not know who in my own family may have read what I have written about legislatures or who will read this book about governors. Whether they read any of this stuff or not, I am thankful to have them around: John, Lisa, Patrick, Kelly, and Tori; Kai; Tony, Kathleen, Ian, and Emily; Lisa, Garrison, Chaz, Dylan, and Mason; Vinnie; and Lynda, of course, as well as Jim, Dorothy, Kent, Susan, Marisa, Carol, Nick, and John. Since they let me do my thing, I have no objection to them doing theirs (even if it means neglecting this work on governors).

1

The Job of Governor

THIRTY-SEVEN GUBERNATORIAL SEATS were on the line in the election of 2010. Six incumbent governors, who were eligible to serve again, had bowed out—either because they didn't think they could win or because they had already been in public office for quite a while. However, there was no lack of candidates for the available positions, including a number of sitting governors who were running for second terms.

None of these men and women had been dissuaded by the difficulty of the job, particularly with the nation and the states experiencing hard economic times. All but four states anticipated lower-than-projected revenues for the fiscal year, forty states had made midyear budget cuts, and overall state spending had been reduced by almost 7 percent. As the gubernatorial election drew closer, thirty-two states were looking ahead to budget deficits for fiscal 2011.

Who would want to be governor under such conditions? Quite a few people, as a matter of fact, including several who might have known better. Five former governors had come back after some years to run once again for the office they previously had held. According to journalists who pursued the story, more former governors than ever before wanted to get back in harness, even though it appeared impossible to come out a winner with such a depressed economy and overstressed fiscal system. Why, in the face of all this, would these former governors still want to run again? Vindication may have been a reason for two of them. Roy Barnes (D-GA) and Bob Ehrlich (R-MD) had been defeated for second terms. Nobody likes to leave elective office involuntarily; individuals would rather exit on their own terms. Three other former governors did not need an assist from voters to prove anything. John Kitzhaber (D-OR) had already served eight years and Terry Branstad (R-IA) had served sixteen. What were their reasons for getting back in the ring? And why try to make their comebacks during a period of economic recession and fiscal constraint?

Probably the most intriguing of the comeback kids was Jerry Brown (D-CA). He had been governor of the largest state in the nation for eight years, had left that office in early 1983, and was about to run again twenty-seven years later. But he had by no means abandoned elective politics. He did eight years as mayor of Oakland and then a stint as state attorney general. Still, why would he want to take on the challenge of governing a state with what many observers believed to be a dysfunctional political system? By the turn of the twenty-first century, California was plagued by a number of structural problems: the initiative, the need for a two-thirds vote in the legislature to pass a budget, limitations on taxes and expenditures, legislative term limits, and polarized political parties. At the same time, the budget deficit was growing by leaps and bounds. In case there was any doubt about a governor's chances of managing to steer the huge ship of state, Gray Davis (D-CA) had been recalled from office by the voters in 2003 and, Davis's successor, Arnold Schwarzenegger (R-CA), had failed to make a big dent in the most imposing problems facing the state. The public had lost confidence in both the Republican governor and the Democratic legislature. Brown, himself, called the job of California governor "a career ender."[1] Yet, Brown ran, which would appear to be an act of deliberate masochism. What was the appeal of gubernatorial office?

One explanation, which applies to newcomers as well as to veterans, is that these individuals have a very healthy (perhaps inflated) sense of self-confidence (a point that I return to in Chapter 3). "I know how state government works, how it should work, and I think I can fix it," Brown said.[2] As governor again, Brown would be able to use his insider's knowledge and the skills he learned to solve the problems California was facing. "It's almost a natural evolution to come back and try to fix things at this time of serious crisis," is the way he felt about taking another shot at the brass ring.[3] In short, California was in crisis, and it was calling out to him for help.[4]

What's So Good About the Job?

Not every governor likes the job. Sarah Palin (R-AK), returning to full-time duty after her run on the national ticket, announced her resignation in July 2009. "Presiding over Alaska," she said, "had become difficult, dull, and unfulfilling."[5] Not every governor likes the job for his or her entire term. It took Jim Edgar (R-IL) some time to adjust, but then he got to enjoy thoroughly being governor. For six or eight months, Mark Warner (D-VA) was frustrated, but "the last three years I was governor, I loved it."[6] In the case of Bob Miller (D-NV), 90 percent of the time he loved being governor, and 10 percent he didn't.[7]

Governors Barnes, Ehrlich, Kitzhaber, Branstad, and Brown, all of whom came back for more, still had things that they wanted to do and the office of governor was where they had to be in order to do them. That office, according to nearly all of those who have held it, is "the best office in American politics." Even in hard times, which most contemporary governors have experienced at least for part of their terms, the job is immensely attractive to both veterans and newcomers to politics. Henry Bellmon (R-OK) started out in the legislature and then was elected as Oklahoma's first Republican governor. He served one term as governor and then two as U.S. senator. Six years later he was reelected governor and served his second term. Bellmon found serving as governor to be a "wonderfully exciting, satisfying experience." "There are tough days in a governor's life," he admitted years later, "but most of the memories are of the good days and fine people who abound."[8]

The only better job might be that of president, which is considered to be at the top of the ladder in the American political system. Many governors aspire to presidential office, and four out of the last six presidents have been governors. Yet aspiring governors realize that there may be a downside to winning the presidency. A few months before he announced his candidacy for the Republican Party's presidential nomination, Rick Perry (R-TX) told a story about George W. Bush (R-TX), who in the winter of 2000 was serving as governor while Perry was serving as lieutenant governor. Bush, who was running for president and confident of victory, called the lieutenant governor into his office. "Perry," he said, "you're gonna love being governor. It's the greatest job in the world." Eighteen months later, Perry received a call from the then President Bush, who chatted at length and asked about what was going on in Austin. They were concluding their conversation, when the president said, "Hey, Perry, you remember that conversation we had in the governor's office about a year and a half ago, and I told you that being the governor of Texas was the greatest job in the world?" Perry said he remembered it. "Well," Bush said, "it is."[9]

Presidents have far more responsibilities than governors and considerably less capacity for meeting them. If one prefers greater control over the environment and greater opportunity to achieve objectives, then being president puts one at some disadvantage. The work that governors have to do is difficult, but not unmanageable. The work of presidents, by contrast, is of a different order entirely. It is a wonder that anyone today can be even moderately successful in that office. Granted, the presidency is the most important job in American politics, but it is not necessarily the best.

In the pecking order of American politics, the job of U.S. senator probably comes closest to that of governor. Conventional wisdom has it that in the larger states, it would be preferable to be elected governor, but in the smaller states the U.S. Senate would be preferred. Politicians, however, tend to run for the seat—whether at the statehouse as governor or at the Capitol in Washington, D.C., as senator—that comes up or becomes open first. Aspirants for high office cannot afford to wait for the most desirable office. They have to strike whenever it is feasible and as early as they can. Otherwise, another aspirant might edge them out.

A few individuals might resist one or the other office as a matter of principle. Alan Simpson, for example, from the very beginning prided himself on being a "legislative man." As a state legislator, he could not conceive of himself serving as governor of Wyoming, although his father had held that office (as well as the office of U.S. senator). Temperamentally, he was suited to and comfortable in a legislative body. So, he chose to run for the U.S. Senate, leaving it to his own son to run (unsuccessfully, as it turned out) for governor. Among successful American politicians, however, Simpson is a rather rare bird.

Some individuals who have held gubernatorial office refuse invitations to run for the U.S. Senate. Larry Sabato pointed out years ago that a number of governors had turned down opportunities for Senate candidacy. This he attributed to the word getting around that governors-turned-senators were often unfulfilled.[10] When Tom Carper (D-DE) was running for the U.S. Senate in 2000, he asked Bob Graham (D-FL) about the difference between the two jobs. Carper recalled that Graham used a football analogy. If you're governor, you are the quarterback calling every play. If you're a U.S. senator, you are the general manager sitting in the box watching the game. Carper asked Graham which he liked better, and Graham said that he preferred being quarterback.[11]

By now, it is common knowledge that former governors are not the happiest of senators. No one listens to them any longer. As governors, they weren't used to that. As governors, moreover, they could lay claim to a number of accomplishments, but when they got to Congress they could lay claim to very little. Dan Evans (R-WA) had three terms as governor before his election to the Senate. He served one term only, leaving in frustration.[12] One former governor, who had thought of running for the U.S. Senate, recalled visiting with a congressman from his state. "Don't come to Congress," he was advised, "if you can't handle deferred gratification."[13]

Twelve members of the U.S. Senate in the 111th Congress had been governors of their states.[14] One of them—Jay Rockefeller (D-WV)—was happy as a senator, because of the broader scope of issues he faced in Washington. All the rest—Lamar Alexander (R-TN), Evan Bayh (D-IN), Christopher Bond (R-MO), Judd Gregg (R-NH), Mike Johanns (R-NE), Ben Nelson (D-NE), Jim Risch (R-ID), Jeanne Shaheen (D-NH), George Voinovich (R-OH), Warner, and Carper—preferred their job as governor to their job as senator. Carper put it succinctly: "My worst day as governor was better than my best day as a United States senator."[15] Nelson was more expansive, but his sentiment was very much in the same vein: "Totally different positions. . . . [A]s governor you're either in charge or they make you think you're in charge. In the Senate, you're not in charge and they let you know it."[16]

Governors have a better life in just about every respect, with the exception of pay. In 2010, U.S. senators earned $174,000 per year (as did members of the U.S. House). The governors of Illinois, Michigan, and New York exceeded that, by a small amount, whereas governors in California, Delaware, Pennsylvania, Tennessee, and Virginia came close. In seven states, governors' salaries were under $100,000. In over two-thirds of the states they earned $100,000–$150,000.

Pay is a relatively small part of the support governors receive. Virtually every governor has an automobile and driver at his or her disposal. Senators do not, although some are chauffeured by members of their staffs. It is convenient for governors to work in the back seat and not have to locate addresses or find parking places when traveling around the state. Brendan Byrne (D-NJ) recalls that, after eight years in office, he was so unused to driving that he had to take driving lessons. He quips about his immediate post-gubernatorial auto travails—getting into the car and expecting it to start without his having put his foot on the gas pedal.

Way beyond automobiles, governors outmatch senators in the perks of office. Four out of five states put airplanes at the disposal of governors. Half provided helicopters. Perhaps the perkiest perk, however, is the governor's official residence. Only a few states do not provide housing for governors and their families. The rest make gubernatorial living comfortable and provide the chief executive a venue for hosting meetings, lunches, and dinners of executive officials and lawmakers, among others. The "mansion," as some call it, or "residence," as governors prefer that it be called, is an important resource when it comes to developing and solidifying relationships that advance gubernatorial agendas.[17]

Two major problems encountered by people in elective office are the limits on privacy and the strains on family life. These problems are worse now than years ago, when one out of three governors felt that the invasion of their privacy was a problem and half felt that interference with their family life was the most difficult aspect of serving as governor.[18] Neither governors nor senators have much advantage as far as privacy is concerned. But governors are better off in terms of family disruption. They are not separated from their families, as are most Washington-based senators, who have to travel hundreds or thousands of miles to get home for long weekends or less often. Although they spend time on the road, governors and their families live in one place, not far from where the governors typically work.

I am not suggesting that governors lead logistically normal lives. They have obligations, such as being in the capital when the legislature is in session. It may be especially difficult for governors of large states with small state capitals, such as Springfield, Illinois. Edgar found it hard to be in the capital when the legislature was in town and also be in Chicago and around the rest of the state. If he was in Chicago when the legislature was in session in Springfield, he would fly back and forth. All the wear and tear from travel took its toll on Edgar.

Still, governors are able, to some extent at least, to set their own schedules. All twelve former governors who were serving in the U.S. Senate in 2008 agreed that they lacked control over their schedules, which they did have as governors.[19] Bill Owens (R-CO), who never experienced the Senate, nevertheless had a good idea of the difference in the scheduling power of the two offices. Governors, according to him, make their own schedules. "As governor," he said, "you can be home when you have to be." Running for governor may be hectic, but being governor is typically at a reasonable pace. When in office, governors exercise some control over their schedules and can give themselves pockets of time, if they so desire. That worked for Edgar. He needed eight hours of sleep; thus, he never scheduled breakfast meetings:

> That was one good thing as governor. You get to dictate the time, and I'm not a breakfast person. I get up, I exercise, I eat breakfast with my wife.

Governors are the only ones in their particular office, at least within their home states, where they have jurisdiction and responsibility. In contrast, two senators (along with from one to over forty members of the U.S. House) represent each state. Moreover, there are 100 members in the U.S. Senate. State by state, the governor is clearly the most important person— one out of one and not one out of a hundred. That gives them stature, more than most people but perhaps less than a few. Toward the end of Owens's two-term tenure, a column in a Denver newspaper referred to the fact that for seven years he "has been the most important person in the state not named John Elway . . . ."[20] In the realm of politics, at any rate, the governor is most important by virtue of the power he or she wields. The power of individual members of the legislative branch—whether at the federal or state level—is far less, even if the legislative branch is a coequal of the executive, a proposition that is examined in the chapters that follow.

"When I was governor, I made decisions," Bayh recalled. "In the Senate I express an opinion."[21] In a similar vein, Edgar remembered talking for years as a state legislator, and even passing bills, but it didn't mean much compared to the far greater control exercised by the governor and the executive branch.

The most significant advantage that governors have over U.S. senators, as well as legislators in their own states, and practically anyone else in public office, is that they can accomplish a lot. They can set their own agendas, which legislators have a more difficult time doing. They can focus more on solving problems than on matters of representation. They can be a formidable force for something they believe needs to be done. As Ehrlich put it, "If you like policy and like to get things done, it's the best job in politics." For most of those who hold gubernatorial office, the job is an immense source of satisfaction.

That is the fundamental reason that governors think their job is the best job in politics. As stated by Bellmon:

> Governors are where the action is. They can make good things happen. They can make a difference for better or worse.[22]

They have control. Their hands are "on the throttle," in the words of Richard Thornburgh (R-PA). The odds are pretty good, but by no means perfect, that they will have substantial success. In the words of Owens, "It is theirs to lose." Not only will they have accomplishments, but they will likely see some early results as well as the expectation of long-term impacts. And they can leave office with the sense, according to Thornburgh, that people will appreciate some of the things they did. In responding to a survey question about what he thought his legacy was, George Nigh (D-OK) listed several accomplishments he wanted to be remembered for. "I'm bragging, but I am proud," he also wrote in response.

Accomplishment is much of what the job is about and much of what makes it a happy place for high achievers to be located.

What They Want to Achieve

Governors have the opportunity to achieve in a wide range of areas, because the role of governor is multidimensional. The governor's responsibilities run the gamut, from the removal of snow on state roads after a severe storm, to naming members to boards and commissions, to enticing businesses to set up shop in the state. The governor's job can be specified in terms of the following opportunities to achieve.

Appointments. Any governor's "What to do" list includes bringing the best people possible into state government, especially those who are appointed to head departments and agencies, and onto important boards and commissions, as well as to the governor's office itself. These are the people who help shape policy, implement policy once it is enacted, and generally carry out the day-to-day business of state government. A governor can derive satisfaction from appointing department and agency heads who manage effectively and avoid controversy. In many states governors also have the authority to appoint judges and prosecutors. Few governors spend the bulk of their time on appointments, but it is an area that concerns all of them.

Management and administration. If a gubernatorial appointee comes under fire or fails to do the tasks that need doing, the governor has the authority to make changes. People can be shifted from one position to another or told to pack their bags and leave altogether. Few governors take management at this level very seriously, except in instances of incompetent or corrupt behavior that comes to light. The administrative responsibilities of governors, however, receive continuing attention. As chief executive, governors oversee the departments and agencies, particularly in terms of rule making, the implementation of policies and programs, the delivery of services, and the budgeting and expenditure of funds. Although lacking in glamour, the gubernatorial role of directing and controlling the bureaucracy is not one that they shrug off. Yet, it is not one for which they receive much credit.

Crisis response. Since 9/11, governors have become even more involved in emergency preparedness and crisis response than used to be the case. Almost every governor is forced to respond to an unanticipated emergency. Hurricanes, tornados, floods, and snowstorms test the ability of governors to satisfy their publics. There is not much that governors do to prepare for such crises; yet, the overall success of their administration and reelection can be affected by how well they manage them.

Promotion. No one can promote the state like the governor can. This entails salesmanship, hawking the economic and other benefits of locating a business in or visiting the state. Governors travel nationwide and around the globe in this promotional work, mainly trying to attract industry and business to start up or expand operations. They also target those firms already in the state who may threaten to relocate. In addition, governors devote themselves to making residents feel good about where they already live. A number of governors work diligently at these tasks, which connect with their economic development objectives. Here, they have a good chance of having something to show for their efforts. Besides promoting the state, governors also work to promote ideas (even if public policy is not involved). For example, they try to change public attitudes and public behavior on matters such as smoking and childhood obesity.

Party leadership. Although not part of the governor's job description, party leadership is nonetheless something that most governors do, at least to some extent. They are almost *required* to lead because, even if their hearts and minds are elsewhere, their parties need and insist on it. The few independents who have served are exempt from these pressures. Especially if governors plan to run for reelection or for other office, they tend to be responsive in this domain. Yet, governors rarely earn a reputation for party-building. Other tasks take precedence.

Policymaking. Most governors emphasize and expect to make their mark in the area of policymaking. This is where the executive and the legislative branches of government, separate as they are by design, are thrown together in the same arena. Here, the governor, in conjunction with the legislature, proposes measures to the legislature, agrees to or rejects measures proposed by the legislature, and decides on budgets to expend funds and figures out how such funds can be raised.

It wasn't always this way. In the nineteenth century and before, governors might advocate for one policy or another, but not for an agenda of multiple policies. They typically reacted to what came their way from the lawmaking body. In 1911, however, Woodrow Wilson, governor of New Jersey at the time, drew up an agenda of bills and tried to get them enacted by the legislature.[23] Since then, governors have become the policy leaders in the states. Coleman Ransone, an early student of the chief executive, concluded in 1976 that, by then, most governors had a set of policies that they wanted to see enacted and they were able to secure passage of a good number that they considered to be crucial.[24]

Modern governors initiate legislation. They shape and manage legislation as it is undergoing the political massaging of the legislative process. They review legislation—and particularly if they haven't initiated it—before deciding whether to sign it into law. Governors today are popularly believed to be the single most significant figures in lawmaking, truly the chief policymakers of the states. They are expected to exercise policy leadership. With few exceptions, they want to do so.

Formulating policy initiatives, including budgets, is where governors achieve their reputations. This is where they put their energies and commit themselves and their administrations. Here is where they can accomplish, where they can succeed, and where people are most likely to take notice. Policy leadership is not the only part of the governor's job. But, as they see it, it is a most important part of their job. It is, moreover, a large part of why they think that being governor is the best job in politics, and why they are probably right.

As Governors See It

What makes the job so appealing to high achievers is that, by exercising leadership on policy and budgets, governors have much better than even odds of accomplishing their objectives. As much as anything else, they want to succeed. A few fail, primarily because of personal (rather than policy) behavior, and are forced out of office. Some are rejected by voters in an attempt to win a second term. A few choose to exit instead of throwing their hat into the ring again. But most, like the five former governors who came in from the cold, want to continue to achieve in the policy arena and are willing to wage a campaign for another stint in office.

This book focuses on the period from 1980 to 2010, which can be considered the contemporary governorship.[25] It examines how governors who held office during these years acted as policy leaders in the states, how and why they managed to succeed, and what they accomplished in the field of public policy. Not including several individuals who held this office for less than a year, 269 men and women were governors of the fifty states from 1980 through the end of 2009. These individuals are listed by state in Appendix A. Of the total, 52 percent were Democrats, 47 percent Republicans, and 1 percent independents.

It would have been ideal if I had been able to spend time observing governors during the course of their work. How many governors, if any, would it have been possible to observe directly? At the very most, only a few. In the interest of achieving broader coverage, I chose to observe instead mainly what governors had to say about their activities in office, and to some degree what other participants in or observers of the policy-making process had to say about them. This study, then, is primarily from the perspective of governors reflecting on their terms in office.

I rely in part on memoirs by governors, biographies of them, or other accounts of their activities. Fifty-one of the governors from the period I am exploring wrote about their experiences in office or are the subjects of books by others. These writings are listed in the References section and are cited where relevant in the chapters that follow. From time to time, I mention a governor who served before 1980, if a memoir or biography was especially informative, as was Lou Cannon's *Governor Reagan: His Rise to Power*.[26] In the last chapter, I consider briefly the new generation of governors, who took over in 2010.

Another source of information is a ten-page survey of governors. The survey was mailed in late 2009 to all former governors for whom addresses were available.[27] The survey was accompanied by a cover letter from Ray Scheppach, then the executive director of the National Governors Association, who in his letter introduced the author and asked recipients for their cooperation. The result, after a few follow-ups, was that seventy-five former governors responded to the survey, a response rate of 44.1 percent. Among the respondents, 49.3 percent were Republicans, 48.0 percent were Democrats, and 2.7 percent were independents. The responding governors are identified in Appendix A. The survey information is specified wherever it is used throughout the following chapters.

Interviews constituted still another source of information for this study. Twenty-three former governors were interviewed in person or by telephone. The interviewees also are identified in Appendix A. The interviews generally ran from about forty to forty-five minutes, although several lasted for more than an hour. The chapters that follow draw heavily on information provided in these interviews. When a governor is specified or quoted, but no specific reference is made to a source, reliance is on information provided in an interview. Interviewees are listed in the appendix.

Several of the governors are represented by two of the sources, only one by all three. Most, however, are represented by only one source. The largest number of governors appear in the survey; the second largest in the memoirs, biographies, and other accounts; and the fewest in the in-person and telephone interviews. All told, by these methods, I have been able to draw on the experiences of 118 of the 269 governors, or 43.9 percent of those who held office during this contemporary period. They include Democrats and Republicans and a few independents, as well as governors from forty-nine of the fifty states.

One-hundred and eighteen is quite a number of governors to keep track of in this account of policymaking leadership in the states. Most of those who responded to the survey receive no mention by name; they are among those reported in a number or included in a percentage. Other governors, however, make several appearances. Twenty or thirty appear frequently and prominently in these pages. Others are mentioned from time to time. The reader may have difficulty keeping even the main characters sorted out by state and political party, let alone those who take the stage only occasionally. As a convention here, each governor is identified by full name, state, and party the first time he or she is mentioned in each chapter, as Jim Edgar (R-IL) or Parris Glendening (D-MD).[28] Upon a second or subsequent appearance in each chapter, governors are furnished less identification, but an effort is still made to make readers aware of where governors are from and, if relevant at that point, the party to which they belong.

The reader may not dispute this focus on governors as policy leaders but may still question the reliance of the author on governors for nearly all of the material on which this exploration is based. The survey and the interviews draw completely on what governors have to say about their own roles in policymaking. The memoirs and biographies vary somewhat, but the bulk of this literature also adopts the perspective of governors. The question for the researcher is, are governors reliable informants? Are they objective? Do they remember what happened years earlier?

Subjectivity and recall present problems for all those who make use of survey research and interview techniques. These problems, no doubt, exist in the present study. Spin and exaggeration are also possibilities when governors review their careers. Still, on the basis of the interviews I conducted as well as some of the accounts by third parties, my judgment is that the governors generally were providing accurate accounts of their policymaking endeavors when in office. Most of them, I believe, could afford to be straightforward, because they had done well. And they readily admitted failures and mistakes they had made.

Any methodological approach has both advantages and disadvantages. Choosing one rather than another involves trade-offs. This study chose to range broadly across states, among governors, and for a substantial period of time rather than to narrow in on a few or several cases, which could have been examined in greater depth and could have been based on a greater array of data sources. This study admits to being governor-centric. In defense of such a one-sided perspective, I would offer that a good sense of governors and of policymaking leadership can be attained by attending to what governors have to say.

Policymaking Success

What makes being governor such a rewarding job is mainly the fact that governors are in a good position to achieve. Among their most visible and their most gratifying achievements are the policies they manage to have enacted into law. With relatively few exceptions (see Chapter 7), governors succeed as policy leaders in their states. They get both the policies and the budgets they want.

Critical to this study and the chapters that follow is specifying what is meant by "success." It is worth some discussion at the outset.

One way to assess gubernatorial success is in terms of whether people approve of the job governors are doing. If they are reelected after four years in office, that is a popular indicator of success. If they win by a substantial margin, they can make a stronger claim to having been successful. By this standard, governors like Bob Ehrlich, Roy Barnes, Bob Holden (D-MO), and Jon Corzine (D-NJ), who lost their bids for reelection, are presumptive failures. Jim Florio (D-NJ) fared even worse, according to an electoral standard. He not only lost his reelection bid, but as a result of his policy initiatives on taxes and guns, Democrats lost control of the legislature for a decade. Electoral defeat does not enhance a governor's reputation nor does it leave a governor unscarred. But it is not the principal measure of how well or how poorly a governor did in promoting his or her policy and budget priorities.

Governors who leave office because of nonfeasance, misfeasance, or malfeasance cannot expect high marks from the public for their performance. They are forced out of office before their terms expire. In California, Gray Davis was thrown out in a special recall election, which brought Arnold Schwarzenegger in as his replacement. Rod Blagojevich (D-IL) was impeached and convicted by the Illinois legislature, ending his second term prematurely. A scandal and potential indictment caused Jim McGreevey (D-NJ) to resign during his first term. Because of the ignominious conclusions of their political careers at the capitol, they are not likely to be remembered as successful chief executives. Yet, they too managed to achieve success on some of their policy initiatives. Even governors who fail politically or ethically should not be denied credit for what they did accomplish. Nonetheless, policy success and political success are not completely independent. Gubernatorial performance on policies and budgets is part of political success, albeit only a part.

Another way of looking at the question of success would take into account what governors achieve in solving the state's problems. This would require that governors: assess what the problems are; design policies that can solve them; get these policies enacted; fund them at the level necessary; implement the enactments; deliver the goods and services; and, finally, have the intended effect on solving—or at least reducing—the problems that existed at the outset. That's a tall order for anyone, even governors. This is not to deny that solving or reducing economic and social problems that confront the state is the ultimate achievement for anyone in public office. However, to assess gubernatorial success by such a standard would require agreement on what the problems are, what constitutes improvement, and how to measure it. In addition, we would want to agree on a way to be sure the policies themselves rather than other factors were responsible for any improvement that we measured. Such agreement is pretty much out of the question. Moreover, few major problems are solved by one administration or even by several administrations. Take education policy, for instance. Over the years, many governors have endeavored to make their name in this field; they wanted to be remembered as "education governors." Yet, none of them would assert that the policies they initiated and the budgets they proposed rid elementary, secondary, and higher education of the problems that schools faced. They do, however, believe that they made inroads, or that substantial gains were achieved during their administrations.

Solving the major problems may be too much to expect of governors. Figuring out what these problems are and whether or to what degree they have been solved may be too much to expect of researchers. The definition of "policy success" used here is one that fits our purposes. It is whether governors got their policy and budget agendas enacted by the legislature. How much of their agendas of initiatives did they get? How much of what they got was modified by legislative action? Also, for present purposes, policy success includes consideration of governors' ability to defeat legislative agenda items that they opposed. Is the legislature able to work its policy, even if the governor objects, or does the legislature have to come to terms with the governor? This, too, has to be taken in account.

One way to assess gubernatorial policymaking success is to establish just what a governor's priorities are and then track them through the legislature. The governor's policy priorities are not always specified. Sometimes they have to be inferred. Compiling a gubernatorial policy agenda would vary from state to state. Determining a governor's budget agenda would also be an elusive business, in part because a governor's budget may be constructed with some items included for bargaining purposes. Several political scientists have focused on an agenda presentation by the governor that is common—or essentially so—in all the states. That is the governor's state of the state address. It is presented annually and is believed to focus on the most important items on a governor's agenda.[29] Items that appear in these addresses are then drafted into detailed legislation in the governor's office or in the legislature itself. According to these scholars, it is the passage of the governor's policy agenda, as it has been translated into bills, that is the measure of success. Kousser and Phillips explain the methodology they used in studying fifty-two state of the state addresses delivered in twenty-seven states. To track the address proposals, the two political scientists consulted statehouse journalism archives to identify the state of the state message bills and chart their legislative histories. Then, they had to determine whether the final disposition of these bills represented a victory, a defeat, or a compromise for the governor.[30] The methodology employed by Kousser and Phillips is impressive in its thoroughness and objectivity. But, as we discuss in Chapter 4, the state of the state is not without its problems as a surrogate for the governor's agenda. Some agenda items haven't been formulated by the time of the address, and some items are included for strategic purposes.

An alternative way to assess gubernatorial policymaking success is to rely largely on the recall and self-reporting of governors themselves. This approach, although more subjective, is the one employed here. It relies on three primary sources of information, as does the entire study: first, the survey responses by seventy-five governors; second, interviews with twenty-three other governors; and third, autobiographies or memoirs by former governors and biographies and accounts by journalists. The obvious problem with a methodology that relies mainly on governors is the tendency for them to accentuate the positive and downplay the negative. They can be expected, looking back on their careers as policymaking leaders, to see success rather than failure. It is probably not an intentional ploy on their parts to mislead the researcher, nor is it deception, but rather that governors have better memories when it comes to victories than defeats. For them, an outcome in which differences are split down the middle may be interpreted as getting some of what they want, a qualified victory but a victory nevertheless. Former governors are likely to see the glass as half full, not half empty.

Responses to the survey of former governors provide us with a number of measures of success, not just one. We inquired as to their success with the legislature on policy issues—whether the legislature enacted nearly all of what they asked for, most of what they asked for, some of what they asked for, or only a little of what they asked for. We inquired as to their success with the legislature regarding budgetary matters—whether the legislature gave them nearly all of what they asked for, most of what they asked for, some of what they asked for, or only a little of what they asked for. We also inquired about their policy success—whether they got most, all, some, or little or none of what they wanted in each of the policy domains in which they proposed initiatives. Finally, we asked if the legislature succeeded in enacting any major policy initiatives that the governors opposed—whether a number of them, a few of them, or none at all.

As we see detailed in Chapter 7, the overall response to these items showed an overall record of success by the 1980–2010 governors. Their responses to the survey were confirmed by information acquired from the interviews with governors and from the biographies and memoirs of governors.

If the reports of former governors are credible, governors have much in which to take pride. Bruce King (D-NM) is a good example. He served three interspersed terms as governor, 1971–1975, 1979–1983, and 1991–1995. At the end of his third term, he tallied up his achievements and concluded, "We left New Mexico a better place when I finally turned the governor's office over."[31] This is because, like other contemporary governors, King committed himself to his policy agenda. With the skills he acquired in the political arena and the advantages inherent in his office, he was able to compile a record in which he could take pride. The overall record of governors, of course, does not mean that the most successful get everything they go after or that the least successful are shut out entirely. The success of governors varies, even though most of them compile a good record according to standards we consider reasonable.

Governors succeed for a variety of reasons that are explored in the pages that follow. They succeed, in part, because they do not place the bar extraordinarily high in assessing their accomplishments. They are practitioners of pragmatism. For them, compromise is part of governing. They believe that a half loaf, or perhaps even a quarter of a loaf, is better than no bread at all.

Take as an example the efforts of C. L. "Butch" Otter (R-ID) to attain $240 million to repair roads in his state. To raise these funds, he proposed raising the gas tax. The house voted the governor's proposal down. A smaller increase in the gas tax also lost, because Republicans didn't want to raise taxes during the recession. Although the legislature would not vote for the gas-tax increase, it found other ways of giving the governor $54 of the $240 million he asked for.[32] If respondents to the survey, along with other former governors, were in Otter's shoes, how would they rate their success on his roads initiative? Would they think that they got most of what they wanted, some of what they wanted, or little or none of what they wanted? Would they consider themselves to be winners or losers on this agenda item? The ratings they give themselves likely would be higher than those given by others. But in the eyes of many, they would have succeeded in obtaining funds for road repairs, albeit not what they asked for and not from the source they would have chosen. It is not that these governors do not admit to losses; they do. But one may suspect that in general they admit to fewer losses than they suffer. That is the way most of them think about their administrations and their efforts.

At the conclusion of their terms in office, many governors produce a document that reports on their accomplishments. Typical is the *Report to the People: The Hunt Administration 1993–2001 Record of Accomplishments*, a pamphlet that details how Jim Hunt (D-NC) improved education, fought crime, and boosted the economy. Much more elaborate in presentation is *Meeting the Challenge: The Edgar Administration 1991–1999*, running 186 pages and including color as well as black-and-white photographs. Jim Edgar's work as governor of Illinois is duly celebrated in this publication. In these cases, the governors' sense of accomplishment is not likely to diminish with the passage of time.

No methodology is ideal. One limitation of putting all one's eggs in a single, formal address basket is that it may ignore or understate the governor's influence on budgetary and fiscal policy.[33] The present study takes into account the governor's success on the budget as well as on policy. Another limitation of relying on a single, formal address is that it overlooks the governor's defensive role. Part of policy leadership is getting the policy one wants. But another part of policy leadership is preventing policy that one doesn't want from becoming law. The governor's strength here is based on the executive's veto powers, but it involves much more than using, or threatening to use, the veto. It often involves a negotiating process in which the governor and legislature reach agreement on a measure with which both sides can live or even one for which both sides can claim credit.

Exploring How and Why Governors Succeed

Being governor is not the best job in politics for every person who holds the position. But it is for the large majority of them. Being governor is no guarantee of policy success for all. But the large majority of governors succeed—at least to some degree in their endeavor to make policy.

I am more concerned with trying to provide readers with a sense of governors and how they do their jobs than in trying to explain the variations in the jobs they do or the success they obtain. The major emphasis in the chapters that follow is on the large majority of governors—successful and relatively successful ones. For the most part, when I refer to governors, it is not to each and every one of them, but to a substantial majority that reasonably defines those serving in 1980–2010. I also look at those governors, albeit relatively few, who do not accomplish much, as well as others who do better. What accounts for differences among governors is explored, along with the overall nature of gubernatorial policy success.

Chapters 2 through 6 describe how and why governors succeed, in terms of the factors that play the most significant roles.

In Chapter 2, I consider the settings in which governors have to operate and that limit what governors can do. The constitutional powers of gubernatorial office matter, as do the powers and independence of the legislature. Even though gubernatorial power varies from state to state, of overriding importance here is the fact that all governors have the upper hand constitutionally and institutionally. Whether government is unified in partisan terms or divided also counts, especially in that it influences how governors determine their policy and budget agendas. The last major givens to be considered here are the fiscal and economic conditions that governors face in their states and how these conditions impinge on policy leadership.

Chapter 3 acknowledges that the individuals who serve as governors are responsible for just what they achieve or fail to achieve. Individuals who are elected governor bring a number of attributes in common to their jobs that tend to contribute to their policy leadership. Their experience weighs heavily, as do the relationships they make on the way to office. Most important is how they view the legislature as an institution and legislators as participants in the process.

Their success depends in large part on what they ask the legislature for and how they ask for it, the subject of Chapter 4. We explore the gubernatorial role in formulating their policy agendas and their budget proposals. The nature and extent of legislative involvement in the formulation process is taken into account.

Chapter 5 deals with how governors lay the groundwork for their initiatives, mainly through the ways in which they relate to legislators and legislative leaders. Their involvement with the legislature is designed to facilitate their effectiveness as policy and budget leaders.

The campaign inside the legislature and on the outside determines whether and to what extent they succeed with their agendas, the subject of Chapter 6. Also explored here are the governor's defensive activities in response to unwanted initiatives from the legislature, including the use of vetoes and line-item vetoes. Finally, the role of compromise in gubernatorial success is examined.

On the basis of the foregoing description and analysis of the factors and processes associated with the enactment of policies and budgets, Chapter 7 details the policy success of governors. On the basis of survey responses, interviews, and information from memoirs and biographies, it is clear that the 1980–2010 governors, as a whole, have compiled a record of considerable success. Nevertheless, all of them have lost initiatives or have had them scaled back, and some of them have suffered substantial defeats. The factors that contribute to success, all of which are raised in earlier chapters, are reprised here.

By way of conclusion, Chapter 8 tries to tie together two strands. First, what legacies do governors leave behind? What do they want to be remembered for, what are they remembered for, and what do they have to show for their policy achievements? Second, assuming that we have accurately portrayed the 1980–2010 generation, can we expect current governors and those in the near future to follow suit? Will they approach their policy leadership roles in a similar fashion? Will they be high policy achievers like their predecessors? Will they also have the best jobs in American politics? Or will politicians have to look elsewhere for the most gratifying employment?

Notes

1. Mark Leibovich, "Who Can Possibly Govern California?" *New York Times Magazine,* July 5, 2009, 28.
2. Dan Balz, "California Governor's Race: Jerry Brown Steps Back in at a Time of Crisis," *Washington Post,* February 10, 2010.
3. Manuel Roig-Franzia, "The New (Same Old) Jerry Brown," *Washington Post,* July 19, 2010.

4. Adam Nagourney, "The Contender," *New York Times Magazine*, May 8, 2011, 48.

5. Scott Conroy and Shushannah Walshe, *Sarah from Alaska* (New York: Public Affairs, 2009), 263.

6. Brian Friel, "The (Red) Governators," *National Journal*, June 27, 2009, 23.

7. Discussion at National Governors Association meeting, February 21, 2010.

8. Henry Bellmon, *The Life and Times of Henry Bellmon* (Tulsa, OK: Council Oak Books, 1992), 212.

9. Peter J. Boyer, "The Right Aims at Texas," *Newsweek*, June 6, 2011, 32.

10. Larry Sabato, "Governors' Office Careers: A New Breed Emerges," *State Government* 52 (Summer 1979): 100.

11. Friel, "The (Red) Governators," 23.

12. Ibid., 21.

13. Discussion at National Governors Association meeting, February 21, 2010.

14. Another former governor, Mike Castle (R-DE), was a member of the U.S. House.

15. Friel, "The (Red) Governators," 24–25.

16. Interview with Nelson. Interviews are not specifically mentioned in the text. Unless otherwise noted, the remarks of or about former governors are from the author's interviews with them or from their responses to a survey sent to individuals who had held gubernatorial office from 1980 to 2008.

17. See Chapter 4.

18. Thad L. Beyle, "Governors' Views on Being Governor," *State Government*, 52 (Summer 1979): 104.

19. Friel, "The (Red) Governators," 23.

20. Mike Litwin, *Rocky Mountain News*, January 19, 2009.

21. Friel, "The (Red) Governators," 20.

22. Bellmon, *The Life and Times of Henry Bellmon*, 212.

23. Alan Ehrenhalt, "Woodrow Wilson and the Modern American Governorship." A paper proposed for the Woodrow Wilson School's Colloquium in Public and International Affairs, *Woodrow Wilson in the Nation's Service*. Princeton University, April 28, 2006.

24. Coleman B. Ransone Jr., "The Governor, the Legislature, and Public Policy," *State Governments* (Summer 1979): 120.

25. These thirty years constitute our cohort of governors. We refer to them as contemporary and as a generation. They came into office as state legislatures had gone through a period of modernization.

26. Lou Cannon, *Governor Reagan: His Rise to Power* (New York: Public Affairs, 2003).

27. These were governors who were elected to office, served at least one full term, and had been in office between January 1, 1980, and June 11, 2009.

28. In the text, governors are referred to by the first names that they have adopted and not by their official first names. Appendix A gives their official first names as well as the years in which they served.

29. Margaret Robertson Ferguson, "Chief Executive Success in the Legislative Arena," *State Politics and Policy Quarterly* 3 (Summer 2003): 166; Thad Kousser and Justin A. Phillips, *The Hidden Power of American Governors.* (Cambridge: Cambridge University Press, in process).

30. Kousser and Phillips, *The Hidden Power of American Governors.*

31. Bruce King, *Cowboy in the Roundhouse* (Santa Fe, NM: Sunstone Press, 1998), 308.

32. Alan Ehrenhalt, "Butch's Battle," *Governing* (June 2009): 11–12.

33. Kousser and Phillips are careful to figure out which items mentioned in the state of the state address are related to the budget, and they assess the success of those items.

2

Playing the Hands They Are Dealt

As governors of South Carolina and Texas, respectively, Democrat Richard Riley and Republican George W. Bush lacked the constitutional, statutory, and raw political power that governors in most other states had. Such weakness institutionally can be expected to diminish a governor's policymaking leadership. Democrat Scott Matheson in Utah faced a Republican-controlled legislature during his entire tenure, whereas Republican Arnold Schwarzenegger in California faced a Democratic-controlled legislature during his years as governor. We would certainly expect such conditions to inhibit optimum policymaking on the governor's part.

In Oregon's election of 1990, when Democrat Barbara Roberts became governor, Measure 5, a ballot initiative, passed narrowly and at the same time the spotted owl became a cause célèbre. Measure 5 required that every penny of local property taxes spent on schools and community colleges had to be reimbursed from the state's general fund. This required Roberts, in her first year in office, to find $500 million in additional funds (to balance a $6 billion biennial budget). Two years later she would have to come up with an additional $1.2 billion. The spotted owl was listed as an endangered species by the federal government, a designation that Roberts as a gubernatorial candidate and environmentalist supported. This meant that the owl's habitat in old-growth forests had to be protected. But these forests were also the source of the most valuable trees for Oregon timber, the state's major industry. The impact on employment and on logging communities was severe, and the new governor received much of the blame for what Roberts referred to as "the worst issue I ever dealt with in my life." These two issues dominated Roberts's four years as governor, but they were not of her choosing. They were forced on the governor by circumstances over which she had no control. But they put the governor on the defensive and diverted her from other policy priorities.

Governors have little or no control over important factors that may contribute to their success, or failure, in office. They have to play the hand they are dealt in terms of constitutional and statutory powers, the independence of the legislature, the partisan division and structure of state government, the fiscal and economic conditions in the state, and other factors as well.

Gubernatorial Powers

Gubernatorial power—that is, the constitutional, legal, and political capacity of governors—has been examined and analyzed by political scientists for almost a half-century. In 1965 Joseph A. Schlesinger developed an index to measure the formal powers of governors in the fifty states. The original index was revised by the National Governors Association, whose index included six institutional powers as well as three others.[1] Probably the most widely used index currently is that constructed by Thad Beyle. It employs six separate measures of the institutional powers of governors: (1) the number of separately elected executive branch officials, (2) tenure potential in terms of length of term and ability to seek another term, (3) appointment power over executive positions, (4) budgetary power, (5) veto power, and (6) party control of the legislature. According to Beyle's calculations, the states with the strongest governors in 2007 were Massachusetts, Alaska, Maryland, New Jersey, New York, and West Virginia.[2]

Whether they are aware of these indexes or not, governors do acknowledge the strength of their office. New Jersey's governors take special pride in their power, as well they might. The authors of the 1947 New Jersey constitution did their utmost to create one of the most powerful executives in the nation. Until recently, the New Jersey governor was the only statewide elected official (other than the state's two U.S. senators). Now there is a lieutenant governor who runs on the same ticket as the governor. According to Tom Kean (R-NJ), the New Jersey governor is "without a doubt, the most powerful chief executive in the fifty states," with "almost total control over the policymaking apparatus."[3] The New Jersey governor has been referred to by George Will as "an American Caesar," enjoying line-item and conditional vetoes and exploiting the appointment powers of the office to trade with the legislature on policy and budget matters.

Maryland's governor is also well endowed, thanks mainly to the executive's budgetary authority, or rather the legislature's lack of authority to do anything but cut the budget. New York's governor also has had a tremendous advantage dating to 1929. That year the state constitution was amended to give the governor primary responsibility for the financial system, while limiting the legislature. Governors such as Al Smith, Franklin Roosevelt, Tom Dewey, Nelson Rockefeller, and Hugh Carey all used their fiscal powers forcefully.[4]

At the other end of the continuum are governors in states such as Texas and South Carolina, who are less endowed. The 1876 constitution of Texas gives the governor little opportunity for strong leadership. A number of important agency heads are elected statewide and not appointed by the governor. The lieutenant governor wields power almost equal to that of the governor, because of his or her control of the state senate. The speaker of the house is the other political leader who shares power with the governor. The Texas governor doesn't even have control of the budget. Constitutionally, responsibility for the formulation of the budget is with the Legislative Budget Board, composed of the lieutenant governor, house speaker, chairs of the house appropriations committee and senate finance committee, and two other legislators. As one Texas insider put it: "Being governor in Texas is a trap. You have all the blame and not nearly enough power."[5]

South Carolina traditionally has also been a weak-governor state, with the budget formulated by the Budget and Control Board. The governor is one member of the board, along with the state treasurer, state comptroller, and two legislators. In the 1980s the governorship was strengthened by allowing an incumbent to run for a successive term and by giving the governor greater control over departments and agencies. Although the office is stronger than it used to be, it is still relatively weak. Similarly, the office of Mississippi's governor, which has been weak, became stronger in the 1980s, thanks to being granted the authority to submit an executive budget.

A principal constitutional restriction on governors is a limit of two successive terms in office. In one state, Virginia, governors are limited to one consecutive term. Even with limits on their tenure, however, Virginia governors manage to lead. Gerald Baliles (D-VA), for instance, was prepared for gubernatorial office, knew what he wanted to achieve, and did not have to worry about running for reelection. "I never found it restricting," was his assessment of the one-term limit.

Governors differ in the formal and informal powers at their disposal. But even the weakest among them are not lacking in tools with which to exercise power. First, they have the wherewithal to initiate policy. For example, the Nevada constitution provides that the governor "shall communicate by message" and "recommend such measures as he may deem expedient." Constitutional provision and political custom allow, if they do not dictate, that governors will present proposals for the legislature to enact. Second, in twenty states only the governor can call the legislature into special session and in ten states only the governor can determine a special session's agenda. A governor can use a special session to focus the attention of both legislators and the public on an issue of his or her choosing. For example, Henry Bellmon (R-OK) called the legislature into session four times during his last term in office. One session, on education reform and taxes to support the schools, lasted eight months.[6] Third, in most states governors formulate the budget, and that is certainly one of the governor's principal powers. Blair Lee (D-MD) regards it as "the most important single thing that a Governor does."[7] Fourth, the veto power and the line-item and conditional or amendatory vetoes are major weapons in a governor's defensive arsenal. Some governors are better endowed than others, but overall relatively few vetoes by relatively few governors are overridden. Fifth, the governor makes appointments—to departments and agencies and to boards and commissions. Legislators are anxious to garner appointments for people from their districts—constituents who want jobs and constituents who want to do public service. Sixth, governors have a variety of ways to acknowledge legislators and others—inviting them to the mansion, giving them a pen at a bill-signing, bestowing on them tickets to a sporting event, visiting their districts, appearing at fundraisers, or otherwise singling them out for special attention.

Coleman Ransone emphasized that a distinction has to be made between the formal and informal powers of governors. Only part of a governor's influence, according to Ransone, derives from formal powers.[8] A strong governor requires some combination of "formal" and "informal" powers; the formal powers are potent policy tools when combined with a governor's electoral mandate and party majorities in the legislature.[9]

Even formally weak governors can exceed expectations by drawing on informal powers. Richard Riley (D-SC) is an example. In his memoirs, he asked how governors with relatively little formal authority govern. His answer was that, in South Carolina, he found that a governor can influence the creation and furtherance of public policy in several ways, including by "influencing the legislature" and by "exerting leadership, which is possibly the most valuable power at the governor's disposal."[10] According to one analyst, Riley succeeded in persuading the legislature to enact his education reform agenda, because, among other things, he had mastered the use of informal powers, such as negotiations, public relations, and strategizing.[11]

Texas governors have an uphill struggle, as far as formal authority is concerned, "but strength or weakness depends on the governor."[12] Opportunities to exercise leadership exist for all governors because of the stature of gubernatorial office, its visibility, and the fact that, to many Texans, state government is personified by the governor. George W. Bush's biographer wrote: "This gives the chief executive an invaluable public forum, a bully pulpit, from which to propose ideas, define and sell his or her vision of the future to the electorate, and bring public pressure to bear on the legislature to enact the governor's agenda."[13] Indiana governors also are weak in terms of formal power, but few think of Mitch Daniels (R-IN) as a weak governor. As elsewhere, in Indiana a resourceful governor can be extremely influential in the legislative process.

Whatever the variations in power among states, within the same states individual governors may differ in how they use the formal and informal powers at their disposal. Take, for example, three of Kentucky's Democratic governors. John Y. Brown offered the legislature a limited agenda and did not engage in the process. Martha Layne Collins was more engaged than Brown but did not intervene in some of the major battles. Wallace Wilkinson, by contrast, was aggressive but not entirely successful with the

Kentucky general assembly.[14] Or take three of Maryland's Democratic governors. Harry Hughes was deferential to the legislature, whereas William Donald Schaefer was quite the opposite. Parris Glendening gave the legislature its due but was firmly committed to his own agenda. These governors, all working under similar constitutional, statutory, and political arrangements, differed in their policymaking leadership and in their effectiveness.

As we shall see, who the governor is makes a difference. But when it comes to dealing with the legislature, which all governors have to do, whoever the governor is and wherever the governor lives, he or she has the advantage. Even relatively weak governors usually have the upper hand over the legislatures. The governor is chief legislator.[15] In the checks-and-balances system of executive and legislature, the one trumps the many. The governor is one, the legislature many. The governor is a single person elected statewide who does not have to share billing with other state officials. In a legislature, there are two houses (except in Nebraska), two parties, and as many as 424 members (in New Hampshire) and as few as 60 (in Alaska).

Compared to the legislature, a governor's decision process is straightforward and simple. Like legislatures, governors are sensitive to their constituencies and circumstances in forming their agendas. They consult, take advice, and then decide. But once governors decide, that's pretty much it. In legislatures, by contrast, the struggle to persuade a majority of members in each chamber to agree on policy is continuing and arduous. Reaching consensus (or majority agreement) can be a formidable challenge in the legislature. The governor can make a decision in one inning; it takes the legislature nine or sometimes extra innings.

Because the governor is a single person elected by voters across the state and the legislature is a collection of individuals elected by people locally, the governor is generally perceived as expressing a statewide point of view. The governor speaks with one voice, the legislature speaks with many—in particular a senate voice and a house voice and a majority-party voice and a minority-party voice. According to Ralph Wright, a former house speaker in Vermont, the governor, being one rather than many, was recognizable by the public. "In any squabble," Wright noted, "the governor had a distinct edge over what amounted to a gang of unknowns in the legislature."[16] The governor has the "bully pulpit" and commands the lion's share of media attention for his or her pronouncements, activities, and agendas. This affords the governor a position to expound administration views and appeal for support for administration policy. The governor has a much better chance of reaching the public than does the legislature, which has practically no pulpit at all, bully or otherwise. The governor has the ability to lead a statewide campaign. Neither the legislature nor anyone in it has similar ability.

Variations in the formal and informal powers of governors from one state to another are less important than differences between the power of the executive and legislative institutions, no matter what the state. Governors can and do fail, but institutionally they have an advantage. As we shall see, most of them make excellent use of the advantage they have.

Legislative Power

The governor's actual power depends partly on the power of others in the political system. An examination of the powers of the governor without an examination of the powers of the legislature would be somewhat misleading, because the potential to utilize political power does not exist in a vacuum.[17] Governors may have the advantage, but they still must share power. Ahlberg and Moynihan, having observed New York government first hand, wrote that, after an election, a new governor has to ask permission of the legislature to enact his or her agenda. Conflict is inevitable.[18] John Martin, speaker of the Maine house, expressed it succinctly. "As long as the legislature controls the budget, as long as the governor has to come to us to get that budget through," he didn't worry too much about the governor; an accommodation of some sort would be reached.[19] The legislature's trump card vis-à-vis governors is the power to say no. "If you want something," said Angus King (I-ME), "they have to pass it." The legislature's power is primarily that of blocking the executive's agenda and secondarily that of imposing its own agenda on the executive. Legislatures can modify, delay, and reject. They can frustrate governors and keep them from doing what they want to do. Any governor who has policy proposals to put into law or budgets to put into effect has to reach agreement with the legislature.

Although the executive was strengthened institutionally in the first half of the twentieth century, legislative strengthening did not occur until the period from the 1960s to the 1980s. Before then, except in states such as California and New York, legislatures were very part-time operations with little capacity to take the initiative or to seriously challenge the executive on many matters. Thanks in large part to a modernization movement that got under way after legislative redistricting in the 1960s, legislatures began to build their capacity and professionalize. Brendan Byrne, who governed New Jersey in the 1970s, observed that when he worked for Governor Robert Meyner in the 1950s, "the legislature had nothing." Even during Byrne's tenure, the New Jersey legislature was hardly equipped to do battle with the governor.[20] Dick Codey (D-NJ), who served part of a term as governor in 2004–2006, had been in the legislature for many years before assuming executive office. He recalled that the influence of the governor's office, vis-à-vis the legislature, had been diminished over the years. The key element was professional staff. Codey's assessment was that "as the legislature got more staff, they grew more independent of the governor's office."[21]

What happened in New Jersey also happened across the nation. Few legislatures were untouched by the modernization movement. Legislatures began to spend more time in session, and standing committees and legislative commissions met between sessions. The lengths of sessions increased, and legislatures that met biennially started meeting annually. Not all legislatures went to annual sessions. In Oregon, for instance, the legislature still meets and budgets biennially, for six months every two years. "It is a lot easier when the legislature is not there every year," said Barbara Roberts. The former governor's assessment of the executive-legislative balance is: "Truthfully, the legislature has not been a coequal branch." Nonetheless, around the country legislator compensation rose, facilities were improved, and—most important—nonpartisan and partisan staffs expanded. By the mid 1980s most of the large states—New York, California, Illinois, Michigan, Ohio, Pennsylvania, and Massachusetts— had nearly full-time and highly professionalized legislatures. These institutions certainly possessed the capacity to try to balance the power of the executive. Legislatures in the smaller states—such as Vermont, Wyoming, Montana, North Dakota, and South Dakota—possessed far less capacity and small nonpartisan staffs.

Coequal or not, legislatures were becoming both more professional and more independent during this period. Kentucky exemplifies the transformation. Until 1980 Kentucky had had two decades of strong governors—Bert Combs, Edward Breathitt, Louis Nunn, Wendell Ford, and Julian Carroll. The last three had to confront a legislature that was gaining a sense of independence. The next three governors—Brown, Collins, and Wilkinson—had to deal with an increasingly independent general assembly, and their job became more difficult as a result.[22] Those legislatures that regarded themselves as separate, independent, and coequal branches of state government insisted on sharing power with the governor. California, Colorado, Florida, Minnesota, Ohio, and Virginia were among the leading independent legislatures. "The more independent and professional the legislature," two political scientists assert, "the harder it is for a governor to dominate on policy matters." Where legislatures meet infrequently and for short periods of time, have little staff support, and are not technologically developed, the governor has an easier time getting his or her policy initiative passed.[23] As we shall see, that is no longer the case.

The period of legislative capacity building was followed by a decade in which twenty-one legislatures had term limits forced upon them by initiatives voted on by the electorate.[24] Fifteen legislatures currently have term limits that restrict members to six, eight, or twelve years in the senate or house. In six other states, legislatures passed statutes rescinding term limits or courts declared term limits unconstitutional. Term limits have weakened legislatures by increasing the turnover and reducing the experience of members. In term-limited legislatures, substantive expertise is diminished, stable leadership no longer exists, and pragmatism is less valued.

In a study spearheaded by the National Conference of State Legislatures, a group of political scientists who explored term limits concluded that legislatures had ceded considerable power to governors as a consequence.[25] Governors, of course, are aware of the effects of term limits. John Engler (R-MI) believes that term limits "killed the legislature" in Michigan, because political factors became so dominant over substantive ones. Term limits, according to Bob Taft (R-OH), strengthens governors by affording them "a clear path" for leadership. No one can stand in their way. But it may be a mixed blessing for governors, said Taft, because it is harder for governors to take on tough issues. Legislative leaders are short-termers, fearful of electoral consequences, and not confident that they can get their members on board. Moreover, it is more difficult for a governor to find knowledgeable legislators to carry issues. In short, the governor concluded, with term limits in Ohio, "It's tougher to find the legislative leadership you need."

Governors already had advantages. But until the imposition of term limits on legislatures, the tenure potential of most governors was shorter than that of a number of legislators in their states. In 1980, for example, New Hampshire and Rhode Island had two-year terms for governors (currently the term in Rhode Island is four years); and governors in Kentucky, New Mexico, and Virginia could not succeed themselves immediately after a four-year term (although currently only Virginia is in that category). Most governors at that time were limited to two four-year terms, whereas legislators' terms were not limited. Legislatures had the advantage of continuity, especially in states where leadership was stable and a core of members typically served fifteen to twenty years. That experience, and the perspective that went with it, contributed to legislative confidence and strength in dealing with the governor. In fifteen states, such confidence and strength has been eviscerated by term limits. Angus King, however, wondered whether the benefits of term limits for governors were illusory. He had to deal with four different speakers during the eight years he served as governor. Power appeared to have evaporated, and both the governor and legislature had to work much harder to get anything accomplished.

Party Control and Partisan Division

All but three governors during the period 1980–2010 have been Democrats or Republicans. The exceptions are King in Maine, Lowell Weicker in Connecticut, and Jesse Ventura in Minnesota, each of whom was an independent. Democratic and Republican governors have natural allies in the legislature. Independents, however, are without party support and have no party in the legislature to try to tell what to do. As governor of Maine, King was without "instant allies" but also, as he points out, without "instant enemies." He governed with a Democratic majority in the house and a Republican majority in the senate. The two parties could have made him fail, but King was fortunate that they didn't. "To their credit," he said, "they were citizens and legislators first and partisans second."

Democratic governors and Republican governors are leaders of their state parties. It is to be expected that Democratic governors have an easier time exercising policy leadership when Democrats control the legislature and Republican governors have an easier time when Republicans control. First, Democratic legislators are more inclined to agree with the policy agendas of Democratic governors and Republican legislators are inclined to agree with the policy agendas of Republican governors. Second, pressure within the legislature tends to produce support for the governor of one's own party, especially given the possibility that the governor will be at the top of the ticket in an election with legislators slated below. Third, it is a natural inclination to support the leader of one's team, unless one's constituency or conscience demands otherwise. Unified government, wherein the party of the governor also has majorities in both houses of the legislature, is likely to be more positive toward the executive agenda. Divided government, with one or both houses controlled by the party other than the governor's, is likely to be less positive toward the agenda.

A governor's party colleagues in the legislature do not want to make "their" governor look bad, if at all possible. Brian Schweitzer (D-MT) was not very popular with the Montana legislature, but Democrats tried to protect him—at least during his first session—as much as they could.[26] A legislature might cut any new governor some slack, but it would go even further with one of their own. In Georgia the governor as party leader is given a great deal of party support. Despite many individuals who had differences with Zell Miller (D-GA), most of the top leaders were willing to go along with him.[27] The majority-party leaders—the president of the senate and the speaker of the house—bear a special responsibility when the governor is a member of their party. They are expected to carry the ball for their governors whenever they can. In Wisconsin, for example,

Democrat Tom Loftus, the assembly speaker, identified himself as a "lieutenant" to Democratic governor, Tony Earl (D-WI).[28]

Yet, as with much of executive-legislative relations, unified government doesn't guarantee a governor's influence. By way of advising new governors, the National Governors Association reports that most experienced governors warn that a legislature of the same party cannot always be counted on and that many governors engage in fierce struggles with members of their own party.[29] Some analysts believe that a majority party that is too large, such as the one-party legislatures in the South years ago, cannot be held together. The more completely a legislature is dominated by a single party, the less organized and cohesive that legislative party is likely to be.[30] Consider the Democrats in the Massachusetts legislature. They comprise a large but disunited majority that has made life difficult for Democratic governor Deval Patrick.[31] However small or large the majority, factionalism in the majority party can always diminish its control and be "debilitating to gubernatorial policy efforts."[32]

Some governors have had a hard time, even with their own party in control. The Republicans had enjoyed large margins in the Idaho legislature but, because the party had been factionalized, C. L. "Butch" Otter (R-ID) didn't really benefit.[33] In New York in 2009, for the first time in ages, Democrats gained a majority in the senate. Since 1939, Republicans had controlled that chamber every year but 1965. They lost control of the assembly in 1974, and Democrats controlled that chamber since then. The assembly Democrats, according to tradition, continued to act cohesively, but the senate Democrats were split and unable to take full charge. David Paterson (D-NY) couldn't restore order and exercise gubernatorial leadership. The narrow Republican victory in the 2010 senate elections removed the Democrats from the feeble control that they briefly had.

Jon Corzine (D-NJ) had a Democratic legislature during his four years in office. But the independence of Democrats in the senate and of the senate president, Codey, who had served as acting governor for about a year prior to Corzine, made for friction. So did a strong, resourceful assembly speaker, Joe Roberts, who, together with his caucus, had their own ideas about where New Jersey might be going on tax policy.[34]

When the legislature is divided, with the Democrats having one chamber and the Republicans the other (as in New York for thirty years from

1979 to 2009), governors use different strategies. Allen Olson (R-ND) changed his approach to the North Dakota legislature when Democrats won the house in the midterm elections. Olson found that, under unified government the first two years, it was more difficult for him to lead because of jealousy between the senate and the house. With the legislature divided, however, as governor he was able to play one body off against the other.[35] Jim Edgar in Illinois held the governorship for eight years. He had a Republican legislature for two years, a Democratic legislature for two, and a Republican senate and Democratic house for four. For him the best situation was divided government, where, as governor, he could work to mediate disagreements among the four caucuses. Bill Owens (R-CO) took pride in working well with both parties in Colorado. He employed different approaches, depending on the political configuration during his eight years as governor. When the Democrats had the senate, "we would triangulate," working with the house and then bringing along the senate.

Dick Thornburgh (R-PA) could be philosophical about the tensions that partisanship injected into the executive-legislative relationship. Pennsylvania is a very partisan state, and Thornburgh had to deal with several configurations of party control. He experienced situations in which both chambers were Republican and in which control of the senate and house were split. The majority party was never separated by more than two or three votes from the minority. The divided-government situation, according to Thornburgh's assessment, had its advantages. It forced both legislative leaders and the governor into "the craft of governing, the making of compromises, the resolution of differences of philosophy."[36] Jim Hunt (D-NC) enjoyed a Democratic legislature for two of his terms. But in his third term, Republicans controlled the house for the first time in the twentieth century. It was a sea change for Hunt, because the Republicans were so partisan after being in the minority for so long that their caucus prohibited the speaker from meeting with the governor.

A number of governors have had to navigate a split legislature, just as many faced a legislature in which both houses were under the command of the opposition party. When Democrat Roberts became governor of Oregon, the house went Republican for the first time in decades. Along with other factors, this made for a tough start. Arne Carlson (R-MN) served as governor for eight years, all of them with the legislature in the hands of the Democrats. Pete Wilson (R-CA) and George Deukmejian (R-CA) had to deal with Democratic legislatures. Francis Keating (R-OK) had a Democratic legislature during his eight-year tenure. In Connecticut, Rhode Island, and Massachusetts, Republicans have had considerable success since 1980 in winning the office of governor, but they then had to face Democratic legislatures.

Governors may well encounter partisan hostility under such circumstances. Tom Kean certainly did, because New Jersey's assembly speaker, Alan Karcher, was combative by nature and partisan by orientation, and because the Democrats generally bought into their speaker's confrontational approach. "We will work with the Governor," Karcher said, "as long as his programs mesh with ours." He advised Kean to expect a "short honeymoon," and that's what the governor got.[37] The Democrats in New Jersey opposed virtually every one of Kean's initial policy proposals and fought almost the entire year over the budget. Their strategy, according to Kean, was to achieve gridlock and go into the elections accusing him of being a do-nothing governor.[38]

Bob Ehrlich (R-MD) faced a similar situation in Maryland, where liberal Democrats, in his opinion, resented his statewide victory and wanted to keep him from accomplishing much. When Ehrlich served in the legislature, the Democratic Party was more diverse, with conservatives and moderates as well as liberals. Indeed, in the 1980s party was not that important in the Maryland legislature, and minority-party members were even able to exercise leadership in both the senate and the house. When Ehrlich was governor, however, the Democrats had shifted to the left and little room existed for the executive and legislature to get together on some critical issues. The Democratic legislature in New Mexico and Republican Gary Johnson also spent eight years opposing one another, and relations between the two branches often turned nasty. As a result, not much got done.[39] When governors of one party and legislatures of the other cannot resolve their differences, gridlock will occur.

But gridlock is by no means unavoidable. After a while, Speaker Alan Karcher realized that he could not best Governor Kean in New Jersey's court of public opinion, and he relented. Kean's agenda was then given an attentive hearing in the legislature. Ronald Reagan, too, fared well when the Democrats controlled the legislature—indeed, better than he did when Republicans were in control.[40] George W. Bush managed to work with the Democratic legislature in Texas. He did better than Bill Clements (R-TX), in part because the legislature—the senate especially—became somewhat more Republican and somewhat more conservative.[41]

The Structure of State Government

Governments are structured differently from state to state, and governors have little choice but to adapt to the systems in which they have to function. Some structural elements, however, hinder a governor's ability to succeed. California exemplifies a state in which both governors and legislatures have been denied the power they need to enact policy. California is not the only state that inhibits elected policymakers, but it is certainly the poster child for those that do. In the words of one observer, in California "the state government and political system are designed to malfunction."[42] Although other states have dysfunctional features, none of them ties the hands of its governors and legislatures with such an array of "fiscal fetters" as does California.[43]

Until Proposition 25 on the 2010 ballot allowed the legislature to pass a budget with a simple majority vote, California had required a two-thirds majority in the legislature to pass a budget. The governor, who formulates the budget, naturally has had a much harder time rounding up two-thirds of the members in support than getting a simple majority. When a legislature is divided sharply along partisan lines, as in California, the minority party has the ability to wrest enormous concessions from the majority (and from the governor), if it commands at least one-third of the votes in either the house or the senate. Arkansas and Rhode Island also require super majorities for passing a budget, thereby restricting the governor's budget power in these states.

California also requires a two-thirds majority in the legislature for raising taxes. Sixteen other states are similar, requiring a super majority for raising some or all taxes.[44] This, too, can inhibit governors who seek to fund policy initiatives and program enhancements by increasing state revenues. This requirement has had substantial effect in limiting the policy possibilities of political leaders. Reagan, for example, had a tax plan that came close, but still fell short of the necessary two-thirds.[45]

The key restriction on the governor and legislature of California is the ballot initiative. The two-thirds requirement for tax increases in this state is a result of 1978's Proposition 13 initiative, which also capped the state's property taxes. The initiative process bypasses the legislature, permitting a proposition that has garnered the requisite number of citizen signatures to go directly to the ballot. Twenty-five other states also provide for the initiative process, but none is as removed from conventional lawmaking as is California's. Here, any statute approved by popular initiative cannot subsequently be amended by the legislature without another vote by the people. According to two critics of the system, a California initiative

> doesn't merely circumvent state lawmakers at a particular time and place. It creates a higher class of law, exempt from independent amendment or fix by the legislature, no matter how problematic or outdated it becomes.[46]

This reliance on the initiative has prompted the chief justice of the state supreme court to conclude that it has "rendered state government dysfunctional."[47]

Direct democracy has limited California's capacity to raise taxes while aggravating the state's "fiscal incontinence." A prime example is Proposition 98, passed by voters in 1988. This proposition guarantees that about 40 percent of every year's budget be dedicated to education, despite the other pressing needs the state may have. Anywhere from 65 to 85 percent of each budget is determined without legislative involvement, as a result of Proposition 98 and a number of bond measures to pay for public projects, amounting to roughly $85 billion since 2000.[48] In effect, the legislature and the governor both have little control over the state's fiscal situation. Just as in California, voters in Florida tied the hands of their elected officials by passing a 2002 constitutional amendment to reduce class size in the schools. It is estimated that, by 2011, the state will have spent almost $15 billion to comply with the class-size mandate.[49]

Like California, Colorado also faces serious constitutional impediments. On the one hand, in 1992 the electorate adopted an initiative, Taxpayer's Bill of Rights (TABOR), that was designed to limit the growth of government. On the other hand, in 2000 the electorate adopted Amendment 23, which was intended to ensure K–12 funding. These constitutional provisions, respectively, limited spending and mandated spending and have helped to make Colorado's fiscal problems worse than would otherwise be the case.

At some point, structural hindrances in state government make it extremely difficult for governors to exercise effective leadership. California is well beyond that point. Governors, like Arnold Schwarzenegger, did not hesitate to bypass the normal lawmaking system and lead initiative campaigns to achieve the policy results they wanted. When the political system is stalemated, tied in knots, or otherwise reeling, voters may turn to another product of direct democracy, the recall, to remove a governor from office before his or her term expires. They did so with Democrat Gray Davis in 2003 and immediately elected Schwarzenegger in his place. In its quest for "bold leadership that might break the logjam and address the state's systematic dysfunction," the public jettisoned one leader and put its faith in another who was also constitutionally prevented from leading successfully.[50]

Economic and Fiscal Conditions

California's inability to agree on budgets, raise taxes, or limit expenditures mandated by initiatives limits the ability of the state's political leaders to exercise policy leadership. The governor, in the role of chief policymaker, can hardly avoid dealing with inherited fiscal problems upon being sworn into office.

Even in states with fewer impediments to gubernatorial leadership, limits of an economic and fiscal nature exist. These limits result from the necessary continuities and commitments in departmental programs and budgets, which are for the most part a given. They limit the governor's freedom of action.[51] Add to this base the growth in state population and the consequent increase in the need for state expenditures. Then factor in the mandates imposed on the states (usually with their acquiescence or support) by the federal government. In the areas of welfare and health, states have had to ante up state funds in order to receive money from

Washington. No program has driven spending as forcefully as has Medicaid, where costs have been rising steadily. Edgar of Illinois remembers having had a tough time as a result of what was required in state matching funds. Partly in jest, he attributes one of his heart bypasses to federal mandates, in particular to Medicaid (he attributes his other bypass to the speaker of the Illinois house). As governor he had no control over rising expenditures during the early 1990s, yet as governor he was responsible for meeting them.

Dollars are always limited for new programs that governors want to undertake. Thus, the choices open to them are constrained by financial commitments that cannot realistically be abrogated and by the inelasticity of state revenues. Governors would like to be able to count on the natural growth of state revenues to pay for programs they want to initiate or expand. Their wishes have been granted during good economic times. In such times, personal and corporate income taxes, sales taxes, and other revenues rise and the state treasury has money on which governors can draw. During poor economic times, however, governors find themselves in a different position. Under such circumstances, they have to concern themselves with fiscal policy above all. Their main options are cutting expenditures, raising taxes, or managing some combination of the two.

Contemporary governors have not been blessed with boon economies. Since 1980 (the starting point for this study) economic conditions in the nation and the states have been sporadic, with ups followed by downs and vice versa. Some men and women have been lucky enough to govern only in up periods, but most were less fortunate in their timing. They faced hard times and fiscal stress during at least part of their single or several administrations. Former governors were questioned in our survey about their state's situation during their years in office. They were asked to locate on a seven-point continuum their state's economy during their tenure—whether it was poor all or most of the time (points 1, 2, and 3), good some of the time and poor some of the time (point 4), or good all or most of the time (points 5, 6, and 7). Four out of five governors reported suffering through part of their administrations: 27 percent believed that they faced a poor economy all or most of the time, 55 percent experienced both good and poor economies, and only 19 percent perceived their state economies as being good all or most of the time they were in office.

The good-time governors benefitted from the economic expansion of the mid-1980s and 1990s, "a period when governors were geniuses," in the words of Maine's King. Substantial revenue surpluses enabled governors to undertake even costly initiatives. In Maryland, Glendening happily enjoyed surpluses for six of eight years of his two administrations, using revenues from a booming economy for school construction, the funding of higher education, and the purchase of open space. When money is plentiful, legislatures also have more spending options open to them, observed George Ariyoshi (D-HI). Like governors, they too have ideas about what ought to be done and what government can do, and they also want credit with the voters for having accomplished something.[52]

The majority of governors experienced mixed economies, and the differences in their agendas in "up" and in "down" times are striking. Mike Dukakis (D-MA) served a first term as governor in 1975–1979 and second and third terms in 1983–1991. When he first took office, unemployment in Massachusetts was over 12 percent, the highest in any of the industrial states. He faced a budget deficit of more than $500 million. Thirteen years later, in his third term, unemployment was 3.8 percent and the state had a $400 million surplus.[53] At the outset, Dukakis had to worry about cutting the budget, raising taxes, or doing both. Later on, his chief problem was not that of inflicting pain, but "the enviable job of allocating the riches among competing constituencies and needs."[54] For Dukakis, life got a lot better. For some other governors, it got a lot worse. Clements had the benefit of good times when he started out as governor of Texas, but during his second term the state's economy declined.[55]

Contrast the two terms served by Frank O'Bannon (D-IN). The new governor's state of the state address in January 1997 reflected flush economic times. O'Bannon called for property tax cuts but also new money for schools, highway construction, and more police officers spread throughout Indiana. During his second term, however, there was no money for major initiatives, new spending, or additional services. With tax revenues sagging, his budget provided only a 2 percent increase for public schools, despite increased costs and inflation.[56]

The majority of governors are confronted by bad economic times, potential budget deficits, or both, because spending commitments tend to exceed revenues, even in decent times. They either have to make do with less or somehow find the dollars to meet their state's obligations. They know what it feels like to confront fiscal problems as soon as they take the oath of office. In New York, Averell Harriman inherited a deficit that had existed for years. Nelson Rockefeller began his first budget message with the announcement that "New York is faced with the most serious fiscal problem of more than a generation." Both governors blamed their predecessors.[57] When Mario Cuomo became governor, he faced a projected $1.8 billion deficit[58], and when Cuomo left office he telephoned his successor, George Pataki (R-NY), to inform him that the state budget was structurally out of balance to the tune of $4 billion.[59] On his first day as governor of New York, David Paterson faced a $4.5 billion shortfall.

In California, Jerry Brown (D-CA) left a $1.5 billion deficit (in a $27 billion state budget) for George Deukmejian, which at the time was deemed to be of unprecedented proportions. Thereafter, Deukmejian passed on a large budget deficit to his successor, Pete Wilson.[60] Richard Celeste (D-OH) took office with Ohio over $500 million in the red[61] and handed it over to George Voinovich (R-OH) with the state $1 billion in the red.[62] Colorado's Owens inherited a $950 million deficit when he became governor in 1999 and over the course of his eight-year tenure saw revenues decline by as much as 16 percent.

Jim McGreevey (D-NJ) had to reconcile the $3 billion tax cut made by his predecessor, Christine Whitman (R-NJ). He faced a $5.3 billion drop in tax revenues, as he started out. In fact, on his first day in office he got a report from his state treasurer that the budget crisis was even worse than it originally looked. "They cooked the books," McGreevey seethed. "They hid the truth and they left taxpayers to foot the bill."[63] It took Edgar a month to discover what James Thompson (R-IL), his former boss and mentor, had left for him. Just after being elected, the new Illinois governor was informed by his transition committee that it had some bad news.

> I said, "What?" "We've got at least a $1 billion deficit." I said, "Is it too late for a recount?" They said, "Yes, you've been certified."

With more debts than revenues, Edgar had little choice. "If the state's broke," he said, "either we raise taxes or we don't spend money." It was just after that that a recession hit Illinois, making things even worse than Edgar imagined at the outset.

Despite constitutional requirements for balanced budgets (in all states but Vermont, which balances its budget regularly, although not mandated to do so), deficits may grow in the period after the budget has been passed and signed into law and before a new governor takes office. Governors like to spend monies available to them before they make their exit. Bob Wise (D-WV) took office and soon figured out that his predecessor had left a mess behind for him. "I felt like I had walked into a restaurant and been handed a bunch of bills for past patrons and past meals," he recalled. The former governors questioned in this study's survey tended to agree. When asked whether their predecessors had left them with a projected deficit or projected surplus, only 16 percent reported a "substantial" or "modest" surplus. Another 26 percent said that they had been left a budget that was in balance. The remaining 58 percent, however, responded that they inherited either a "modest" or "substantial" deficit.

Governors have to manage the effects of an economic downturn or unsustainable spending. Indeed, their administrations and policy leadership are shaped in large part by the fiscal conditions they inherit. Insofar as possible, they want to escape political blame for something over which they had no control. James Blanchard (D-MI) left Engler a hefty deficit, but one that was not obvious to the public. One of the first actions the new governor took was to have his fiscal people go over state fiscal information with a fine tooth comb. "If we don't disclose it now," Engler commented, "we'll own it later." It was better, he believed, to put the blame where it deserved to be, on his predecessor. Other governors, too, will lay blame on their predecessors, with the hope that it gives them the time they need to address the immediate problems. Inevitably, governors in these circumstances get more involved in the budget process at the very outset than they might ordinarily choose to be. For Henry Bellmon it was a particularly wrenching experience. Oklahoma had been living through an oil boom with income from the severance tax and from petroleum-related tax increases, producing plentiful revenues for the state and allowing for taxes to be reduced a dozen times. But when the oil boom played out and revenues declined, and after surplus revenues had been used to avoid a tax increase, the new governor and legislature had to find a way to make up a large revenue shortfall. This became Bellmon's central focus during his first legislative session and for months thereafter. Other major issues that the governor wanted to tackle had to be deferred. It took even longer for Benjamin Cayetano (D-HI), who served two terms. Economic revival and balancing the state budget overshadowed other issues for six out of his eight years.[64]

For governors under fiscal duress, budget involvement usually means that they have to lay aside any plans to increase funding for their priorities. Such plans have to be put on hold. Bill Clinton (D-AR) ran into a fiscal brick wall at the outset of his first term. He had hoped, right from the beginning, to have made a dramatic difference in public education, but "the economy finally caught up with us," he recalled.[65] The downturn for Harry Hughes occurred two years after he took office in Maryland. Facing a deficit in 1981, Hughes scaled back plans for new spending—no pay raise for state employees, no increase in welfare benefits, and no new state aid for education, all of which he would have favored were it not for the recession.[66]

The first resort of most governors who face deficits is to cut the budget. This can be extremely agonizing—for Republicans as well as Democrats. During his eight years as governor, Ohio's Voinovich had to cut the state budget four times. "Those were very bad times," he remembers. "I went through hell." Typical was the action of McGreevey in New Jersey. At his first cabinet meeting, he blocked as much of the new spending as he felt he could and ordered department heads to make cuts of 5 percent across the board. Then he had to lay off 600 technical workers; gut the "smart growth" office; freeze aid to municipalities; reduce college funding; end future school construction programs; and postpone dam repairs, park improvements, and new tuition assistance grants. McGreevey's campaign promise to eliminate tolls on the Garden State Parkway had to be postponed, because "we simply couldn't afford to lose the revenue."[67]

For Edgar, the budgetary pain continued for a while. He had no cushion at all when the recession hit in 1991. Every month the Illinois revenue estimates came in, and every month they were lower. Edgar had to keep cutting the budget. He did not give higher education, which was especially close to his heart, any increase. The legislature took issue with his continuing cuts and the governor kept explaining, "the money is just not there." Halfway through the year, he had to call the legislature back to Springfield to cut the entire budget again. Arne Carlson had to take money from Minnesota state agencies to pay for the governor's office. "It was that bad," he remembered.

If governors are willing to raise taxes, they may not have to cut as deeply. And if they raise taxes, they can produce the wherewithal to fund at least a few of their initiatives. Most governors, however, are against raising taxes, particularly if they have promised not to do so in their election campaigns. Mario Cuomo had promised not to raise any of the three broad-based taxes in New York. So his agenda became one of "survival," which meant that government had "to do more with less."[68] A decline in revenues in Texas faced Clements with the choice: cut services to meet revenues or raise taxes by $5.8 billion to support current service levels. He chose to cut services.[69] A similar choice faced Georgia governor Zell Miller in 1991. He, too, determined not to raise taxes.[70]

No governor tried to hold the no-taxes line more than Democrat Dukakis in his first term as governor of Massachusetts. He pledged himself to resisting any tax hikes. Even though Democratic legislative leaders urged the new governor to face reality and abandon his pledge, he held fast, telling reporters, "We have made a commitment and we have the will to keep it," even though he didn't know how. Eventually, Dukakis did agree to raise taxes, along with making substantial cuts in state services, including welfare.[71]

Other governors at some point also find that they have no recourse. Elected on a pledge not to raise taxes, Norman Bangerter (R-UT) managed to keep his pledge during his first two years, despite a decline in revenues. Only when the budgetary situation continued to worsen did he propose a tax increase.[72] During George Nigh's (D-OK) first term, Oklahoma had an oil boom. He lowered taxes. During his second term, Oklahoma had an oil bust. He raised taxes.[73]

The conventional wisdom is that governors run a great risk if they raise taxes. Nevertheless, most governors have managed to survive the tax increases they initiated. Marc Racicot (R-MT), for example, inherited a $200 million budget deficit. He cut the budget by $99 million and raised taxes by $99 million. His strategy worked, and he had a smooth two terms as governor. Indeed, he may have been the most popular governor in Montana's history, with approval ratings climbing as high as 83 percent and at 70 percent when he left office in 2000.[74] New Jersey's Kean never suffered with the public because of tax increases. His approval ratings stayed consistently high. When he reluctantly consented to raising taxes, he not only closed the budget gap but also helped create future surpluses that would fund his initiatives.[75] The governor had ensured that there would be money in the bank with which to work.

Other governors have had to postpone their policy ideas or scuttle the more expensive ones. They believed themselves to be hogtied. When he was elected governor, Booth Gardner (D-WA) was committed to raising teacher salaries and reducing class size in the early grades. But projected revenues were not congenial to his plans. He had to conclude that after meeting fixed costs and costs previously mandated by the legislature, he would have to make incremental improvements rather than rely on "some bold, short-time expansion of the state budget."[76] When Indiana ran out of money, O'Bannon could not only not start anything new or respond to opportunities that arose, he couldn't even grapple with the normal operations of state government.[77] Carlson had to shy away from proposing policy changes that cost money for practically his entire two terms as governor of Minnesota.[78] When the economy goes south during the final years of a governor's administration, as in the case of Jim Hodges (D-SC), it is disheartening. In looking back on his four years as governor of South Carolina, Hodges recalled regretfully that "there were things that we wanted to accomplish that we didn't."

If they cannot fund their initiatives, governors then will pursue policies that don't require funds. Carlson took on restructuring property taxes, a bear of an issue in Minnesota and everywhere else. Engler also put property tax reform on the front burner in Michigan. And with the economy soft and people anxious, Engler felt that he had to try to reform the fiscal system as well. The poor economy helped shape Engler's initiatives from 1991 to 1994. He advocated a "taxpayers' agenda" that called for cutting taxes and downsizing government. He pushed welfare reform and continued with budget-cutting programs until the economy began to recover. His triumph occurred when voters approved his plan to cut property taxes and raise the sales tax in order to finance the public schools in Michigan.[79]

For Thornburgh, a poor economy put pressure on him to develop an economic development plan for Pennsylvania, which would reduce the cost of state government and keep taxes down. Harry Hughes limited the objectives of his administration when there was a dearth of money. He wanted changes for Maryland that he considered "important," but "not costly"—raising the penalties and lowering the threshold for convicting drunken drivers, establishing a state energy corporation, requiring motorcycle riders to wear protective helmets, and removing state circuit court judges from the partisan election process.[80]

If the governors who served during the 1980s and 1990s were limited by the economic and fiscal conditions in the nation and in their states, toward the end of the period under study the governors were in even worse shape. David Paterson attributes the recent plight of governors and legislatures to "a culture of overspending." As he looked at New York's fiscal history from an executive perspective, he was bipartisan in his criticism:

> The Democrats were in charge of the first half of that trend, and we were accused of taxing and spending; and the Republicans were in charge for the second half, and they did it with borrow and spend, but where we agreed was, we kept spending.[81]

To keep the budget in technical balance, the governor and the legislature in New York managed from year to year to close the expenditure-revenue gap by moving money from off-budget accounts and other revenues into the general fund.[82] Other states worked in similar fashion. They resorted to a whole bagful of tricks and gimmicks to balance their budgets and to push debt into the future.

As of 2010, California was in the midst of a systemic crisis, accelerated by the recession that began in 2009 but grounded on "two decades of poor judgment, reckless mismanagement, and irresponsibility."[83] As the year drew to an end, the office of legislative analyst estimated that the state would face annual shortfalls reaching $20 billion each year through 2015–2016. Governor-elect Jerry Brown, who was well aware of the state's terrible fiscal situation when he declared for a third term, after being briefed, commented that the fiscal situation was "as bad as you could imagine."[84] Although California's problems were in "a league of their own," similar pressure and similar behavior also existed elsewhere. The Pew Center on the States, in a November 2009 report, indicated that in addition to California, nine other states were in bad fiscal shape. They were, in order of peril: Arizona, Rhode Island, Michigan, Oregon, Nevada, Florida, New Jersey, Illinois, and Wisconsin. Colorado, Georgia, Kentucky, New York, and Hawaii were not far behind.[85] Only a few states—such as Montana, North Dakota, and Idaho—were without serious budget problems.

Other Conditions and Events

Governors have no control over the economic or fiscal conditions that befall them. Yet their potential agendas are significantly affected by such conditions. Even less predictable happenings can make a difference to the policymaking leadership of the nation's governors. Some events are unexpected, such as natural and other catastrophes that enable governors to respond forcefully and win public approval or to respond inadequately and sink in the polls.

In 1978 Dukakis faced a once-in-a-century blizzard that dumped nearly three feet of snow and paralyzed Massachusetts for a week. The governor quickly took charge and was perceived by the public as forceful and effective. Dukakis benefitted from sustained media coverage that most elected public officials can only dream about.[86] Thornburgh also came out ahead, as a result of his effective handling of a near nuclear disaster at Three Mile Island. The credit that he gained with Pennsylvania's public helped him throughout his tenure. Shortly after Oklahoma's Keating was sworn in as governor, the bombing of the federal building in Oklahoma City occurred. "The public had a view of me as a crisis manager," he said. That perception carried forward and proved to be hugely useful to him. After his response to the bombing, Keating couldn't seem to do anything wrong, as far as Oklahoma citizens were concerned.

Crises are by no means a single-edged sword. Governors can lose as well as gain. Despite enabling governors to reap benefits from their management, crises can also sap energies that otherwise would be devoted to policy. Events over which governors have no control, at the very least, distract them from what they had intended to do. During his four years as governor of West Virginia, Wise had to handle eleven federal- and thirty state-declared disasters. It put a strain on his policy leadership. Voinovich had to respond to a prison riot, as well as a 1997 Ohio supreme court school-funding decision that upset his calculations.[87] In Oregon a former mill worker, angry at her position on the spotted owl, filed three petitions to recall Roberts as governor. Although none of the petitions made it to the ballot, they did receive enough support from the public to hurt the governor politically. In her opinion, it was "distracting, politically demeaning, and totally disrespectful." Her standing with the legislature took a hit. In South Carolina, Hodges felt that he had to deal with the ongoing controversy of the Confederate flag flying from the capitol dome. He managed to resolve the dispute, but the battle "stole the political oxygen out of the air," making it difficult for him to accomplish what he had intended to do. Few events are as debilitating as the automobile accident that almost killed Corzine halfway through his term as governor of New Jersey. It took him months to recuperate and resulted in him having little time and little energy for legislative initiatives. During a relatively long hiatus, the absence of gubernatorial leadership in New Jersey was telling.

Notes

1. Joseph A. Schlesinger, "The Politics of the Executive," in *Politics in the American States*, ed. Herbert Jacob and Kenneth N. Vines (Boston: Little, Brown, 1965); see also Thad L. Beyle, "The Institutionalized Powers of the Governorship," *Comparative State Politics Newsletter* 9 (1988): 29.
2. Thad L. Beyle, "The Evolution of the Gubernatorial Office: United States Governors over the Twentieth Century," in *A Legacy of Leadership: Governors and American History*, ed. Clayton McClure Brooks (Philadelphia: University of Pennsylvania Press, 2008), 207.
3. Thomas H. Kean, *The Politics of Inclusion* (New York: Free Press, 1988), 63.
4. George J. Marlin, *Squandered Opportunities: New York's Pataki Years* (South Bend, IN: St. Augustine's Press, 2006), 67–68.
5. Mike Shropshire and Frank Schaefer, *The Thorny Rose of Texas: An Intimate Portrait of Governor Ann Richards* (New York: Carol, 1994), 226.
6. David R. Morgan, Robert E. England, and George G. Humphreys, *Oklahoma Politics and Policies* (Lincoln: University of Nebraska Press, 1991), 102–3.

7. Blair Lee, in Alan Rosenthal, *Governors and Legislatures: Contending Powers* (Washington, DC: CQ Press, 1990), 134.

8. Coleman B. Ransone Jr., "The Governor, the Legislature, and Public Policy," *State Governments* (Summer 1979): 118.

9. Eric B. Herzik, "Policy Agendas and Gubernatorial Leadership," in *Gubernatorial Leadership and State Policy*, ed. Eric B. Herzik and Brent W. Brown (Westport, CT: Greenwood Press, 1991), 27.

10. Richard W. Riley, "Overcoming Restrictions on Gubernatorial Authority: The Unique Problem of Some Governors," in *Governors on Governing*, ed. Robert D. Behn (Lanham, MD: University Press of America, 1991), 33.

11. Dan Durning, "Education Reform in Arkansas: The Governor's Role in Policymaking," in Herzik and Brown, *Gubernatorial Leadership and State Policy*, 123.

12. Jan Reid, "The Case of Ann Richards: Women in Gubernatorial Office," in Brooks, *A Legacy of Leadership*, 190.

13. J. H. Hatfield, *Fortunate Son: George W. Bush and the Making of an American President* (New York: Soft Skull, 2001), 146–47.

14. Penny M. Miller, *Kentucky Politics and Government* (Lincoln: University of Nebraska Press, 1994), 140–45.

15. The following paragraphs are drawn from Alan Rosenthal, *Engines of Democracy* (Washington, DC: CQ Press, 2009), 275–80.

16. Ralph Wright, *Inside the Statehouse* (Washington, DC: CQ Press, 2005), 88.

17. Donald A. Gross, "The Policy Role of Governors," in Herzik and Brown, *Gubernatorial Leadership and State Policy*, 3.

18. Clark D. Ahlberg and Daniel P. Moynihan, "Changing Governors—and Policies," in *The American Governor in Behavioral Perspective*, ed. Thad Beyle and J. Oliver Williams (New York: Harper & Row, 1972), 97.

19. John Martin in Alan Rosenthal, ed., *The Governor and the Legislature: Eagleton's 1987 Symposium on the State of the States* (New Brunswick, NJ: Eagleton Institute of Politics, 1988), 55.

20. Brendan Byrne interview, Governors Project archives, Eagleton Institute of Politics, Rutgers University, October 30, 2007.

21. Dick Codey interview, Eagleton Institute of Politics Governors Program, Rutgers University, March 23, 2010.

22. Miller, *Kentucky Politics and Government*, 136, 138.

23. Lee Bernick and Charles W. Wiggins, "Executive Legislative Relations: The Governor's Role as Chief Legislator," in Herzik and Brown, *Gubernatorial Leadership and State Policy*, 88–89.

24. The only state that was not compelled by an initiative, or threat of an initiative, to adopt term limits but that did so of its own accord, was Louisiana. Here the legislature decided to enact term limits in response to what it perceived to be the popular will.

25. Karl T. Kurtz, Bruce Cain, and Richard G. Niemi, eds., *Institutional Change in American Politics: The Case of Term Limits* (Ann Arbor: University of Michigan Press, 2007).

26. Greg Lemon, *Blue Man in a Red State: Montana's Governor Brian Schweitzer and the New Western Populism* (Helena, MT: TwoDot, 2008), 99.

27. Laura A. van Assendelft, *Governors, Agenda Setting, and Divided Government* (Lanham, MD: University Press of America, 1997), 74–75.

28. Tom Loftus, *The Art of Legislative Politics* (Washington, DC: CQ Press, 1994), 67.

29. National Governors Association, *Transition and the New Governor: A Planning Guide* (Washington, DC: National Governors Association, 1998), 32.

30. Malcolm E. Jewell, "The Governor as a Legislative Leader," in Beyle and Williams, *The American Governor in Behavioral Perspective*, 136.

31. Alan Ehrenhalt, "Butch's Battle," *Governing* (June 2009): 12.

32. Herzik, "Policy Agendas and Gubernatorial Leadership," 28.

33. Ehrenhalt, "Butch's Battle," 11.

34. Discussion with Bill Castner, former chief counsel to Governor Corzine, November 11, 2009.

35. Response from survey.

36. Thornburgh in Rosenthal, *The Governor and the Legislature*, 39–40.

37. Alvin S. Felzenberg, *Governor Tom Kean* (New Brunswick, NJ: Rutgers University Press, 2006), 199.

38. Kean, *The Politics of Inclusion* 84–85.

39. Bill Richardson, *Between Worlds: The Making of an American Life* (New York: Penguin Group, 2005), 302.

40. Lou Cannon, "Preparing for the Presidency: The Political Education of Ronald Reagan," in Brooks, *A Legacy of Leadership*, 147.

41. Carolyn Barta, *Bill Clements: Texian to His Toenails* (Austin, TX: Eakin Press, 1996), 339, 405.

42. Troy Senik, "Who Killed California?" *National Affairs* (Fall 2009): 55–56.

43. Joe Mathews and Mark Paul, *California Crackup* (Berkeley: University of California Press, 2010), 80–81.

44. Pew Center on the States, *Beyond California: States in Fiscal Peril* (Washington, DC: Pew Center on the States, 2009), 65.

45. Lou Cannon, *Governor Reagan* (New York: Public Affairs, 2003), 335.

46. Mathews and Paul, *California Crackup*, 63.

47. Quoted in *New York Times*, October 11, 2009.

48. Senik, "Who Killed California?" 55–58.

49. Pew Center on the States, *Beyond California*, 42.

50. Senik, "Who Killed California?" 63.

51. Norton Long, "After the Voting Is Over," in Beyle and Williams, *The American Governor in Behavioral Perspective*, 85.

52. George R. Ariyoshi, *With Obligations to All* (Honolulu: Ariyoshi Foundation, 1997), 153.

53. Charles Kenney and Robert L. Turner, *Dukakis: An American Odyssey* (Boston: Houghton Mifflin, 1988), 194–95.

54. Richard Gaines and Michael Segal, *Dukakis and the Reform Impulse* (Boston: Quinlan Press, 1987), 222.

55. Barta, *Bill Clements*, 336.

56. Andrew E. Stoner, *Legacy of a Governor: The Life of Indiana's Frank O'Bannon* (Bloomington, IN: Rooftop, 2006), 239–241, 305–306.

57. Ahlberg and Moynihan, "Changing Governors—and Policies," 97–98.

58. Robert S. McElvaine, *Mario Cuomo: A Biography* (New York: Scribner's, 1988), 310.

59. Marlin, *Squandered Opportunities: New York's Pataki Years,* 60.

60. James Richardson, *Willie Brown: A Biography* (Berkeley: University of California Press, 1996), 295.

61. Richard F. Celeste, "The Governor as CEO," in Behn, *Governors on Governing*, 99.

62. Joe Hallett, "The Voinovich Years 1991–1998," *Plain Dealer,* January 3, 1999.

63. James E. McGreevey, *The Confession* (New York: HarperCollins, 2006), 411–13.

64. Benjamin J. Cayetano, *Ben: A Memoir From Street Kid to Governor* (Honolulu: Watermark, 2009), 474.

65. Charles F. Allen and Jonathan Portis, *The Comeback Kid: The Life and Career of Bill Clinton* (New York: Carol, 1992), 60.

66. Harry Roe Hughes, *My Unexpected Journey* (Charleston, SC: History Press, 2006), 151.

67. McGreevey, *The Confession*, 412–13.

68. Cuomo, quoted in McElvaine, *Mario Cuomo: A Biography*, 310–11.

69. Barta, *Bill Clements*, 339–40.

70. Richard Hyatt, *Zell: The Governor Who Gave Georgia HOPE* (Macon, GA: Mercer University Press, 1997), 266.

71. Kenney and Turner, *Dukakis*, 90, 108; Gaines and Segal, *Dukakis and the Reform Impulse*, 117–20.

72. Rosenthal, *Governors and Legislatures*, 99.

73. Response from survey.

74. Lemon, *Blue Man in a Red State*, 59.

75. Felzenberg, *Governor Tom Kean*, 210.

76. Booth Gardner, "Schools for the 21st Century," in Behn, *Governors on Governing*, 122.

77. Stoner, *Legacy of a Governor*, 306.

78. Daniel J. Elazar, Virginia Gray, and Wyman Spano, *Minnesota Politics and Government* (Lincoln: University of Nebraska Press, 1999), 131.

79. Gleaves Whitney, *John Engler: The Man, the Leader & the Legacy* (Chelsea, MI: Sleeping Bear, 2002), 293–94.

80. Hughes, *My Unexpected Journey*, 151.

81. Rob Gurwitt, "The Ordeal of David Paterson," *Governing* (March 2009): 30.

82. Ibid., 32.

83. Senik, "Who Killed California?" 54.

84. *State Net Capitol Journal*, November 15, 2010, 2.

85. Pew Center on the States, *Beyond California*.

86. Kenney and Turner, *Dukakis*, 107.

87. Hallett, "The Voinovich Years."

3

What Governors Bring to the Table

IT IS UP TO GOVERNORS to exploit the constitutional and institutional advantages available to them. And it is up to them to surmount the political, economic, and circumstantial obstacles that stand in their way. Whether they manage or not depends in large part on the stuff governors bring to office with them.

A few governors demonstrate personal shortcomings and are compelled to leave office. Whatever they may have achieved by way of policy in their interrupted administrations tends to be overlooked because of their dramatic exits. Evan Mecham (R-AZ), John Rowland (R-CT), Eliot Spitzer (D-NY), Jim McGreevey (D-NJ), and Rod Blagojevich (D-IL) are governors who had to leave their positions as a result of criminal or other scandals in which they were implicated. Even with their failings, these individuals were not without policy influence when in office. They, too, had policy successes before coming under fire and having to leave. The large majority of governors, however, serve out their terms. Most run for reelection if they can.

A new governor, having won a statewide election, is welcomed to office with good will. Legislators cannot fail to be impressed; one thing they understand is votes. They are impressed by winners—governors who win in landslides, especially, but even those who just squeak by. Governors may act as if they have a mandate from the electorate, as Angus King (I-ME) points out. But for their part, legislators don't think in terms of gubernatorial mandates, only that they are dealing with the governor. King was reelected overwhelmingly, but the legislature did not regard his victory as a mandate for one initiative or another. He had to make his case. "Hey guys, I just won by a huge margin, I mean, trust me," is the message Jim Edgar (R-IL) tried to send to the Illinois legislature. "But they didn't buy it," so he had to do it the old-fashioned way, persuading lawmakers of the merits of his initiatives rather than of the mandate he won in being reelected by the voters of Illinois. At least as governors experience their relationships to the legislature, their election victories are not mandates for one policy or another.

Personalities

In politics friendships matter, so amiability should be a valuable personality characteristic for a governor. No doubt it helps if governors are likeable. Many are. Take Frank O'Bannon (D-IN). He is described as a gentleman, low key, genuine, and well liked by everybody.[1] But not being likeable doesn't disqualify governors who have other attributes. Before becoming governor of New Jersey, McGreevey had gotten a reputation among insiders as "a young man in a hurry." He had to compensate for the reputation he earned on the way up, so he made especial efforts to win over those who were inclined to dislike him.[2] McGreevey held his own, although he would never have won a popularity contest. A governor doesn't have to be personable, as long as he or she has other qualifications. John Engler (R-MI) was not particularly well liked, but he was very effective nonetheless. People didn't take to his style or persona, and he did not appear to care. His lack of popularity did not prevent him from dominating policymaking in Michigan during his twelve years as governor.[3]

Whereas many governors enjoy the friendships that come by way of politics and endeavor to cultivate closer relationships with legislators, a number of governors are standoffish when it comes to socializing or connecting with legislators. Their focus is almost entirely on business. Dick Codey (D-NJ), a legislative leader and former governor of New Jersey, characterized Jim Florio (D-NJ) as someone who talked policy almost around the clock. Typically at leadership meetings, the conventional New Jersey governor would start off with, "Did you see the Giants game, the Mets game, or whatever?" Florio would start with, "Dick, let me talk to you about the gun bill." It was strictly policy, despite his being Italian American, being from Brooklyn, being an amateur fighter. Small talk was not part of Florio's persona. Codey summed up, ". . . and you had to accept it."[4] Others adapted to Florio's style, not expecting him to behave like one of the boys or be just like them.

"By far the most common criticism voiced during my tenure," wrote Dick Thornburgh (R-PA), "related to my personality and style of governing." Thornburgh was thought to be aloof and definitely was not considered by people in politics to be very sociable.[5] Yet, he governed effectively. It was his way and not the way of the Harrisburg political community. Bob Graham (D-FL) took a similar tack. He studied, learned the issues, and worked to persuade others of the rightness of his position. Personal friendships and loyalties were much less important to him than the merits of each and every case.[6] Governors who are wonkish do risk estrangement from legislative leaders and legislative rank and file, who tend to be more political. Parris Glendening (D-MD), a self-described policy wonk, insisted that good policy could be made to be good politics. He was not a glad-hander and not comfortable with small talk. "I was not loved," he recalls. Indeed, Mike Miller, the senate president, once referred to Glendening as "alien." But the governor did know the legislative process and he had the political skill to steer his political initiatives through it.

If there is one characteristic that governors seem to have in common, it is self-confidence. Simply put, by the time individuals achieve gubernatorial office, if not long before, they have accomplished quite a bit in politics or in other areas of life and have developed a positive sense of self. If they are endowed with fame, fortune, or family, as a number are, they are likely to have an extra dollop of self-confidence. Arnold Schwarzenegger (R-CA), with body-building, hit films, and *Terminator* stature already under his belt, began his administration with understandable bravado. Jesse Ventura (I-MN), the professional wrestler, and Jon Corzine (D-NJ), the managing partner of Goldman Sachs, shared the strong belief that they were up to the job, whatever the job. Bill Weld (R-MA) was the nineteenth Weld to go to Harvard, where two buildings were named for the family.[7] Pierre (Pete) du Pont (R-DE), scion of a chemical manufacturing empire, also took on the job with no reservations about his ability to master it. Joe Brennan (D-ME) remembers an occasion when he had been governor and was in Washington, D.C., with du Pont, who was then a congressman from Delaware after having been governor, and Jay Rockefeller, who was then a U.S. senator from West Virginia. Du Pont and Rockefeller were in the midst of an argument about some political point, when Rockefeller pulled back, looked du Pont in the eye, and with a trace of a smile on his face, said, "Pete, if it wasn't for your name, you wouldn't be here." Du Pont's wealth didn't hurt his career, nor did Rockefeller's hurt his.

A sense of personal strength is not surprising. Governors have been elected to the highest office in the state. Most have already served in other elective office and already have had a chance to influence public policy. During their stints as governors, they are likely to add to earlier achievements. Their self-confidence grows with their experience. A can-do personality is nourished by achievement, which further strengthens self-esteem. Former governors who were surveyed or interviewed for this study overwhelmingly saw their careers and accomplishments in a positive light. Such an attitude can, of course, go too far. If governors lose touch with reality or if healthy self-confidence becomes hubris, then they risk derailment.[8] Gubernatorial self-confidence is linked to a fundamental sense of optimism. "Effective leaders," according to Florida's Graham, "truly believe that they have an opportunity to make things better."[9] Governors are optimists; they feel that they can exercise control. They have the power to do so. And nearly all of them have the abilities and skills to govern effectively. These abilities and skills have been acquired during their prior careers, on the road to gubernatorial office.

Experience

Despite the foregoing mention of governors who came from the private sector or from the field of entertainment, relatively few arrive without prior political experience. Thad Beyle, a political scientist who has been tracking governors for many years, examined their experience from 1900 to 2006 (a period during which the states elected 1,005 men and women to the office of governor) and found that only 10 percent had no prior experience as elected officials. Only 16 percent could be labeled pure amateurs in a more recent period.[10]

These political amateurs often come from business backgrounds, including a number from positions as CEOs. Business might be considered useful experience, especially since a governor frequently is compared to the CEO of a company. Bill Clements (R-TX) exemplifies the governor as CEO. Coming from a big business background, he saw himself as the chief executive officer. For him, state government was just another big business.[11] He stands in sharp contrast to Dolph Briscoe, another governor and a former Texas legislator. Clements wanted to shake up the system, whereas Briscoe was comfortable with the way things worked in Austin. Briscoe got along with business lobbyists at the capitol, whereas Clements told them to stay away from his office. Briscoe was typical; Clements was an outsider who rejected traditional political practice.[12] Experts are of the view that governors who have developed skills running large businesses will be better able to run the departments and agencies of the executive branch. But because the governor has to manage does not mean that a manager has to be governor.

In their relationship to one another as policymakers, however, the governor is not a CEO and the legislature is not a board of directors, as the two branches are portrayed on occasion. Thornburgh recalled the observation of his predecessor, who had gone right from business to the office of governor. He told Thornburgh: "I thought that I was the CEO and they were the board of directors, but I never had to deal with a board of directors in which half the members were working for the competition.[13] Whereas the CEO is definitely the boss, the governor is not—at least in terms of dealing with a legislature in a constitutional system of separated powers. The house speaker, Tim Ford, described Kirk Fordice (R-MS): "He's used to getting his way in a business world by being the boss and I think he's learned that's not the way the state has to operate."[14]

Corzine's chairmanship at Goldman Sachs did not prepare him for politics in Trenton. At first he insisted that it did, but after leaving office he acknowledged that being a CEO doesn't equip anyone for the grind of governing.[15] Business experience can be helpful, particularly if it is leavened by experience in politics or elective office. Maine's King had varied positions, including that of a businessman. But because of his involvement in politics, he was never under the misimpression that governing is just like running a business. He knew just what he was up against. Another governor with political and business experiences, both of which prepared him well, was Mitt Romney (R-MA). His work heading up the organizing committee at the 2002 Winter Olympics and at a major consulting firm,

Bain & Co., put him in good stead when he became governor.[16] A number of governors have been in business and also served in legislatures. The combination seems to have been strong preparation for those who have gone this route. Victor Atiyeh (R-OR), for instance, ran his family's rug business before he was elected to the legislature. By the time he became governor, he had thirty-five years in business and twenty in the legislature. "That is the kind of background corporations look for when they select their chief executives," wrote Atiyeh. Although such qualifications may not play a part in the electorate's choice for governor,[17] they do provide worthwhile training for executive office.

Public office prior to the governorship would appear to be beneficial, but not all public offices provide equally useful training. Perhaps one of the least useful avenues of preparation is law enforcement. Jennifer Granholm (D-MI) was a federal prosecutor and also a state attorney general. The combination does not appear to have helped her relate to the Michigan legislature. A number of other governors have had prior careers as prosecutors. Thornburgh of Illinois has reflected on his experience in this field. In fact, his record as U.S. attorney, prosecuting public corruption, including several prominent Democratic legislators, helped propel him to the governorship. "The Pennsylvania General Assembly was somewhat chastened and defensive when I took office," he wrote.[18] Nevertheless, once his administration got under way, his earlier prosecution of legislators did not seem to handicap him. That may be as a result of Thornburgh's ability to resist generalizing from the prosecutions of legislators he had undertaken to the entire legislature. Despite a few corrupt legislators, he "didn't want to tar them all with the same brush."

Weld also made an adjustment, after seven years with the U.S. Department of Justice, including a stint as U.S. attorney for Massachusetts, through which he gained national recognition for fighting public corruption. He had even conducted a criminal investigation of Whitey Bulger, the brother of the senate president. In fact, in his campaign for governor, he ran on a platform that was highly critical of the legislature. But upon taking office he soon realized that he had to totally change his approach. As prosecutor, Weld recalled, he had to isolate himself from others; as governor, he had to reach out. He learned the difference between the "terror power" of the prosecutor and the "benefit power" of the governor soon after the election, when he started getting telephone calls from supporters asking for help. Weld left his old office behind and adapted to his new one.

As far as elective public office is concerned, service in the U.S. Senate or U.S. House does not appear to be as valuable preparation for the office of governor as holding an elective position in-state. Corzine was first elected to the U.S. Senate but was frustrated in a legislative role. He chose to give up his seat in Washington to run for the governorship. Neither his experience on Wall Street nor his tour as a senator in Washington, D.C., prepared him for dealing with politics, and particularly legislative politics, in the Garden State. By contrast, holding office within the state holds out the promise of more applicable political learning before becoming governor. Edgar, who was elected to the Illinois legislature and as secretary of state before being elected governor, describes himself as a "creature of state government." He knew the people and he knew the issues, both of which put him in good stead later on. Andrew Cuomo (D-NY) became intimately acquainted with Albany when his father governed and later as attorney general. He was ready to take over when his time came:

> I know these guys. I know them very well. I've played with them. I know this game. I know it extraordinarily well.[19]

Within a state, the office of lieutenant governor is among the natural stepping stones to the office of governor. With few exceptions (such as Texas), the position of lieutenant governor is a weak one, dependent on the governor for authority. But this position gives incumbents a chance to observe or engage in policymaking processes and is useful in that respect. However, executive positions, such as mayor, may not be the best preparation for governors. Being a mayor, and especially of a city with a strong executive and a weak council, does not equip one to deal with an independent state legislature. Mel Martinez (R-FL), as mayor of Tampa, could issue commands and make things happen overnight. He couldn't do the same with the Florida legislature and had to figure out what levers to pull if he wanted to exercise influence on the legislative branch of government. William Donald Schaefer (D-MD) came to the office of governor from that of mayor of Baltimore. He didn't trust anyone in Annapolis and had little tolerance for a legislature that might try to slow the process by which Schaefer was used to getting things done.[20] In Annapolis, like in Baltimore, Schaefer tried to steamroll anything that got in his way. It didn't work well with the Maryland legislature, and as it turned out, Schaefer was much happier being mayor of Baltimore than governor of Maryland.[21] Pete Wilson of California got used to being mayor of San Diego, where he dominated a deferential city council. When he arrived in Sacramento, he expected legislators to show him similar deference. But they didn't, and it took him a while to adapt to the rough-and-tumble of legislative politics and all the deal making that was required.[22]

There are exceptions, however. At least one governor with mayoral experience appeared to benefit as a result. George Voinovich was mayor of Cleveland, and also a county commissioner and state auditor, before becoming governor. He also had had a four-year stint in the Ohio house earlier in his career. Whether or not the Cleveland mayor typically dominated over the city council, Voinovich as mayor quickly learned the lesson that governing requires working with others. He made it a practice to go to the office of the leader of the city council rather than expect that the leader would come to him. That was good preparation for the office of governor.

In the view of governors, themselves, the best preparation for their policymaking role is having served previously in the legislature.[23] Of the governors from 1980 through 2010, who are the subjects of this study, 52 percent had served previously in the senate or house, or both chambers, of their state legislature. All four governors of Florida and Vermont had been legislators, as had five out of six governors of Idaho and West Virginia, and four out of five from Minnesota.

This is not to say that a governor cannot succeed in policymaking without first being in the legislature, only that it helps. When asked what had prepared him for working with the Maine legislature as governor, Joseph Brennan (D-ME) mentioned his eight years in the legislature, including six in leadership. Mike Beebe (D-AR) served twenty years in the senate, where he achieved a leadership role before being term-limited out. Then, as attorney general, he continued to function as de facto legislative liaison for Governor Mike Huckabee (R-AR). According to one journalist: "There are numerous explanations for why Beebe has done so well [as governor], but one seems to stand out. He is the first Arkansas governor with legislative experience elected in more than 30 years . . . ."[24]

The major benefit of prior experience in the legislature is knowledge, and knowledge in several arenas. In Beebe's case, former governor David Pryor (D-AR) explained that "he knows more about the governing process, the levers of power and the budget than anyone [in the legislature]."[25] Knowledge of the budget and the budget process, from the legislative perspective, is an asset for any governor. A number of governors, such as Benjamin Cayetano (D-HI), Roy Romer (D-CO), and Mike Hayden (R-KA), served on budget committees while in the legislature. Hayden recalled that as chair of the ways and means committee, he got into the minutia of the budget. He continued to do so as governor, although probably he should have been operating at 10,000 feet. "A lot of facts, in the end, didn't make a difference," said Hayden, "but I could discuss the budget with any legislator, even the chair of ways and means." That certainly helped him in the process. Furthermore, to understand the process, as many former-legislator governors do, is also to respect it. After being through it repeatedly, Frank Keating (R-OK) said, "I wouldn't dis it." This attitude is conducive to good executive-legislative relations.

Knowledge of the issues is another asset for an individual who is starting out, or even ending a four-year term, as governor. Knowing the issues and how they developed and changed and who is on which side is of tremendous help to a governor. Knowledge of government, particularly the departments and agencies of the executive branch, is another benefit of having been in the legislature. Zell Miller (D-GA) had been a legislator and then lieutenant governor and consequently "understood the inner workings of state government probably better than any governor" Georgia ever had.[26] Gerald Baliles (D-VA) prides himself on his understanding of state government that he acquired in the legislature and as attorney general. "When I got to the governor's office," he said, "I knew the state, the issues, and the people in the general assembly."

Engler is an exemplar of someone whose legislative service was the strongest preparation possible. He is quick to acknowledge how useful his background in the process, the rules, and the substance of issues had been to him. Probably the best example of how Engler was groomed for gubernatorial office by his two decades in the legislature was his handling of the Michigan state budget, as complex as any task faced by legislators and by governors. By the time he became governor, Engler knew the details of every program in the budget and how well these programs performed. He knew this because he had been working with the state budget for so many years.[27] It is important for governors to have an ability—partly instinctive and partly learned—to judge what can get done and how it can get done. Engler credits his legislative service for knowing just what is possible in various situations.

Probably as important as any other intelligence for a governor is that of knowing the legislators themselves—who they are, where they are from, and what they want. Governors who have come out of the legislature have had a real advantage here. George Deukmejian (R-CA) is described as being "more attuned to legislators and their egos than any of his modern predecessors or his successor." He was simply one of them.[28] Engler's twenty years in the Michigan legislature—as rank-and-file member and leader, and in the minority as well as majority—did much to shape him as governor. "I could walk in everybody's shoes," he reflected. Bob Wise (D-WV), who had been a member of both Congress and the West Virginia legislature, felt that he "knew the thought processes of legislators," because when he was one of them, he thought the same way that they did. As governor, Edgar of Illinois could also put himself in the shoes worn by legislators—worrying about how one of their votes could be taken out of their entire record and made the center of a media campaign against them.

In reviewing his experience in the legislature, Jim Hodges (D-SC) realized how valuable it was in giving him an understanding of "where they were coming from." As governor, he knew 170 legislators by name, which was a step in the right direction, although "it doesn't keep them from calling you a son of a bitch." Not only did he feel that he knew legislators' personalities, districts, and relationships, but he also felt he had "a real understanding of legislative leaders and the pressures they face." All of this was no guarantee, but it did make for understanding and ultimately the ability to figure out "how I can move legislators from opposition to support."

Having been one of them—a legislator, that is—does not guarantee that the experience works to the governor's advantage. A few governors are exceptions, individuals who have never been entirely comfortable while serving in the legislature. They didn't like the game as it was being played. No one had as shaky a beginning with the legislature as ex-legislator Mike

Dukakis (D-MA), who took office with a rhetorical bow to the Great and General Court, as the Massachusetts legislature is formally titled. Although he declared himself a product of the legislature, he did not think, feel, or act like a legislator and refused to take the legislative culture or legislators' needs into account. A former member of Dukakis's legislative staff, who was elected to the legislature the same year his former boss won his race for governor, recalls that he was ecstatic that he would be in the house "with his pal Mike down the hall in the corner office." But he soon found out that he could not rely on or have much contact with the governor. As he put it years later: "I couldn't get the time of day."[29] That was certainly not in keeping with a Massachusetts culture which at the time verged on cronyism.

Friends

Former legislators who ascend to gubernatorial office bring with them not only knowledge, but also friendships. The friendships come in handy, but again are no guarantee of success. If they have been out of the legislature too long before becoming governor, the friendships they thought they had may no longer exist. Wise had been in Congress for eighteen years, between his service in the legislature and his being elected governor of West Virginia. Having been out of the legislature and out of the state for some years, by the time he had been sworn in as governor, his relationships had cooled. Wise recalls, "Legislators can be cold to someone who has been in Washington for so long." Bob Ehrlich (R-MD) could reminisce about how he used to play Thursday night pick-up basketball with colleagues when he was a legislator in Annapolis. He went off to Congress in Washington, D.C., not many miles away. When he returned as governor, the basketball games had stopped and his popularity sagged. Democrats in the traditionally Democratic state neither expected nor welcomed a Republican as governor. "I thought I was going back to the place I had left, but no," Ehrlich declared. Annapolis had gotten more partisan and former ties had loosened. Most governors, however, have remained in their states and the ties are still close to legislators with whom they had served.

Since governors and legislators have different and, in some respects, competing roles, friendships do not always carry the day. But, at the very least, legislative friends will give the governor and his policy and budget proposals the benefit of the doubt. Personal relationships, cultivated when they were in the legislature, made life easier for both Engler and Bill Owens (R-CO). And Tony Earl (D-WI), who had made close friends when he served in the Wisconsin legislature, relied on them when he became governor. His political personality, and his enjoyment of politics, politicians, pinochle, and Pilsner, according to his friend and assembly speaker, Tom Loftus, continued to bolster his popularity with former colleagues when he was the chief executive.[30] For Gary Locke (D-WA), his eleven years in the legislature and the lasting friendships that resulted made governing easier. People who had served together were more inclined to try to resolve their differences.

Some governors, like Hayden and Ned McWherter (D-TN), were especially expert in cultivating and maintaining friendships with legislators. When he ran for governor of Kansas, Hayden involved fifty members of the house in his campaign, further solidifying his legislature connections. McWherter's close ties derived from his personal style when he was speaker and the length of time he held office. But they were solidified by his empathy for individual legislators and what they needed for themselves and their constituencies. Indeed, as governor, McWherter remained so close to his former colleagues that he was characterized by some as continuing to be speaker of the house rather than governor.[31]

Governors may make enemies of legislators as well as friends on their way to gubernatorial office. The relationship between Miller, when he was lieutenant governor, and Tom Murphy, the speaker, in Georgia, did not portend well when the former ascended to governor. The two men had clashed repeatedly, with Miller, as presiding officer and leader in the senate, representing that body's perspective and Murphy the house's perspective. Not only in Georgia, but throughout the states, senate and house leaders conflict with one another. It is natural. In many places, in fact, the divide between the two chambers has been greater than that between the two political parties. Yet, when Miller was sworn in as governor, Murphy switched gears. Respecting the office of governor, he reached out to Miller. He was no longer an antagonist. The relationship between the governor and the speaker became that of two independent policymaking leaders attempting to get along—and for the most part succeeding.[32]

Staff

Governors lean heavily on the legislative friendships they have made because of their own service in the senate or house, or otherwise. The "otherwise" might pertain to a relative in the legislature. In the case of New Mexico's Bruce King, it was his son, Gary, who was a representative when his father became governor. The son could be depended upon to keep an eye out for his father's administration in the house.[33] But the governor needs more than legislative friends and a legislative relative here and there. A few governors lean on their lieutenant governors for advice, and they benefit greatly. Weld, for example, came from outside the mainstream of Massachusetts politics. But his running mate, Paul Cellucci, had valuable experience inside. He was the one who counseled Weld on how to handle the legislature.

A governor needs more. To get his initiatives through the legislature and to be able to decide whether to sign or veto bills that emanate from the legislature, governors need a solid team to help them out. "There is nobody smart enough or who has enough time to do it all themselves," said Edgar of Illinois. Thus, staffing one's office is one of the first things new governors do.

Typically, somewhere within the governor's office a professional staff has particular responsibility for the administration's relations with the legislature. The point person here is given the generic title of legislative director by the National Governors Association. The role involves the following:

- Overseeing the development of the legislative program
- Coordinating the lobbying activities of the administration
- Negotiating with the legislature
- Coordinating department and agency proposals

- Mobilizing support for the governor's legislative program
- Advising the governor and members of the administration on probable legislative reaction to executive proposals
- Monitoring legislation
- Recommending whether to sign or veto legislation

The legislative director, according to the National Governors Association, also works closely with the budget and policy directors in the governor's office.[34]

The location of this directorate varies among the states and, to some extent, among individual governors from the same states. The survey undertaken for this study indicates that 35 percent of governors assigned this function to their legislative liaison, whereas 30 percent assigned it to their chief of staff and 6 percent had the counsel to the governor doing it. Another 25 percent had some combination of chief of staff, legislative liaison, and counsel responsible for legislative liaison. The job gets done according to how the governor wants it to be done, and the organization, assignments, and individual personnel are subject to change, even within a single administration. It is interesting to note, however, that Democratic governors are more inclined than Republican governors to lodge the liaison function with their chief of staff, at the control center in their office. The size of the staffs who work on legislative liaison also vary, mainly according to the size of the states. Large-state governors generally have more staff to do the job.

The main point is that governors tend to appoint people to these positions who have experience with the legislature. Some bring on board members of their staffs from the time they were members of the legislature. Engler brought over people who had worked for him in the senate; his top liaison as governor was his former administrative assistant. Others range farther. Brennan brought two assistant attorneys general with him from his prior position as attorney general. Wise hired the West Virginia house majority leader and a former senate president to work on his staff. Martin O'Malley (D-MD) gave the liaison job to a staffer who had worked earlier for the senate president and then for a previous Democratic governor. All of these staffers not only had knowledge of the legislature, but they had its respect as well.

Among the most experienced people who governors hire are legislators themselves. Some governors make their key appointments from these ranks. Republican Henry Bellmon, after his election, realized that he needed someone who had good rapport with the Democrats in the Oklahoma legislature, and yet someone who would be loyal to him. He found a former Republican senator with twenty-four years of experience.[35] After having served as speaker of the assembly, New Jersey's Tom Kean organized his office as governor with a troika arrangement. One of the top three was Cary Edwards, a former legislative leader, who was given responsibility as chief counsel for legislative affairs. Edwards had to work with a legislature controlled by the opposite party but still was able, according to Kean, "to craft an astounding series of legislative accomplishments."[36]

If a governor is lacking in legislative experience, it is imperative that he or she bring in people who do have legislative experience—as elected members or as key legislative staffers. Angus King, an independent, recalled that the first, fundamental decision he made after being elected was to bring on a mature legislative liaison team. He recruited a former Democratic legislator and a former Republican legislator, both of whom had served on the appropriations committee, as well as a former lobbyist for the association of Maine municipalities. The day after he was elected governor, Brian Schweitzer (D-MT) hired a twenty-six-year veteran of the legislature, who had been speaker and floor leader, as chief policy advisor and to work with the legislature.[37] In Texas, although Republican businessman Clements hired relatively few insiders, he did bring two former Democratic legislators on as legislative director and assistant director.[38]

Legislators and legislative staff would appear to be best positioned by virtue of their experience and their relationships. Nevertheless, some governors organize their offices and hire people who do not fit the conventional mold, but who turn out to be effective. When he became governor, Ronald Reagan knew virtually no one in the California legislature. Even so, he hired a businessman as his first legislative secretary. The appointment worked out, and the office was considered to be a strong one.[39] It took Florida's Bob Graham a few years to organize his legislative directorate, with Charlie Reed at the helm as chief legislative lobbyist and then chief of staff. Reed's experience was not in the legislature, but as a professional educator. Nonetheless, he proved to be a gem in the job and, unlike

Graham, had bear-hugging, back-slapping skills and was also adept at the political deal.[40]

A few governors, however, fail to make the kinds of appointments that can help them in their legislative dealings. They start out with people who have little experience with or understanding of the legislature. George Pataki's (R-NY) top aides at the outset had limited knowledge of how New York's state government worked. The only exception was an aide whose job was that of director of state operations instead of that of liaison to the legislature.[41] During the first years of his administration, Corzine also lacked staff with legislative experience in the governor's office. He was more intent on sending the message to Trenton's political community that he would do things differently. The first chief counsel, who in New Jersey typically spearheads legislative liaison, was neither a former legislator nor a former legislative staffer, but rather a federal prosecutor. At best, Corzine's administration was balkanized in its dealings with the legislature. It lacked a legislative quarterback and legislative heavyweights—people with close, long-term relationships, who knew how to get things done.[42]

After trial and error, governors do make personnel adjustments. Corzine's office staff was reshaped, and by the time he left, he had a chief counsel who for years had worked in the legislature and had served as chief of staff to the assembly speaker. It took Republican Fordice only one legislative session to realize that he needed "insiders" to compensate for his "outsider" approach to the Mississippi legislature. He brought two former Democratic legislators on board; they understood the process well and had excellent contacts.[43] The initial staff of Harry Hughes (D-MD) was also light on statehouse experience. But when legislators kept complaining that they were not getting enough personal attention from the governor's office, Hughes brought in a former member of the Maryland general assembly to take charge.[44] Barbara Roberts (D-OR) had what she regarded as a superb policy staff, which handled most of her office's dealings with the legislature. But her chief of staff was abrasive and not well-liked. She was replaced, but not until the third year of Roberts's term.

Having the right staff to deal with the legislature does not mean that governors can or do forsake personal involvement. When asked in the survey how much they were personally involved in dealings with the legislature and how much they relied on staff in their office, governors indicated a high degree of personal involvement. On a scale of 1 (involved personally) to 7 (relied mostly on staff), governors scored a mean of 3.07, closer to the personal-involvement than to the staff-reliance end of the scale. Only six governors indicated a greater reliance on staff than personal involvement (four of the six were Republicans), whereas in the case of eighteen governors the reliance on staff and themselves was equal. By contrast, forty governors indicated that they were more personally involved than staff-reliant. As might be expected, the longer governors were in office, the more likely they were to rely on staff. But even those in office longer than eight years continued to be personally involved in day-to-day legislative business. Most governors were like South Carolina's Hodges. They relied on staff for many of the day-to-day dealings with the legislature because, like him, they had "plenty of other things to do."

A few governors did delegate the most important matters to their staff. Reagan, as governor of California (and later as president), is a prime example of a chief executive whose practice was to delegate much of the operational business of office. He strongly preferred not to deal with detail. Lou Cannon, his biographer, wrote:

> Reagan was by inclination and sometimes by necessity a delegator. He performed best when he had a chief of staff who understood his modes of behavior and could fill in the details in a manner consistent with Reagan's objectives.

In these respects, the governor had a perfect team in Ed Meese, his chief of staff, and George Steffes, his legislative liaison.[45]

Although most governors give their staff pretty free rein, they stay in relative close touch with what they are doing. During his second administration, Dukakis had John Sasso as his chief secretary (as the chief of staff position is called in Massachusetts). Sasso strategized for Dukakis, spoke for him, and negotiated with legislative leaders for him.[46] In New Jersey, Kean used former legislator Cary Edwards as legislative spear carrier. Edwards made the most of his charge, taking control of the state budget and more than doubling the staff (to twenty-six assistant counsels) in his office.[47] And Bill Owens, in his eight years as governor of Colorado, had two strong and effective chiefs of staff who exercised considerable authority on his behalf. "Legislators could work with these chiefs of staff, because they knew the two of them spoke for me," Owens explained.

However much they delegated to staff, a number of governors, like King in New Mexico, chose to stay at the center of things, in part because they enjoyed the legislative process and the legislature. King, for example, used his knowledge of the body in which and the people with which he once served to great advantage. "I often said," he wrote in his memoirs, "that by looking at the name of the sponsor and the title of the bill I could get as good a general idea of its contents as many people would have after reading it." In briefing his department and agency heads, he would comment on the legislators they would be facing when testifying on their budgets and he would coach them on approaches that would appeal to each legislator. King had the same type of control over legislative liaisons. He had two lobbyists working to link the governor to the legislature. These two former legislators "carried the word directly from me to the appropriations committee." If an agency head, after budget hearings, reported trouble, the governor would instruct one of his two lobbyists to visit quickly with the legislators in question and take care of any problem.[48]

Orientations

Their political personalities, along with their experiences, shape how governors conceive of their role vis-à-vis the legislature. Not all of them define it the same way or on the same dimension. Two political scientists provide help. They have examined the gubernatorial role in terms of what they call "assertiveness."[49] At one end of an assertiveness-passivity continuum is the governor who narrowly defines his or her role in the legislative process and as a consequence is more restrained in policymaking leadership. Governors range along this continuum for a variety of reasons. Harry Hughes exemplifies them. Philosophically, he believed that the legislature should play the principal role in the lawmaking process, with the governor's role more limited. John Y. Brown (D-KY) took a similar tack, with the legislature as the policymaking board of a government that ran according to business principles. Oklahoma's Bellmon seems to have started out this way. Despite his prior experience in the legislature, the new governor was somewhat shocked when he discovered the legislative leadership expected him to present a package of proposals. Up until then, he had given little thought to preparing a legislative program. "I believed the governor's job was to be the state's chief administration officer, not to propose new legislation," Bellmon wrote. "I felt that was the job of the legislature . . . ." However, Bellmon quickly came to realize that the job of proposing legislation was a shared responsibility, one that he could not avoid.[50] Some governors are purposeful in their strategy of turning over the reins to the legislature. Bruce King of New Mexico was one of them. He had learned over the years not to lead too strongly, lest he "dampen the spirits of the legislators." Left alone, the legislature would come up with its own initiatives, ones that he would have chosen and could heartily endorse. "So I didn't try to direct the legislature on topics that I knew were going to come out about as I wanted them, anyway," King reasoned.[51]

At the other end of the "assertiveness" continuum are those governors who believe that policymaking is the prerogative of the executive and expect their legislatures to approve their policy initiatives, adopt their budgets, and uphold their vetoes. They do not welcome assertive participation by the legislature. One extreme example of an executive-supremacy governor is Schaefer of Maryland. He was zealous in advancing his agenda and intolerant of any disagreement from the legislature. His eight years in office were marked by almost continuous battles between him and a legislature under the control of the same political party.[52] Chris Christie took office after having served as a U.S. attorney and having prosecuted and convicted a number of New Jersey legislators. His words and his tone rankled the legislature, and the new speaker of the assembly took him to task. "He's talking to the Legislature as if he's still prosecutor and we're the defendants."[53]

Generally speaking, governors are not at either extreme, but they do feel that they have responsibility for policy leadership. In our survey, former governors were asked to characterize their approach to policymaking on a continuum ranging from 1 (legislature should exercise policy leadership) to 7 (governor should exercise policy leadership). The midpoint, 4, would have the legislature and governor sharing equally in policy leadership. The mean of the 73 respondents is 5.63, with Republicans opting for gubernatorial leadership slightly more than Democrats. Not one of the governors chose response options 1, 2, or 3, which would have indicated that they felt the legislature should lead. One out of six of them chose 4, or a balance of shared leadership. The other 84 percent opted for 5, 6, or 7—that is, gubernatorial leadership—with as many as 21 percent selecting the extreme of the leadership-choice continuum. According to governors, policy leadership is their responsibility.

One reason that governors assume responsibility is that they cannot escape it. "When you're a governor," said Mike Castle (R-DE), "you have a true sense of responsibility for everything that's happening in the state."[54] Unlike legislators who are responsive mainly to the districts that elect them, governors have a statewide constituency and a statewide perspective. "I might have felt differently if I had still been one of the 76 members of the legislature," wrote Ben Cayetano, but as governor of Hawaii, his perspective was necessarily broader. "The proverbial buck for the stewardship of the state stopped at my office on the fifth floor of the State Capitol."[55]

On fiscal matters, especially, governors believe they, and not their legislatures, are the ones willing to make tough decisions. They recognize that legislatures don't like to raise taxes or cut spending, and legislatures tend to go over budget. "When deadlocked at the end of the day," said Bob Holden (D-MO), "the governor has to keep the budget balanced." Joe Brennan recalls that when he was a liberal legislator in Maine, he had very little idea of how to pay the bills for programs that were designed to solve problems. However, as governor he learned to be fiscally responsible. If the budget is to be in true balance, so that expenditures and revenues are equal to one another, governors have to do the job. That is because legislatures tend to add to the governor's budget rather than subtract from it. As Stephen Merrill (R-NH) put it: "The legislature is elected to spend on programs they believe in. A governor is elected as a CEO, to lead and balance the budget."[56]

Edgar elaborates on the point that spending is "just their [legislatures'] nature, while doing what has to be done is gubernatorial nature." At the outset, Edgar wasn't viewed as a fiscal conservative, but by the end of his first term he was. Kean also points to the tendency of legislators to overspend. In his view, legislators may "talk economy, but vote for every spending measure that might conceivably benefit a constituent." It is up to the governor to exert fiscal discipline. "If the governor won't say no, no one else will."[57] A subtheme is that legislatures are more politically oriented, whereas governors are more policy oriented. Legislators, as individuals, simply do not have the courage it takes. "They worry about every vote they make," according to Edgar. Even legislators who have been around twenty years "still get scared about every vote." Although legislators avow the coequality of their branch of government, they still expect governors to lead and to make the hard decisions. Legislators appreciate governors who are willing to take the heat for them. In the eyes of governors, legislators are thankful that, when it comes to fiscal policy, in particular, the governor will be blamed, and not them.

Just as the large majority of governors have a sense of their own responsibility for policy leadership, they also have a sense of the legislature as an independent branch of government with which the executive must share power. The two orientations might appear to be contradictory, but they are not. At one extreme are the few governors like Maryland's Hughes, who are not only willing to share power, but who also defer to the legislature's leadership.[58] At another extreme are the few governors like Maryland's Schaefer, who are contemptuous of the legislature and insist that everything be done their way.[59] Between these two extremes are the many governors who have served in the legislature (and a number who have not) who understand that, even with gubernatorial leadership, there has to be a sharing of power.

One reason that governors believe in sharing power with the legislature is that they realize they have to, if they are going to get anything done. "If you don't get the legislature on your side," commented Arne Carlson (R-MN), "it's not going to happen." Any governor who came up through legislative ranks knows this. McWherter of Tennessee, at heart a legislative man, was not the only governor to recognize that the legislature wants to be informed and consulted, and it wants to participate. The governor, to achieve his goals, had to have the support of the legislature.[60]

New Jersey's Kean was in the legislature when it was modernizing and struggling for independence from the governor. He appreciated how legislators felt about their domain and their insistence on being treated as an equal branch.[61] Furthermore, Kean understood that even a powerful governor could not go it alone. The legislature can bottle up the governor's agenda, cut funding for the governor's priorities, and harass the governor's appointees. "Life is much easier when the governor and the legislature are working together . . . ," Kean concluded.[62] Angus King was of like mind. He acknowledged that the only absolute power the Maine governor possessed was the pardoning of criminals and the setting of the annual herring quota. To get anything else done, the governor had to enlist the legislature.

Respect is another important element in the orientation of governors toward the legislature. Not every governor feels respectful, and not every governor shows respect for the legislative institution and its members. Neither Maryland's Schaefer nor Minnesota's Ventura respected the legislature. Schaefer tried to undermine the authority of the senate president with his colleagues, and suspended communications with the speaker of the house for a period of almost six months.[63] Ventura prided himself on being a political outsider and was characterized as a governor without any friends in the capitol and a governor who "was determined not to make any."[64]

Others may not have been as publicly disdainful of the legislature, but they too showed little regard for the institution with which they had to deal. Hugh Carey (D-NY) compared the members of the state legislature unfavorably to his former colleagues in Congress.[65] Gary Johnson (R-NM) had a stormy relationship with the legislature during the eight years he was in office. Buddy Roemer (R-LA) was condescending toward lawmakers and was impatient with the slowness of the legislative process.[66] Jeb Bush (R-FL) had no problem with a compliant Florida house, but he "ridiculed and marginalized" and bullied his fellow Republicans in the senate.[67] And although Schwarzenegger liked to hobnob with California legislators, his public utterances showed disdain for members. A prime example was the phrase "girlie men," which he directed at Democratic legislators who could not agree on a state budget.[68] Still other governors, while by no means disrespectful, were far from comfortable with the legislature and its ways. Neither Christine Whitman (R-NJ) nor Jon Corzine were at ease when the legislature was in Trenton. Madeleine Kunin (D-VT) could not accept the wheeling and dealing that were part of the life even of a citizen legislature, like Vermont's.[69]

It helps, moreover, if governors actually like legislators and dealing with them. Frank Keating (R-OK) was not one to look down his nose at legislators, as did a few of his colleagues. He liked and respected them. Of course, it is not always easy for governors to act in friendly fashion when their initiatives are under attack. Thus, it is natural for even the most respectful governors to complain that when the legislature was in session the governor's life was miserable. In fact, there is a saying that when you see a governor smiling, you know the legislature has left town. According to Edgar's recollections, on some occasions he wished that Illinois legislators would just stop asking questions and on other occasions he hoped that they would just go home. For Edgar, like many of his gubernatorial colleagues, the legislature was "a pain in the neck, but a necessary pain."

Many governors actually enjoy the push and pull. Zell Miller loved the legislative process when he was in the legislature, and he loved it as governor.[70] John McKernan (R-ME) took particular pleasure in the legislative part of the job. Bill Clinton (D-AR) was all over the place, testifying before committees and rounding up votes, when the Arkansas general assembly was in session. John Waihee (D-HI) also relished the give-and-take of the process and was referred to as the "twenty-sixth senator" and the "fifty-second representative."[71]

Most governors bring to office a respect for the legislature and legislators, as well as an understanding of the problems the institution and individuals face. These governors do not think, as some do, that they are smarter than legislators. They do not feel superior. They understand that legislators have, and should have, different perspectives than they do, since they respond to different constituencies and are subject to different demands.[72] To signal his own feelings as governor, as the 1997 Georgia legislature drew to a close, Miller spoke from the podium in the senate chamber: "This will always be my home," the governor told the assembled senators.[73] As the reader might imagine, the governor received a warm response.

Pragmatism

Glendening's assessment is that, as a species, governors are the most practical and least ideological of all the people in politics. Actually, the same governor can be ideological on the one hand and pragmatic on the other. Take Owens of Colorado, who has been described as "the smart politician who is also a principled conservative."[74] Engler of Michigan was an ideological conservative both as legislative leader and as governor. But he led pragmatically and was willing to settle for less than the ideal. Other governors also eschew ideological extremes. Most crowd the center, so pragmatism comes easily to them. Colorado's Romer exemplifies such a governor. For him, the issue is what works, or what works best.

The large majority of governors who are pragmatists above all else strive to find consensus. That means recognizing the legitimacy of other people's views. Mario Cuomo (D-NY), for example, worked as a conciliator, governing more by mediation than by confrontation. He was adept at finding whatever common ground existed.[75] On his part, George Ariyoshi (D-HI) was careful not to dramatize the situation or exacerbate differences. He avoided telling the legislature to do what would have been impossible for it to do. Nor did he imply that legislators were lacking moral fiber if they did not respond to his leadership. Also, he did not raise public expectations without having a pretty good idea that a range of solutions was available.[76]

Governors want to accomplish something; they want to solve problems, get things done. To do so requires that majorities in the legislature go along. Building majorities usually requires compromise by governors. Governors demonstrate a genuine willingness to compromise—to play by the legislature's rules, split the difference, settle for half a loaf, trade a *quid* for a *quo*, ask for what they can get. They have what political theorists Amy Gutman and Dennis Thompson refer to as the "mindsets of political compromise," which includes adapting one's principles and respecting one's opponents.[77] This doesn't mean that they will compromise on every disagreement. It does mean that they are disposed to settling, if at all possible. "There are things you can give on and things you can't give on," according to Romer. "You give on what you can." Even governors who consider themselves ideological, like Ehrlich of Maryland, are disposed to bend in order to get things done. "Compromise where appropriate and fight like hell where appropriate," is Ehrlich's formulation. Pragmatism, therefore, encompasses both principle and compromise, staying with one's values, holding one's ground, but giving way when one must and where one can. It is not the easiest distinction to make, but governors are able to draw the line and they do so. Some, like Ehrlich, draw it closer to the principled end, whereas others, like Romer, draw it closer to the pragmatic end.

Just about all of them, however, recognize that whatever the issue, they will run into opposition in the legislature. Moreover, legislators can be expected to be critical of the governor, to second-guess his or her proposals or strategies. It is their political disposition to be critical. Whether they stand fast or give way and whether they win or lose, few governors let the fights they engage in with legislators become personal. "I understand you have to vote against me," Virginia's Baliles would say, "but I need your vote on this other issue."

Adaptability

Speaking for neophytes in elective office, Dick Thornburgh admitted to having no real preparation for being governor. Nor did he think other political office provided the learning that was necessary. "We all learned on the job," he said. Speaking for those who were well prepared, Edgar maintained that he probably had as good a resume as anybody ever elected as governor of Illinois, and yet, "I didn't have a clue. Until you're sitting behind the desk, and the stuff starts flying at you . . . ." It is no surprise that governors learn on the job. They learn with the experience they gain in gubernatorial office. Different governors process their experiences differently. Joe Frank Harris (D-GA), like many other governors, gradually came to feel more comfortable and more confident during the course of his eight years in office. He wrote:

> There is much less pressure in the second term because you're more experienced in your position and you've got more confidence not only in what you have achieved, but in what you feel you're able to achieve. You've also had some successes that help to bolster that confidence.[78]

Governors learn by being in office and doing the job, and they change with the passage of time and the accretion of experience. "I started out as a young whippersnapper," Jim Hunt (D-NC) recalled, "but I matured quickly." Hunt was a student of the policymaking process and read about it as he engaged in it. By the time he started his second term, he was in his own estimation a better prepared governor. It took a while, but Corzine caught on. Year by year, he became a little more comfortable dealing with legislative leaders in New Jersey. He started out as a politically awkward chief executive, but he improved, at least somewhat, in the course of time.[79] Clements had a stubborn streak, but he too was able to change. He learned from his mistakes. According to his press aide, after a shaky beginning Clements realized "what old politicians knew—you can't do much with force with the Legislature, you have to sweet talk 'em." The governor was able to adopt a more agreeable style in dealing with Texas legislators.[80]

Governors, of course, shift gears from one year to the next or from their first term to the following one. In the survey, former governors were asked whether their approach to the legislature had changed during their tenure in office. Only 5 percent reported "significant change," but 40 percent said they had made some change. Almost half the governors who responded to the survey had shifted in their approach to the legislature. Those governors were asked to specify the reasons for the shift. The predominant reason was a change in partisan control of the legislature. If the governor's party lost control, then the governor would increase his or her involvement with the new majority, the opposition party. Or, as in the case of Hodges of South Carolina, the governor would use the veto more and put greater reliance on appealing to the public. For some governors, like Edgar, control by the opposition meant that the governor became more involved personally than when his or her own party controlled the legislature. It might even result in a governor's switching from an offensive to a defensive stance, as Jim Folsom (D-AL) was compelled to do, or simply becoming more cautious, as in the case of Jim Blanchard (D-MI). John Spellman (R-WA) was faced with a highly charged situation when a legislator changed allegiance and the governor's party lost control of the senate. The result was that Spellman had to meet with both caucuses and not just with the majority caucus, which had previously been that of his own party.

It doesn't require a partisan upheaval for governors to change their approach. A change in legislative personnel may do it. A new speaker in Oklahoma proved very difficult for George Nigh (D-OK) to work with, so the governor relied more on the senate than on the house. Mike Leavitt (R-UT) also altered his approach, because of a change in legislative leadership. One governor—Bill Graves (R-KS)—began to reach out to the minority party when his relationships with new leaders of his own party became strained. On occasion, a governor benefits from new leaders replacing old ones. During the early days of his administration, Deval Patrick (D-MA) feuded openly with the leaders of the senate and the house. When both leaders left, the governor developed a much friendlier relationship with their successors.

Effective governors are constantly alert for means by which they can improve their relations with the legislature. Like Clements of Texas, they may become more personally involved and less reliant on staff. Or, like John Sununu (R-NH), they decide that it would be better to consult more. Or, like a number of governors, they change the staff members who handle their legislative affairs. Glendening had an arms-length relationship with the Maryland General Assembly during his first term as governor. During his second term, however, he decided to give legislators his personal attention, consult more, and give greater deference to the senate and house leaders.

Most governors who change do so at the margins, but Dukakis is the classic case of a governor who fundamentally changed his approach to the legislature. It occurred after Dukakis, in running for reelection as governor, was defeated in the 1978 Democratic primary. However, he came back four years later to win a second term (and then a third term) as governor of Massachusetts. The first term, known as "Duke I," was a disaster as far as his political leadership was concerned. Severely chastened by the defeat of his agenda and his subsequent repudiation at the polls, he made a 180-degree course correction. His second term, "Duke II," featured a more accommodating, practical style on his part. "He did the exact opposite of what he'd done in his first term," is the characterization of the senate president, Kevin Harrington. Dukakis himself explained:

One of the things I learned in my first administration is people can be very intelligent, very thoughtful, very honest, and so on, but if they don't have the political skills in the best sense of the word, if they can't work with the legislature . . . .

His first term, he acknowledged, had been characterized by "arrogance and cockiness" toward the legislature. During his second term, his style was very different, as were his dealings with legislators. He engaged in the nitty-gritty of statehouse politics, apparently relishing the give-and-take that he had disdained earlier. He listened to legislators, partnered with legislative leaders, and even made use of patronage.[81]

Most governors adapt readily to the legislature and the circumstances they confront. They learn the easy way; Dukakis learned the hard way. But like others, adapt he did and with demonstrable results.

Notes

1. Andrew E. Stoner, *Legacy of a Governor: The Life of Indiana's Frank O'Bannon* (Bloomington, IN: Rooftop Publishing, 2006), 75.
2. James E. McGreevey, *The Confession* (New York: HarperCollins, 2006), 211.
3. Gleaves Whitney, *John Engler: The Man, the Leader & the Legacy* (Chelsea, MI: Sleeping Bear Press, 2002), 396.
4. Dick Codey interview, Eagleton Institute of Politics Governors Program, Rutgers University, March 23, 2010.
5. Dick Thornburgh, *Where the Evidence Leads* (Pittsburgh: University of Pittsburgh Press, 2003), 107.
6. S. V. Date, *Quiet Passion: A Biography of Senator Bob Graham* (New York: Penguin, 2004), 101.
7. By contrast, William Bulger, the president of the Massachusetts senate, with whom Weld struck up a productive friendship, was an Irish politician from South Boston. Bulger's brother, Whitey, was one of Boston's most notable gangsters.
8. On Dukakis in his first term, see Richard Gaines and Michael Segal, *Dukakis and the Reform Impulse* (Boston: Quinlan Press, 1987), 110.
9. Bob Graham, "A Magical Vision and Other Ingredients of Leadership," in *Governors on Governing*, ed. Robert D. Behn (Lanham, MD: University Press of America, 1991), 59.

10. Thad L. Beyle, "The Evolution of the Gubernatorial Office: United States Governors over the Twentieth Century," in *A Legacy of Leadership: Governors and American History*, ed. Clayton McClure Brooks (Philadelphia: University of Pennsylvania Press, 2008), 212-213.

11. Carolyn Barta, *Bill Clements: Texian to His Toenails* (Austin, TX: Eakin Press, 1996), 221.

12. Ibid., 222.

13. Thornburgh in Alan Rosenthal, ed., *The Governor and the Legislature: Eagleton's 1987 Symposium on the State of the States* (New Brunswick, NJ: Eagleton Institute of Politics, 1988), 36.

14. Laura A. van Assendelft, *Governors, Agenda Setting, and Divided Government* (Lanham, MD: University Press of America, 1997), 135, 136.

15. Andrew Romano and Michael Hirsh, "America, Inc.," *Newsweek*, February 22, 2010, 38.

16. Ibid., 38.

17. Victor G. Atiyeh, "The Role of Business Management Techniques in State Government," in Behn, *Governors on Governing*, 110.

18. Thornburgh, *Where the Evidence Leads*, 106.

19. Quoted in *New York Times*, October 25, 2010.

20. C. Fraser Smith, *William Donald Schaefer* (Baltimore: Johns Hopkins University Press, 1999), 276; Alan Rosenthal, *Governors and Legislatures: Contending Powers* (Washington, D.C.: CQ Press, 1990), 72.

21. Smith, *William Donald Schaefer*, 357.

22. James Richardson, *Willie Brown: A Biography* (Berkeley: University of California Press, 1996), 358, 360.

23. Larry Sabato, "Governors' Office Careers: A New Breed Emerges," *State Government* 52 (Summer 1979): 95.

24. Alan Greenblatt, "The Job of a Lifetime," *Governing* (June 2009).

25. Ibid.

26. Van Assendelft, *Governors, Agenda Setting, and Divided Government*, 70.

27. Whitney, *John Engler*, 326–27.

28. Richardson, *Willie Brown*, 296.

29. Charles Kenney and Robert L. Turner, *Dukakis: An American Odyssey* (Boston: Houghton Mifflin, 1988), 118–19.

30. Tom Loftus, *The Art of Legislative Politics* (Washington, D.C.: CQ Press, 1994), 67–69.

31. Van Assendelft, *Governors, Agenda Setting, and Divided Government*, 103.

32. Richard Hyatt, *Zell: The Governor Who Gave Georgia HOPE* (Macon, GA: Mercer University Press, 1997), 181, 183–90, 267.

33. Bruce King, *Cowboy in the Roundhouse* (Santa Fe, NM: Sunstone Press, 1998), 295.

34. National Governors Association, *Transition and the New Governor: A Planning Guide* (Washington, D.C.: National Governors Association, 1998), 42.

35. Henry Bellmon, *The Life and Times of Henry Bellmon* (Tulsa, OK: Council Oak Books, 1992), 168.

36. Thomas H. Kean, *The Politics of Inclusion* (New York: Free Press, 1988), 73–74.

37. *Independent Record* (Helena, MT), June 15, 2010.

38. Barta, *Bill Clements*, 220.

39. Lou Cannon, *Governor Reagan* (New York: Public Affairs, 2003), 195.

40. Date, *Quiet Passion*, 107–8.

41. George J. Marlin, *Squandered Opportunities: New York's Pataki Years* (South Bend, IN: St. Augustine's Press, 2006), 72.

42. Discussion with Edward McBride, former chief of staff to Governor Corzine, November 11, 2009.

43. Van Assendelft, *Governors, Agenda Setting, and Divided Government*, 145.

44. Harry Roe Hughes, *My Unexpected Journey* (Charleston, SC: History Press, 2006), 146–47.

45. Cannon, *Governor Reagan*, 144, 150.

46. Kenney and Turner, *Dukakis*, 185.

47. Alvin S. Felzenberg, *Governor Tom Kean* (New Brunswick, NJ: Rutgers University Press, 2006), 190.

48. King, *Cowboy in the Roundhouse*, 198.

49. Lee Bernick and Charles W. Wiggins, "Executive Legislative Relations: The Governor's Role as Chief Legislator," in *Gubernatorial Leadership and State Policy*, ed. Eric B. Herzik and Brent W. Brown (Westport, CT: Greenwood Press, 1991), 83.

50. Bellmon, *The Life and Times of Henry Bellmon*, 208.

51. King, *Cowboy in the Roundhouse*, 196–97.

52. Smith, *William Donald Schaefer*, 356.

53. Quoted on politickernj.com, no date.

54. Brian Friel, "The (Red) Governators," *National Journal,* June 27, 2009, 20.

55. Benjamin J. Cayetano, *Ben: A Memoir From Street Kid to Governor* (Honolulu: Watermark Publishing, 2009), 454.

56. Response from survey.

57. Kean, *The Politics of Inclusion*, 63.

58. In his memoirs, Hughes rejects the criticism that he abdicated leadership to the legislature. He does admit that, at first, he may have gone too far in this regard, but later he restored the balance. Hughes, *My Unexpected Journey*, 211–12.

59. See Smith, *William Donald Schaefer*, 289–90.

60. Ken Renner, in van Assendelft, *Governors, Agenda Setting, and Divided Government*, 109.

61. Panel on Governor Kean, Governors Project archive, Eagleton Institute of Politics, Rutgers University, April 15, 2009.

62. Ibid.

63. Rosenthal, *Governors and Legislatures*, 74.

64. Dan Creed, *Governor Ventura: "The Body" Exposed* (Madison, WI: Hunter Halverson Press, 2003), 128.

65. Daniel C. Kramer, *The Days of Wine and Roses Are Over: Governor Hugh Carey and New York State* (Lanham, MD: University Press of America, 1997), 148.

66. Leo Honeycutt, *Edwin Edwards: Governor of Louisiana* (Baton Rouge, LA: Lisburn Press, 2009), 275.

67. S. V. Date, *Jeb: America's Next Bush* (New York: Penguin, 2007), 129.

68. Louise Krasniewicz and Michael Blitz, *Arnold Schwarzenegger: A Biography* (Westport, CT: Greenwood Press, 2006), 134.

69. Ralph Wright, *Inside the Statehouse* (Washington, D.C.: CQ Press, 2005), 179.

70. Hyatt, *Zell*, 121.

71. Rosenthal, *Governors and Legislatures*, 70.

72. On Hunt, see Jack D. Fleer, *North Carolina Government and Politics* (Lincoln: University of Nebraska Press, 1994), 103–4.

73. Hyatt, *Zell*, 404.

74. John J. Miller, "America's Best Governor," *National Review*, September 2, 2002, 18.

75. Robert S. McElvaine, *Mario Cuomo: A Biography* (New York: Scribner's, 1988), 339–40.

76. George R. Ariyoshi, *With Obligations to All* (Honolulu: Ariyoshi Foundation, 1997), 152.

77. Amy Gutman and Dennis Thompson, "The Mindsets of Political Compromise," *Perspectives on Politics, American Political Science Association* 8 (December 2010): 1125.

78. Joe Frank Harris, *Personal Reflections on a Public Life* (Macon, GA: Mercer University Press, 1998), 166.
79. Discussion with Bill Castner, former chief counsel to Governor Corzine, November 11, 2009.
80. Barta, *Bill Clements*, 249, 365.
81. Kenney and Turner, *Dukakis*, 134–35, 175–82, 201.

4

How Governors Put Together Their Policy Agendas

"THE GOVERNOR'S REAL POWER," according to Angus King (I-ME), "is that of setting the agenda." Policy agendas are not solely the prerogative of governors. Senate and house leaders have measures they want to enact. Majority-party caucuses may develop agendas either as the session begins or as it progresses. Standing committees, and particularly their chairs, have their own ideas about what they want to recommend in their jurisdictional areas. In addition, the agendas of individual legislators consist of the bills they sponsor and want to see enacted.

Everyone in the policymaking enterprise is entitled to an agenda. Yet not all agendas are created equal. The governor's agenda is far and away the most equal of all. That is because constitutionally and politically governors are expected to propose measures that require the legislature to enact law. (Governors also can and do use executive orders, rather than statutes per se, to effect public policy.) Legislatures, on their part, can also propose policies, but it is much more difficult for them to capture the attention that the governor does with his or her proposals. Legislatures, moreover, deal with multiple agendas, and the challenge before legislators is to sift and sort among them. Just about any interest group, executive department or agency, standing committee, or individual member has the means to put something on the legislature's agenda. For an item to be taken seriously, however, it has to build support in either one or both chambers. Among other things, because governors are one and legislators are many, the governor's agenda typically gets major consideration by the legislature at each session. Political scientists who have studied the subject are in general agreement that "no other individual has the potential to play as important a role" in state policymaking.[1] Most governors do take the lead in framing issues, setting the agenda, and influencing policy outcomes by using the powers and tools at their disposal, even though each governor faces constraints as well as opportunities.[2]

By contrast to legislatures, where control over a policy agenda is diffuse, governors can be selective in what policies they propose as legislation. Governors are required only to take a position on the state budget, which most of them formulate and submit to the legislature. Outside of their budget responsibilities, which restrict them, they have discretion to pick and choose. Their tendency is to attend to issues of larger dimension and to those that lend themselves to thematic treatment. The tendency of legislatures, by contrast, is to take anything or almost anything that comes their way, including of course whatever the governor transmits to them as part of the chief executive's policy agenda.[3]

Governors have a wide range of options when it comes to their agendas. They decide on the domain of public policy—whether to hone in on education, economic development, the environment, or whatever. They decide on the direction, innovative or conservative, and the scope, broad or narrow. They decide on who will benefit and to what extent. They decide on the specifics as well as on the general shape of policy.

Whatever their thrust, the agenda is theirs. Governors are counseled by their membership organization, the National Governors Association (NGA), to set the policy agenda themselves and not let the legislature or the media do it.[4] They have little difficulty taking that advice to heart; formulating an agenda comes naturally to them. The legislature, of course, introduces more bills, but the bills introduced by or on behalf of the governor are the major ones. On the survey to which former governors responded, they were asked, "Roughly speaking, what proportion of the major items enacted by the legislature during your tenure as governor were initiated by you and what proportion were initiated by the legislature itself?" On a seven-point scale, ranging from 1 (all major enactments initiated by governor) to 7 (all major enactments initiated by legislature), with 4 at a midpoint of equal initiation, respondents scored a mean of 2.82. Of the seventy-five governors responding, fifty-three were at the gubernatorial side of the continuum, whereas eighteen were at the midpoint, and only three on the legislative side. In Alabama, Tennessee, and Vermont, initiatives by the legislature reportedly outnumbered those by the governor. Republican respondents were somewhat more apt than Democratic respondents to report gubernatorial initiation during their terms in office.

Jim Hunt (D-NC), for one, didn't have any doubts as to the source of policy initiatives. "They [legislators] would have a few things," he said, "but I was such an activist, I overwhelmed them." Not all governors were as active as Hunt, but still their role was the central one in the policymaking process. When the two partners in state governance stand up to dance, it is typically the governor who leads and the legislature that follows.

What Is the Governor's Agenda

The NGA counsels new governors on their opportunities "to present and advocate a legislative program," informing them that they have at their disposal the inaugural address, the state of the state message, the budget message, and special messages they convey to their legislatures.[5] NGA adds, governors can formulate and advocate for policies and programs without messaging the legislature in a formal manner. One of the questions that political scientists wrestle with is, how can a governor's agenda be determined? Unless an investigator confines his or her examination to a limited period of time in a single state, it may be difficult to spot a governor's fingerprints in legislation that is introduced. Governors keep track of their initiatives, and some issue scorecards at the end of the year or of their terms that record the degree of their success, agenda item by agenda item. But such data are scattered among the states and among the governors.

As noted in Chapter 1, political scientists, who have been investigating gubernatorial agendas in all fifty states, recently have used state of the state addresses to specify the issues that comprise a governor's policy agenda.[6] Most compelling for research purposes, these addresses are offered everywhere, or practically everywhere, have been offered for years, and are publicly available.[7] Because they are delivered at the beginning of the legislative session and contain specific policy and budgetary proposals, they ought to be reasonable approximations of the governor's policy agenda.

Without doubt, governors make use of the state of the state address to lay out their policy agendas. Some are more devoted to the use of this address than are others. Madeleine Kunin (D-VT) expected her agenda to receive widespread attention when she presented the state of the state speech before a joint session of the general assembly, "when all 180 members . . . , as well as many of the citizens of Vermont, focused on each word."[8] Jim Hodges (D-SC) was another governor who laid out program objectives in his state of the state address. According to him, it provided a good road map of where he wanted to go.

As a surrogate for the governor's policy agenda, the state of the state address is not without drawbacks, however. First, the identification of items in the address as administration bills is fraught with difficulty. Enunciation of policy initiatives in an hour-long address is very general in nature. Bills introduced in the legislature are very specific. It is a daunting task to match the bill to the item and to be sure of the correspondence. A bill on the same subject may go in a different direction than an idea put forward in a speech. Margaret Robertson Ferguson's method of tracing items is as follows: After identifying specific proposals from each state of the state address, she coded them and then tagged bills introduced in the legislature in these policy areas as potential gubernatorial bills. She reviewed the synopsis of each of these bills to verify its match with the governor's enunciated preferences. Using this method, she identified 1,092 governor-endorsed bills.[9] Kousser and Phillips went through a similar process in identifying gubernatorial agendas. They analyzed state of the state addresses of governors in twenty-seven states in 2001 and 2006, identifying individual agenda items—a total of 612 policy proposals and 476 budget proposals. They assessed the policy significance of each proposal. Then, they relied on journalistic accounts and state legislative databases to track agenda items through the lawmaking process.[10]

Second, the state of the state address does not account for all the governor's initiatives. As I mentioned earlier, virtually every governor has had to respond to unforeseen circumstances, even crises that require a legislative fix. Governors cannot anticipate what they will have to go to the legislature for during the period between messages. Unforeseen circumstances result in some message items' being deferred while other items take command of the governor's attention.

Third, the state of the state does not necessarily consider many of the most important policy initiatives of governors—the budget. Dollar allocations to departments, agencies, and programs are part and parcel of public policy. In most respects, there is little policy without the funds to implement it. Dick Thornburgh (R-PA) did not even deliver a state of the state, but only a budget message. For him, "the budget was key." Add to this the fact that the authorization of policies is often written into state budgets rather than in stand-alone legislation. In Wisconsin, in particular, but in other states as well, the budget bill has come to be the vehicle for a number of policy initiatives. Both the governor and legislators themselves enhance the chances of their policy proposals by putting them in an omnibus budget bill, a bill that has to be passed in one form or another. Ben Nelson (D-NE) acknowledged the close tie-ins between his legislative policy goals and the budget. South Carolina's Hodges also recalled how much he had done through the budget. "In state government," he said, "everything goes through the budget process." Jim Edgar (R-IL) went even further. He referred to the agenda in the state of the state address as "irrelevant." According to him, governors put things in that message because it is expected of them, but "the budget address is the one that really mattered." That is because the budget is where the money can be found. Still, it is necessary for governors to provide a legislative agenda, even though "some of it was just BS." At the end of the session, governors can claim that they got all or most of what they went after in the state of the state.

Fourth, just as governors cannot be expected to include afterthoughts or emergency or crisis proposals in their opening addresses, they cannot be expected to be committed to all the items they do include. Most governors will pay lip service to measures that, for an assortment of reasons, they may not pursue. These items carry political or symbolic weight but are not really expected to be the focus of the legislative process. Legislators, nonetheless, may introduce bills in these domains. These initiatives are really not those of the governor. Moreover, like Edgar, other governors anticipate that the media will measure their success by how much of their state of the state wish list they get passed. These governors will tilt their formal addresses toward those measures that are likely to receive legislative approval. But their real agenda may be communicated by other means and on other occasions.

The present study does not rely on the state of the state address as an indicator of the governor's policy agenda. Instead, reliance is on governors, themselves, for information as to what measures were on their agendas. This method, like others used here, depends primarily on the recall and veracity of respondents. Do men and women who held office thirty years ago, or even ten years ago, remember just what policies and programs they advocated as governor? Interviews with governors, which constitute one source of information for this study, suggest that governors generally do recall the major items on their agendas even after the passage of considerable time. Can former governors—or governors who have written memoirs or their biographers—be trusted to report honestly on their agendas? Again, on the basis of interviews with a number of former governors, it appears that they have little that they wish to hide and they look back on their policy leadership with pride. For one reason or another, they may omit some initiatives from their four, eight, or more years in the governor's office, but my belief is that they are for the most part accurate in specifying the major items on their agendas. The methodology employed here is admittedly an imperfect one. Yet, I believe that it brings us closer to an understanding of what measures get on the governor's priority list and how such measures get there.

Initiatives on the Agenda

In response to the open-ended survey question, "What do you consider to have been your main policy priorities during your time in office?" the seventy-five respondents wrote in a total of 325 items or an average of 4.4 initiatives per governor. No doubt, many of the respondents did not include everything on their agendas, but only what they remembered as the major items. They could not be expected, in response to a questionnaire, to write down everything that might have been mentioned in a public address or communicated directly to the legislature during their terms in office.

Not only in their recall later on, but also in the moment itself, governors focus on relatively few items. Sometimes differences in the degree of focus or concentration are reflected in the state of the state address as presented by various governors. Mario Cuomo (D-NY), for example, gave lengthy addresses that included dozens of separate policy recommendations. By contrast, George Pataki (R-NY) delivered shorter, more thematic speeches, concentrating on a few key policy initiatives.[11] Cuomo was rather unusual among governors, insisting on casting the widest of nets. When asked what he wanted to do when he became governor, Cuomo said, "I wanted to do everything." He explained, "The difference between me and a lot of other executives was that they pick one or two priorities and get identified with them. . . . But we do all these things simultaneously." For Cuomo, everything he did he regarded as a priority.[12]

Among the relatively few governors who start out wanting to do everything, most quickly learn from experience that they can't. Bob Graham (D-FL) started out ambitiously. He had trouble narrowing his focus; ideas constantly churned in his head. He would take notes and give his aides instructions on how to follow up. It appears that he never slowed down enough to set his priorities. "He didn't recognize you couldn't heal the world in sixty days," one of his aides recalled. His chief of staff, Charlie Reed, described how Graham kept generating new priorities. The governor would call Reed every Sunday night at 11:30, having come up with lots of "to do" things after he watched the 11 o'clock news. Graham's aides did their best to rein him in. "We had the biggest fights to try to get him to narrow his agenda down," said Tom Herndon. "He just would not hear of it." Eventually, Graham learned to focus, at least somewhat. "In the end, instead of sixty things on his agenda, he had eighteen, when he should have had six," said one of his aides.[13]

If there is anything on which both experts and governors agree nowadays it is that one's policy agenda has to be limited, perhaps not to as few as six items but certainly to a manageable number. Two students of the subject acknowledge that the range and number of issues on the agenda may be quite variable, but "almost every governor has a small number of issues of policy initiatives that define his or her term of office."[14] For decades the NGA has been giving advice, tendered by veteran governors, to those about to enter office:

> Success in the governorship depends first and foremost on focus. The term should be committed to a limited number of issues and concentrate on them throughout.

The recommendation is that the new governor should at the outset select no more than three or four issues on which to concentrate, although other items will arise and have to be added as the term progresses.[15]

This advice has been taken to heart. At a seminar for new governors, Jim Hunt related to Jim Hodges that during his first term he wanted to be the education governor, the transportation governor, and the health care governor. However, Hunt continued, he couldn't do it all, or do it all well, so he decided to focus. Hodges took Hunt's advice and made a single subject—education—his primary focus. John Engler (R-MI) remembered going to NGA's new governors school, where Pete du Pont (R-DE) gave some advice that he would never forget. Du Pont said, "Being governor is the greatest job in the world. You can do anything you want—but you can't do everything."[16] "It is important to have a clear set of priorities," recommended Bob Taft (R-OH), "but not too many." Christine Whitman (R-NJ) was asked early on, what are your ten top priorities? "Ten is too many," she replied. To the follow-up, what isn't too many, she responded, "Four." The economy, education, cities, and juvenile justice were the four she mentioned.[17] Though limited in number, her priorities ranged broadly and could encompass quite a number of gubernatorial proposals.

Note that there is a difference between agenda priorities of the governor (as stated in an address or as recalled in later years) and the legislation introduced to implement such priorities. For example, in his 1992 state of the state address, Zell Miller (D-GA) enunciated four priorities as "making our children's education better, our streets and neighborhoods safer, our environment cleaner, and our economy stronger." These priorities were translated and specified in over forty bills introduced in the legislature.[18] Depending on whether one is examining agendas from the perspective of declaration on the one hand or that of bills on the other, a governor's agenda will vary in the quantity of its proposals.

The former governors who were surveyed reflected substantial agreement with the prescription of NGA and their colleagues noted previously. In response to a question about how many important policy items they had on their agendas for legislatures to deal with each year, 47.1 percent said they had only 1–5 items, 28.6 percent said 6–10, 18.6 percent said 11–20, only 5.7 percent reported over 20, and none said over 30. The outliers, with 21–30, were George Allen (R-VA), Michael Leavitt (R-UT), Bob

Miller (D-NV), and Harry Hughes (D-MD). One year, Hughes recalled, he had more than thirty initiatives on his agenda in addition to a gas tax and it turned out to be the most successful year of his first term.[19] All told, three out of four governors limited their agendas to ten or fewer items each year. Republican governors advanced slightly fewer proposals than Democratic ones.

The budget is definitely a policymaking priority. Governors are virtually unanimous in their agreement that the budget has to be their principal focus. Andrew Cuomo (D-NY), just before his election in 2010, declared that he was "very big on focus" and that the budget was going to be his vehicle for policy and the subject of his major focus.[20] Bob Ehrlich (R-MD) was just as definite in his view: "The budget is the most important thing governors do." His predecessor, Parris Glendening (D-MD), was in total agreement that the budget is the governor's major policy document. No governor paid more attention to the budget than Thornburgh. Upon taking office in 1979, he had to submit a budget to the Pennsylvania legislature in early March. It was the top priority for him:

> Because all of an administration's priorities are, sooner or later, reflected in the budget figures, the budget process is far more than just making sure all the numbers add up. It is at the very heart of the craft of governing.[21]

Governors probably have an even greater advantage when it comes to the budget than they do when it comes to their other policy initiatives. Constitutionally, governors have the responsibility for formulating budgets in the large majority of states. What they put into the budget is what gets delivered to the legislature and what gets introduced by way of appropriation or budget bills. In several states, governors do not have sole authority for budget formulation. In one fashion or another, they share authority with the legislature in Arizona, Arkansas, Colorado, Mississippi, New Mexico, North Carolina, Texas, and Utah.

In Texas, for instance, the Legislative Budget Board presents its budget bill, whereas the governor presents the budget document. The two formulations compete in the process of legislative review. In North Carolina the legislature prepares its own budget and considers it along with the budget submitted by the governor. Arkansas also has a hybrid process, whereby the Legislative Council, a senate-house interim committee, puts together one budget while the governor puts together another. Both are considered by the legislature's joint budget committee. The Mississippi legislature also receives two budget proposals—one from the Joint Legislative Budget Committee and the other from the governor, with the former being followed more closely than the latter. The Colorado legislature has a Joint Budget Committee, which receives the governor's budget recommendations, has briefings, holds hearings, and then constructs its own budget, which becomes the focus of the budget process in the legislature.[22]

Even in these states, where the legislature is the governor's budgetary equal if not superior, the governor's power has been enhanced of late. These governors may not play the dominant role that governors in most states play, but they share with the legislature in the initiation of budget proposals. Take the Colorado governor, for example. Roy Romer (D-CO) knew the strength of the legislature's Joint Budget Committee, since he had served on it when he was a member of the legislature. Thus, he realized that he had to work to sell the committee on his budget proposals. It would have been easier, he admitted, if he could have done the budget from the governor's office, but he felt that the process made for stability and that participants felt an obligation to make it work. As far as Romer was concerned, it did. His successor, Bill Owens (R-CO), was similarly inclined. He felt that, although governors in his state did not have the advantage of controlling the formulation of the budget that the legislature considered, they were able to influence and even shape the product of the Joint Budget Committee.

Governors acknowledge the responsibility they have for formulating a state budget, even when the formal power is not exclusively theirs. In the survey, they were asked who, during their years in office, was responsible for the formulation of the state budget. Response options were on a six-point scale, ranging from 1 (the legislature played the predominant role) to 7 (the governor played the predominant role), with 4 signifying that an equal role was played by each. William Winter (R-MS), who was in office when the Mississippi state supreme court strengthened the governor's office on separation-of-powers grounds, did not submit a budget to the legislature. Only Otis Bowen (R-IN) indicated that the legislature played a greater role than the governor in the formulation of the budget. Another ten respondents ascribed an equal role to the two branches of government. The remaining 81 percent thought the governor dominated, including 24 percent who were at the extreme end of the scale in believing that the governor was totally dominant. The longer governors had served, the more dominant they reported they had been.

Although governors and legislatures have discretion over only 5 to 15 percent of the budget (whereas the rest of the budget is absorbed by mandated expenditures), this affords them the ability to prioritize, especially when the economy is in good shape.[23] Depending on the fiscal climate and revenue projections, governors can decide, at least initially, where expenditures will be increased and where they will be reduced, what new initiatives will be funded, and whether changes in taxes will be sought. At this stage, governors know what some of their policy goals are and what it will take in the budget to achieve them. Under an executive budget system, the governor defines the agenda, deals the cards, and dictates what game is to be played.[24] Even in states where governors do not formulate the budget, they are not without influence on the shape of the budget that is formulated.

If governors are facing fiscal difficulties, they are constrained severely in shaping their budgets and compiling their policy agendas. Many governors find themselves in such circumstances at one time or another during their administrations. They try to do more with less, like Cuomo when he was elected governor in New York.[25] They lay off state employees and remove people from relief rolls, as Mike Dukakis (D-MA) was forced to do.[26] They raise taxes, like George Nigh (D-OK) did. Alternatively, they defer new policy initiatives—in Arne Carlson's (R-MN) case for six years and in Zell Miller's case for only a short time.[27] At the very least, in bad times governors adjust their policy agendas accordingly.

Take Booth Gardner (D-WA), who later wrote about his budget priorities for state spending in the 1987–1989 biennium. He was committed to improving teacher salaries and reducing class size in the early elementary grades. But projected revenues were, in his words, "not that congenial." His conclusion was that after meeting fixed costs and accommodating expanded costs mandated by the legislature in previous years, "paying for improvements in our education system would have to be done incrementally and not through some bold, short-time expansion of the state budget.[28]

However constrained they may be by fiscal conditions and however many detours they have to take, governors continue to formulate policy agendas for their administrations. Former governors were asked in the survey to list their main policy priorities while in office. Of those responding, 92 percent listed education as one of their priorities. Those measures, coded as education, included school finance, reform, teacher pay, higher education, and the like. Many governors wanted to be recognized for their contributions to education in the state. Among the most prominent in the 1980s and 1990s were Lamar Alexander (R-TN), George W. Bush (R-TX), Tom Kean (R-NJ), Dick Riley (D-SC), Bill Clinton (D-AR), Booth Gardner, Jim Hunt, and Roy Romer. Governor after governor prided himself or herself on being the "education governor." When their state economies are favorable, almost every governor chooses to pursue a program of education improvement.

The second most popular priority is the economy and economic development, which can encompass educational improvement. A skilled workforce that derives from educational improvement is considered by governors to be one of the most important avenues to building the state's economy. Almost nine out of ten Republican governors and about half the Democratic governors emphasized measures in this area. Dukakis was acclaimed for the economic turnaround in his state, known as the "Massachusetts Miracle," which helped him win the Democratic nomination for president in 1988. During Hunt's sixteen years as governor of North Carolina, economic development, along with education, were major thrusts of his administration. During Gerald Baliles's (D-VA) four years as governor, most of his major initiatives (such as transportation, education, and the cleanup of the Chesapeake Bay) were in some way tied to economic development. Along with education, the economy was also the emphasis of Angus King, as it was for Joe Brennan (D-ME) before him. Few governors have paid as much attention to the nitty-gritty of economic development as George Voinovich (R-OH). He addressed problems of workers' compensation, agribusiness, technology, and tourism, and he reorganized the state's environmental protection agency to facilitate development. Voinovich took special pride in having helped business by building more turnpike exits than were built by all the Ohio governors before him.

Other policy domains were mentioned, as well—environment and energy by 47 percent, transportation by 34 percent, health by 32 percent, welfare by 22 percent, and criminal justice by 15 percent.

What is striking about the governors' survey responses is the issues that are missing from their priorities. Hot-button issues are not to be found. Guns are mentioned by only two of the responding governors; abortion, gay rights, immigration, and the death penalty are not mentioned at all. In these areas, bills were introduced by legislators. Governors may have backed legislator sponsors, negotiated modifications, or simply gone along with what legislative majorities endorsed, but these issues were not on their policy agendas. They responded to such issues but did not raise them. Their policy work was, in a sense, more mundane—the business of attending to the overall welfare of the state, concentrating on the "bread and butter" issues of state government.

Education is the major enterprise conducted by government in the states, requiring the largest portion of expenditures from revenues available. Starting in the 1970s, the nations' governors, especially those from the South, became more involved in education. They saw education reform as a means to improved economic development in their states. Then, following the publication of A Nation at Risk in 1983, governors made even greater efforts to improve education.[29] In any case, education has been perceived to be a less divisive issue than others, and the political risks of advocacy in this domain have been relatively low. It is not surprising, therefore, that so many governors put education on their want lists.

If education is one slice of "bread" on gubernatorial agendas, the economy and economic development is the other slice. "Governors have become the preeminent economic boosters of their states," one scholar wrote, "with a panoply of policies to promote business and create employment."[30] In the 1980s the pressure grew for governors to take a leadership role in this domain, as a consequence of the national recession that hurt the economies of many states. When NGA surveyed the governors and their aides in 1982, it found that in every region of the nation, except the West, the "economy/jobs" was the top issue. That same year, when Jim Blanchard (D-MI) was elected in Michigan, he announced his three top priorities—jobs, jobs, jobs.[31] Nowadays, the economy and its development is practically part of a governor's job description. Providing for a healthy economy and substantial economic growth is the governor's most direct route to increasing employment, productivity, and the standard of living. An important byproduct of a healthy economy is the enhancement of revenues that are available for other programs and services, including, of course, education. It is little wonder, then, that governors choose to press forward here.

The Multiple Sources of Initiatives

When political scientists write about the agenda-setting process, they note that ideas for legislation come from various sources, including interest groups, constituents, legislators, executives, and bureaucrats. In a conception as broad as agenda setting, it is easy to become bogged down in an attempt to answer the question, who thought of the idea first?[32] That question is almost impossible to answer. It is just as difficult to locate the precise source of each of the major policy proposals that comprise a governor's agenda. Gubernatorial policy initiatives come from just about everywhere and advance from stage to stage for a multiplicity of reasons. There is nothing neat about the processes by which governors decide on what to push by way of legislative programs. Some governors go through a more formal culling of ideas than do others, but the origins of these ideas are virtually impossible to trace with precision. An item in the survey made an attempt, however. It listed eleven sources of policy initiatives and asked whether items on the governors' policy agendas came from each source "to a large extent," "to some extent," or "to very little extent." Responses here, supplemented by interviews and memoirs and biographies, provide at least a general sense of some of the main tracks along which policy ideas run.

Policy proposals may not be born during the candidates' political campaigns for governor, although most policy proposals that governors advance are forged during their campaigns, at least in general terms. The "promises" and "commitments" made to the electorate during campaigns serve as the primary source and substance of their first year's agenda.[33] Indeed, almost nine out of ten survey respondents indicated that the items on their policy agendas came ("to a large extent" or "to some extent") from campaign promises, and as many as 65.5 percent of them recognized that their agendas derived "to a large extent" from what they had advocated during their campaigns for governor.

Governors take their campaign promises seriously. Nebraska's Nelson campaigned on what he referred to as "the three E's"—education, the environment, and economic development—and won a close race running on those issues. It occasioned little surprise that he dedicated his agenda to them. North Carolina's Hunt believed in establishing a contract with the electorate. "I always ran on what I was going to do," he said. That way people would know just what would happen if Hunt got elected. Joe Frank Harris (D-GA) took a similar tack. His administration's priorities were determined in his campaign. For him, there were two basic issues— education and economic development.

Those who win by large majorities consider them as mandates for their proposals. But even when governors win by less, they interpret their election as a mandate for their policy ideas. "I won in Texas by 352,000 votes," George W. Bush told the media, interpreting his election as a conservative "mandate." It was clear, the governor said, that "when you stand up in front of the Legislature and outline a legislative agenda that was endorsed by the will of the people, that helps remind people that this is what Texans want. . . ."[34] Tommy Thompson (R-WI) campaigned on the idea of cutting welfare benefits and putting the savings into job training; Dick Riley took office pledged to improve education; and Deval Patrick (D-MA) promised safe streets, better schools, and a reduced property tax. Christine Whitman campaigned on a pledge to cut taxes by up to 30 percent and reduce spending; and George Pataki had as a major issue of his campaign returning the death penalty to New York.[35] Mike Beebe (D-AR) made one of the more focused promises—that he would reduce the sales tax on groceries.[36] Bob Taft was even more down to earth—he would improve the trails in state parks.

The issues that governors run on as candidates are seldom new to them. They aren't invented for the statewide election campaign. In most cases, these are issues and ideas that the candidates have been thinking about and promoting for some time. They are embedded in their political philosophies or derive from prior political experiences. Kunin explained her policy heritage:

My political priorities stemmed from various experiences and observations, and they expressed the totality of who I was and how I had lived my life. In that respect I was no different from any other politician. Each one of us extracts policies from the mosaic of our lives.[37]

Glendening's agenda was also rooted in his life experiences. By the time he was elected county executive in Maryland's Prince Georges County, he had defined an agenda for himself. He was anti-tobacco, having seen his mother, a smoker, die of lung cancer and his brother, also a smoker, die of a heart attack at an early age. His gay brother died of AIDS, which became a continuing concern of Glendening. The environment evolved as one of his priorities over the years, in part because he watched the Everglades deteriorate during the time he was growing up in Florida. As governor, he translated his environmental concerns into the protection of Chesapeake Bay and smart growth programs for Maryland. Another of Glendening's priorities was education, which had made a big difference in his own life. He was very conscious of being the first one in his family to go to college. As governor, he funded education most generously and accelerated school construction by tapping into surpluses in the state's general revenue fund. Guns became an issue for him later on, as a result of gun violence in the cocaine wars of Prince Georges County.

Other governors also recalled specific linkages to the policy concerns they brought into office. Early encounters with education had an impact on a number of them. Tom Kean had been a teacher for twenty years before becoming governor, so when he assumed office the issue naturally became his top priority.[38] South Carolina's Riley became interested in education policy as a parent of children in the public school system, where his wife worked as a volunteer.[39] When his daughter was five years old and ready to attend kindergarten, Frank O'Bannon (D-IN) began to recognize the value of getting an early start on education. It was natural that as governor he made full-day kindergarten the centerpiece of his state of the state address and one of the principal goals of his first term in office.[40]

If individuals have served in executive or legislative branches of government previously, chances are good that their agenda items have been bouncing around long before their election as governor. Georgia's Miller knew from his experience as a legislator and lieutenant governor what he wanted to do as governor.[41] "By the time I became governor, I had eight years in the legislature, four as attorney general, plus an avid interest in government," said Brennan of Maine. Many of his policy initiatives as governor were hatched from ideas that came to him well before he took office. It was the same for Mike Hayden (R-KS). His three major initiatives—highway construction, mental health, and funding for the state water plan—all gestated before he was elected governor. John Engler started to think about Michigan's welfare system in the early 1970s, years before welfare reform was high on the national agenda.[42] Bob Wise (D-WV) brought college scholarships and health care, which he promoted in Congress, to the governor's office in West Virginia. "I knew what I wanted to do as governor," Kean wrote in his memoirs. Of course he knew. He had studied the office and the issues for almost a decade and a half before he became governor.[43]

In addition to what they would like to do, there are things governors feel they have to do. Engler, for instance, did not think that he could ignore the problem of property taxes in Michigan. Local schools were dependent on property taxes, which appeared to be on an upward trajectory beyond control. Either the governor would get something done or the courts would intervene, as they had in so many other states. Engler felt that he didn't have much choice. Governors who come to office in economic hard times and those who inherit deficits from their predecessors are not entirely free to choose. At the very least, they have to balance the budget. If things are bad enough—as they were in Arnold Schwarzenegger's (R-CA) California and Chris Christie's (R-NJ) New Jersey—they may be pushed to take on a longer-term structural deficit. For example, one month into the transition period, Christie was told that without serious action the state would fail to meet its payroll two months into his administration. The governor-elect figured that the only way to get control of state spending and local taxes was to reduce pension and health care benefits for public employees. To do this, he advanced a number of measures, including a cap on local expenditures.[44] Jim McGreevey (D-NJ) had pledged not to raise taxes. But Moody's Investor Service criticized the state, because cutting out fat would not be enough to make ends meet. Moreover, Moody's downgraded the state rating from Aa1 to Aa2, which meant that New Jersey would have to pay higher interest rates on borrowing. McGreevey felt that he had to resort to higher taxes—not on property or income, but on corporations operating within the state.[45]

Some new governors feel compelled to distance themselves from their predecessors. Jim Edgar had worked as a legislative liaison on the staff of Jim Thompson (R-IL), and Thompson had appointed him secretary of state. With Democrats charging, "We had Big Jim, now we got Little Jim," Edgar's challenge was "to convince voters after fourteen years of Jim Thompson that I was not more Jim Thompson." Jay Rockefeller (D-WV) undertook a competition with Arch Moore (R-WV), who preceded him as governor. Moore had tried to remove a sales tax on food, but failed. Rockefeller promised to remove it during his first campaign, but he too failed. Two years later he resurrected his proposal, and this time he prevailed. At the signing of the law, he reminded everybody present that he had been successful in getting the food tax removed and Moore hadn't. His biographer wrote, "One could easily suspect that Jay's true purpose was to accomplish something Moore couldn't."[46]

Blanchard pointed out that every new governor wants to do his or her own thing, and not build on or tear down what old governors did.[47] Nevertheless, a few may want to extend a predecessor's policy initiation or accomplishment, on the one hand, or erase it, on the other. According to survey responses, three out of ten governors sought legislative action to extend or expand major programs or policies enacted by their predecessors. Gary Locke (D-WA) followed in the footsteps of his Democratic predecessor on welfare reform policy. Taft adopted a report on education standards commissioned by his predecessor and completed it on his watch. Four out of ten survey responses revealed that governors sought to repeal or significantly change programs or policies enacted by their predecessors.

The departments and agencies of state government are not a principal source of agenda items. Only one out of five governors reported that departments and agencies in their administration furnished them such items to a large extent. Typically, department and agency bills proceed on a different track than the governor's initiatives. In New York, for instance, governors request "program bills" from the agencies. These proposals are usually of lesser or narrower import. They may be classified as governor's "program bills" or as "departmental bills."[48] Still, they would not be thought of as initiatives of their own by New York's governors. Only a few of the numerous departmental and agency proposals in states throughout the nation are at the core of a governor's legislative package. Governor Kay Orr (R-NE) illustrates the point. Her administration was responsible for about 80 to 100 bills—measures of a housekeeping nature, fine-tuning of previous legislation, or providing for reauthorization of some program. Governor Orr concentrated on a handful of issues, whereas the others were pushed by Nebraska's executive departments and agencies.[49]

Finally, whatever their overall usefulness, transition teams do not directly contribute to many gubernatorial agendas. According to Bob Wise, "a transition team cannot develop an agenda for you." That is because a governor needs an agenda a while before he or she is sworn into office. The campaign lays it out. Georgia's Harris wrote: "I guess our administration was somewhat predetermined coming out of the campaign, because that's when our priorities were established, the priorities upon which we campaigned, received the majority of votes, and got elected."[50] This affords governors a "mandate" of sorts. If the campaign had been about issues, the candidates took opposite positions, and the winner won by a large margin and also helped his or her party win seats in the legislature, then the legislature will recognize a solid mandate. Otherwise, as in most cases, the governor's mandate will be to govern, which includes proposing an agenda that the legislature will take seriously.[51]

How Agendas Are Developed

"You campaign in poetry, you govern in prose"—this observation of Mario Cuomo implies that the eloquent rhetoric of running has to be translated into the gritty practicalities of an agenda and the particularities of legislation. It begins with the shaping of an agenda from the values, ideas, and commitments that governors carry with them. Kunin wrote of the governor going through a creative process, like an artist, taking an idea that is about to emerge, articulating it, and readying it for action.[52] The formulative process surely contains some of that. Governors have to begin by thinking through what they want to prioritize and in what form. With Miller, the selection process raised the following sorts of questions: Which is most important among the possible items? Which will do more for people in Georgia? What do people want most?[53]

Here is where the governor's staff comes into the equation. On the survey, governors were asked whether their policy staffs had furnished items for their agendas. Nine out of ten respondents responded that they had, either to a large extent or to some extent, with 51 percent indicating that they contributed to a large extent. Some staffs play a significant role in determining what gets on the policy agenda. Kirk Fordice (R-MS) had no prior experience in office, so his staff had considerable discretion in finding issues that met some combination of the following criteria: were consistent with the governor's philosophy as a business-oriented conservative, reflected true reform, were things people wanted, made sense, could be paid for, and constituted good policy.[54] Most governors, however, are managers of the process rather than consumers of what their staffs devise. In line with a policy-management perspective, they use staff to increase the flow of information, they encourage a strategic outlook, and they involve themselves throughout. Take the approach that Riley used in South Carolina. About six months before each state of the state address, his staff focused on the year ahead. Staffers concerned primarily with education, industrial development, environmental issues, and other matters presented ideas and suggestions while the governor listened. This process resulted in the development of Riley's policy agenda.[55]

Among others, Cuomo addressed issues in a very organized way—the premises, the problems, the principles, and the recommendations.[56] One of the most rational processes of developing an agenda is that used by Thornburgh in Pennsylvania. His staff examined every proposal. First, a proposal went through a policy shop, which would make an assessment and offer a "pure" policy recommendation or set of options. Second, the lawyers would review it and warn of legal, especially constitutional, problems. Third, the budget office would look at costs and potential sources of revenue. Fourth, the legislative implications would be reviewed, including potential support and opposition. Fifth, the press office would consider the media's likely reaction. Sixth, a political assessment would determine whether the policy was consistent with the governor's overall philosophy and his campaign themes and would gauge how key interest groups would react. The procedure was never as orderly as this description suggests, but it did save the Thornburgh administration from a number of mistakes.[57] "We stubbed our toe," said Thornburgh, "when we didn't go through the checkpoints."

The developmental process can involve outsiders as well as the governor's own staff. Governors may invite academic experts to help them with the details of their policy agenda. In South Carolina, Hodges teamed up with a Duke University policy expert, who had experience working with a number of Democratic governors. They put together an educational plan, the components of which had been adopted as an "It's All About Our Schools" program in states around the country. Maine's Brennan established a commission to examine education and followed up its report with an initiative on merit pay for teachers. Kunin set up a summer study commission on school funding to help her out. Several legislators were members of the commission. She also created a commission on Vermont's future, which came up with recommendations that were then transformed into legislation. Georgia's Harris appointed an education review commission at the start of his term as governor. It was made up of thirty-five people, representing diverse backgrounds. The commission made recommendations for revising the curriculum and the funding formulas of the state.[58]

Thornburgh turned over the task of working out his new jobs and economic growth agenda to the state planning board and assigned one of his top aides to work with the group. The board took two and one-half years—of data gathering, study, and meetings across the state—to produce recommendations, which his administration then pursued for a number of years.[59] Oklahoma's ranking of forty-fifth in per-capita income prompted Frank Keating's (R-OK) drive for economic development. He asked the economics departments at the two state universities to figure out the reasons for the state's poverty. They informed him of the following: economic development was hurt by not having a right-to-work provision, the welfare system discouraged work, the power of trial lawyers made for high litigation costs, the transportation system was inadequate, the schools did not have academic rigor, and the state had too high a divorce rate. These issues became Keating's agenda.

All of this is part of the process by which governors put together their policy agendas. When they reach out, as in the examples provided by

Kunin, Harris, and Thornburgh, their intention is not only to come up with worthy proposals but also to begin building support for them. The more people who have their hands on what eventually becomes a gubernatorial agenda priority, the more support is built along the way. Participants on the committees and commissions, many of whom represent key groups in the state, develop within themselves a sense of ownership while they are helping to shape policies for the governor.

The Political Calculus at Work

NGA advises governors to consult with legislative leaders and other legislators as part of "selling the Governor's legislative program." It is useful, according to the association for governors, to discuss their priorities and solicit ideas at an early stage, identifying common ground before one side or the other becomes frozen into a position.[60] In the survey, former governors were asked to what extent they consulted with legislative leaders of their own party and of the opposition party when they formulated their policy agendas. As expected, they were more likely to consult with leaders of their own party; 71 percent said they consulted with their own party's leaders "all of the time" or "often," while 34 percent said they consulted with the other party's leaders as frequently. "Consultation," however, covers a wide range.

Some governors consult little or not much at all. Lowell Weicker (I-CT), Ben Cayetano (D-HI), Frank Murkowski (R-AK), and Joe Frank Harris rarely, if ever, consulted with leaders of either party when putting together their agendas.[61] In North Carolina the legislature rarely had a role in helping Hunt shape his initiatives. It either went along with them, which was usually the case, or it didn't, which happened only a few times.

On occasion, the legislature turns down a governor's overtures and refuses to be consulted. When Henry Bellmon (R-OK) invited senate and house Democratic leaders to breakfast and asked them to make suggestions for his budget and policy program, they declined, saying that they were legislators and Democrats and that he should develop his own proposals. They would help pass his program, but only if they felt it was good for the state.[62]

In some cases, a governor doesn't consult, because he or she doesn't want to lose the element of surprise. Christine Whitman was not disposed to consult, even with leaders of her own party that controlled the New Jersey legislature. After one document on her tax-cut plan had become public, she decided to keep the proposal a secret. "It's not that I like sneaking up on people," she said. "There are just times—on an issue that's very important to me or to the administration—I do want that opportunity to present it in the context in which I would like to see it." Until she revealed the tax cut in her budget address, everyone, including Republican legislators, would have to be patient. Whitman's exclusion of people who helped her get elected rankled Republican legislators.[63] Nonetheless, she got her program to reduce taxes through the legislature. Some governors, when they want to move quickly and when legislators generally know the direction in which they are going, are also less inclined to consult. They may be confident enough that the legislature will follow their lead without much consultation.

Most governors, however, do consult. When they fail to do so, they usually regret it later on. For example, because of his preoccupation with education issues, Bill Richardson (D-NM) forgot to clue in legislators on his plan for personal taxes. As a result, lawmakers were unprepared to deal with his proposal. Richardson wrote:

> There was someone to blame for this debacle, and I looked at him every morning when I shaved. In the aftermath, I vowed never to make that mistake again.[64]

For some governors, consultation is a one-way street. Traffic runs from governor to legislators, but not the other way. Thornburgh, for example, believed in keeping legislators informed. The policy initiatives and budgets were his, not theirs. Still, Thornburgh wanted legislators to feel that they were part of the process by which the governor's initiatives were developed. Their views would be taken into account. Those views usually pertained to the political ramifications of a proposal, rather than to its substance.

Other governors listen to legislative leaders. This practically ensures that they will have support for their proposals. Former governors call this "giving the legislature ownership." Maine's Brennan put it this way: "Involve people, involve them early, and make it seem like it was their idea." "We always tried to sit down with them and make them feel like they were part of it," recalled Edgar of Illinois. On Chicago school reform, for instance, Edgar met with Republican legislative leaders, who managed to put some provisions—but not major ones—into the governor's initiative. As a result, they felt like it was theirs. "I got the credit . . . they all voted for it and felt good, and we all did work together on it."

Governors who are probably most effective at gaining legislative support are the ones who are willing to surrender some control. They not only want to give the legislature a sense of ownership, they actually want the legislature to have ownership, even co-ownership. George Ariyoshi (D-HI) could probably have gotten his way with a Democratic legislature. But he let lawmakers know that he wanted to develop ideas collaboratively with them. Sometimes he would not even make a formal proposal, but instead gave them a lot of room to shape ideas and also to receive credit. "An idea that was mine," Ariyoshi wrote, "would become ours, and sometimes it would become theirs alone."[65] Democratic governor Romer had to face off against a Republican legislature in Colorado. He let it be known that he was available to work with the legislature and tended to highlight general areas that he thought needed action, rather than drafting proposals. He gave lawmakers ample leeway to work out the details.[66] Perhaps no governor, however, was as willing to delegate to the legislature as was Ned McWherter (D-TN). He was comfortable leaving a lot of major decisions up to the legislature and just as comfortable permitting the legislature to reshape proposals he had made.[67] Once he decided on an initiative, he would ask legislators to refine and perfect the proposal.

Budgeting is a particular area in which governors listen carefully to what legislative leaders have to say. Most governors have the authority to formulate budgets, but only a minority hold power as tightly as possible, excluding legislators from the initial stages of budget formulation. Republicans Tommy Thompson and Bob Ehrlich were among them, examples of governors who believed that the budget was theirs and theirs alone to assemble. Thompson did not invite leaders of the Democratic majorities in the Wisconsin senate and assembly to meet with him on the budget. Ehrlich regarded negotiations on the shape of the budget to be internal—among the departments and agencies of the executive branch—rather than between the governor and the Democratic legislature in Maryland.

He did acknowledge, however, that Maryland's supplemental budget was "where the games are played." The supplemental is a relatively small add-on, but one where the legislature seeks funding for its priorities. That's where the legislature comes in, according to Ehrlich's views.

It is not necessarily difficult for governors and legislators to reach agreement on the policy agenda. On many occasions, the governor and the legislature see eye to eye, at least in general terms. If the executive and legislative branches are under the control of the same party, agreement comes somewhat more easily. Governors are new to office every four or eight years, but legislatures are continuing bodies. Frequently, a governor's agenda priorities have already been on the legislature's agenda, especially since many items find their ways onto a committee, caucus, or leadership priority list. For example, the Texas legislature had been working toward welfare reform, "home rule" school districts, and juvenile justice reform well before Bush raised the issues in his 1994 gubernatorial campaign. Democrats criticized Bush for claiming credit for these initiatives, with one commenting that "he got on board a train that was already leaving the station."[68] (Of course, the train might not have reached its destination had the governor not gotten on board.) Indeed, when Bill Clements (R-TX) came into office, his agenda was far more conceptual than practical. His staff identified bills, already in the legislature, that matched the new governor's priorities. Thus, a legislative program was fashioned out of much that was already there.[69] On some measures, legislators and governors agree. They are aligned, such as on welfare reform in Illinois, Michigan, Wisconsin, and other states during the 1990s.

Some governors will go for broke, no matter what their chances might appear to be. Dick Snelling (R-VT) believed that it was the governor's job to take risks. "It is incumbent upon the governor to frequently stick out his neck and do something which is very, very unpopular, but important to the state."[70] Ehrlich, a Republican, put medical malpractice on his agenda, even though he expected it to be rejected by the Democratic legislature in Maryland. Riley, in South Carolina, was not afraid of losing, because he believed he was right and would prevail in the end.[71] Ronald Reagan epitomized those governors who aimed high but expected to settle for less. According to Lou Cannon, "The genius of Reagan as a politician was that his reach almost always exceeded his grasp, and that he didn't seem to mind." As California's governor, he sought more than was obtainable, and then signed off on the best deal he could get.[72]

However, most governors, most often, calculate what is politically possible before they commit to a policy agenda or to a budget. They anticipate the reaction of the legislature, based on their political intelligence and on their consultations with legislative leaders and other members. What they ask for in the first place depends in part, and sometimes large part, on what they think they can get. Ordinarily, if they face a legislature, or even one chamber, controlled by the other party, pragmatic governors calculate that they can get less. And they ask for less.

Romer, a Democratic governor facing a Republican legislature in Colorado, proved to be most effective at moving his agenda. Most important, he made the correct choices. He chose a few issues on which he couldn't win, but he chose many more on which he could. "You either pick a policy you can move on, and you move," he said. "Otherwise you don't move." This meant steering away from ideological issues as much as possible (recognizing, however, that the issue of more versus less government involved just about everything). Water policy, agriculture, energy, and the environment could be handled without sharp partisan divide. This also meant looking for existing or likely agreement in the legislature, such as on workers' compensation. The next steps involved identifying lawmakers who were interested in what the governor had in mind and then crafting an initiative in a way to get a broad base of members of each party.

Even with one's own party in control of the legislature, governors may opt to steer a cautious course. Maryland's Glendening would have liked to limit the purchase of guns to one per month. Mike Miller, the senate president, advised Glendening, "It's dead. Don't even put it in the state of the state." The governor took the advice. Ohio's Taft watched his step because "I was interested in getting stuff done." So, he brought forward proposals that the legislature could be expected to support. Taft had to scale back. He wanted to improve the quality of teachers. He acknowledged that tenure and other sensitive issues were important if teacher quality were to be improved. "But we didn't want to start a war." So his proposal concentrated on improving the education and training of teachers.

Governors have to know what agenda items to choose and when to choose them. By the time they take office, most individuals are skilled at making political choices—like Edgar, who had to work with both Republican and Democratic legislatures in Illinois. "Certain things I could do with a Republican legislature, such as reforming Chicago's schools," he explained. "But when it was necessary to raise taxes, it could only be done with a Democratic legislature." He was able to get much of what he wanted from both legislatures.

Agendas in a State of Play

The discussion thus far may lead one to believe that, at whatever time a governor's agenda starts being assembled, the time comes when the agenda is complete. The agenda's completion, it is popularly believed, occurs with the state of the state address or with the governor's budget message. Agenda setting, however, is by no means such a determinate process. Governors continue to reshape the agendas they have already molded and add items that they had not anticipated when they began the process. The need for the process to remain open has several sources.

First, and most important, governors encounter unanticipated crises or other events, some of which require legislative fixes and all of which divert the governor's attention from his or her previous priorities. As Thornburgh explained, there is not much time to calculate chances of success, but "when things are forced on you, then you just had to act." For Edgar, as for many others, "events set the agenda." When former governors were asked on the survey about the various sources of their policy agendas, four out of five indicated that, to a "large extent" or to "some extent," emergencies that arose were responsible for their initiatives. Lamar Alexander (R-TN) described the uncertainty of gubernatorial planning:

> Some days I'm trying to get the road program passed and a prison riot breaks out. . . . Someone is indicted. . . . It's like driving a team of mules with half pulling one way and half pulling the other, all with blinders on, and people shooting at you from all sides.[73]

John Ashcroft (R-MO) expressed his frustration with the frequency, complexity, and force of unexpected and uninvited issues that confronted him as governor. He didn't want to operate in the style of "Ready—Fire—Aim" as governor, but it was difficult for him to avoid it.[74]

Crises, in particular, demand the governor's attention, and they get it. As governor, Cecil Andrus (D-ID) was reminded frequently of the old adage that "there's nothing like a hanging in the morning to focus the mind."[75] Kean recalled that at the outset of his administration in New Jersey, "In the middle of all the planning and focus, we had a crisis every few days."[76] "Much of one's agenda," Wise said, "comes from events that governors can't control, such as economic conditions and natural disasters." During his first year as governor, Wise called six special sessions of the West Virginia legislature, including ones needed to shift budget items after 9/11, to enact legislation to forgive loans after floods, to respond to a demonstration at the capitol by coal truckers, and to avert the imminent shutdown of the state's three trauma centers. These are what South Carolina's Hodges refers to as "the events of the day." For him, one such event was 9/11, which resulted in a decline in state revenues and an increased focus by the governor on security matters. These "events of the day" can, and do, divert the governor from the legislative agenda he or she has settled on and may result in other items rising to priority status.

Thornburgh gave a telling account of how governors get distracted from their agendas day in and day out. As governor, he had agreed to visit a university class that had been studying the welfare reform initiative in Pennsylvania. Based on their study, the students were prepared to make recommendations to the governor. The day he visited, however, Thornburgh preempted the students' agenda, by starting out:

> Whew, what a day! I just had a call from Three Mile Island and had to dispatch the state police to deal with some antinuclear demonstrators there. As I left the office, I heard from one of our correctional institutions where a hunger strike is being carried on by some inmates who claim their religious practices are being inhibited by the administration's policy. Then, just as I got into the car to come here, an aide broke the news that he had me scheduled to meet with the United Way in Philadelphia and an Erie County Republican gathering on the same evening.... Now, what is it that you're here to talk about?

During this account of his day, the students could see how the relative priority of a policy briefing could be crowded out of the governor's agenda. The important subject to which they had devoted weeks of study turned out to be a mere blip on the screen of that day's pressing problems.[77]

Any number or variety of events can impact the governor's policy agenda one way or another. Court decisions require response, and often education funding is involved. When the Arkansas Supreme Court ruled that the state's formula for distributing education aid was unconstitutional, Bill Clinton had to take action, resulting in a major reform package.[78] School funding was an issue for Taft in Ohio, because of the court's requirement for equalization. The Montana Supreme Court forced Brian Schweitzer (D-MT) to call a special session of the legislature to deal with school funding.[79] Bill Clements had to call the legislature back into session by order of the state supreme court in order to address school funding disparities in Texas.[80]

Prisons have caused concern for a number of governors, including Clements. A suit led to a court order requiring that Texas relieve prison overcrowding. The governor had to ask the legislature for emergency funds to construct new prison dormitories.[81] Maryland's Hughes felt that he had to allocate state funds for the construction of new prisons to house a growing convict population and other programs to rehabilitate them.[82] A number of governors had to handle a savings and loan crisis. Hughes was one of them. He worked with legislative leaders to fashion a package of seven emergency bills designed to solve the problem in Maryland.[83] Three Mile Island took Thornburgh completely by surprise. Less than three months into his administration, an accident occurred at the nuclear power plant, requiring all of the new governor's energy. In retrospect, Thornburgh acknowledged that it helped his administration hone its skills; nonetheless, it was a tremendous distraction from the policy agenda he had shaped.[84]

From Three Mile Island, Thornburgh learned not to be surprised by the unexpected. That's much of what he got—long gas lines, water shortages, floods, transit strikes, subway crashes, and hostage-taking in the state prisons.[85] All these events affected the governor's policy plans and created an agenda that had not been planned ahead. Jay Rockefeller also met with a series of mishaps—frozen rivers, frozen pipes, a natural gas shortage, and a winter storm of blizzard proportion. Rockefeller is said to have told his staff during that period that the Lord must have been a Republican. The time that Rockefeller had to devote to weather problems left him little for his legislative agenda. So, instead of an agenda, he gave about half his proposals to legislators to advocate and the rest he kept for himself, to be used at a June special session.[86] It was not the way he would have preferred it to be.

Virginia's Baliles counsels governors that they have to be "strategic," "methodical," and flexible when opportunities arise. In other words, they have to plan carefully but adjust constantly. The objective is to cross the goal line, which is more likely by weaving and spinning than by running straight ahead. However they run, they have to be able to stay on their feet and keep their legs moving. Persistence is necessary. Carroll Campbell (R-SC) pursued one of his priority issues—restructuring government—for three years before he could get a win.[87] Riley lost his tax equity package in the South Carolina legislature. Rebounding from the defeat, the governor and his staff decided on a different educational reform plan and figured out how to build support for that plan. Within a few months they were putting together the Education Improvement Act package that eventually constituted Governor Riley's legacy to his state.[88] Incrementalism was the *modus operandi* of the large majority of governors, even for Mario Cuomo, who is celebrated for his vision and his rhetoric. After the 1985 legislative session, Cuomo referred to how the process works by accretion: "Pick up a little piece here, a little piece there, and you have to keep working at it." It took him five years to get a Medicaid change, nine years to get the legislature to vote on life imprisonment without parole, and a long time to get a tax cut he sought. "So," Cuomo summed up, "you don't get everything the first shot."[89] It all requires resilience, which governors have in great supply. It also takes hard work, which governors are more than willing to do.

Notes

1. Lee Bernick and Charles W. Wiggins, "Executive Legislative Relations: The Governor's Role as Chief Legislator," in *Gubernatorial Leadership and State Policy*, ed. Eric B. Herzik and Brent W. Brown (Westport, CT: Greenwood Press, 1991), 73.

2. Herzik and Brown, *Gubernatorial Leadership and State Policy*, ix.

3. Alan Rosenthal, *Governors and Legislatures: Contending Powers* (Washington, D.C.: CQ Press, 1990), 96.

4. National Governors Association, *Words of Wisdom on Transition & Governing Topics* (Washington, D.C.: National Governors Association, n.d.).

5. National Governors Association, *Transition and the New Governor: A Planning Guide* (Washington, D.C.: National Governors Association, 1998), 93.

6. Eric B. Herzik, "Policy Agendas and Gubernatorial Leadership," in Herzik and Brown, *Gubernatorial Leadership and State Policy*, 25–37.

7. Thad Kousser and Justin A. Phillips, *The Hidden Power of American Governors* (Cambridge: Cambridge University Press, in process).

8. Madeleine M. Kunin, *Living a Political Life* (New York: Vintage, 1994), 382.

9. Margaret Robertson Ferguson, "Chief Executive Success in the Legislative Arena," *State Politics and Policy Quarterly* 3 (Summer 2003): 167.

10. Kousser and Phillips, *The Hidden Power of American Governors*.

11. Robert B. Ward, *New York State Government* (Albany, NY: Rockefeller Institute Press, 2002), 54.

12. Robert S. McElvaine, *Mario Cuomo: A Biography* (New York: Scribner's, 1988), 315–16.

13. S. V. Date, *Quiet Passion: A Biography of Senator Bob Graham* (New York: Penguin, 2004), 107, 109.

14. Bernick and Wiggins, "Executive Legislative Relations," 75–76.

15. National Governors Association, *Transition and the New Governor*, 25–26.

16. Gleaves Whitney, *John Engler: The Man, the Leader & the Legacy* (Chelsea, MI: Sleeping Bear Press, 2002), 167.

17. Patricia Beard, *Growing Up Republican* (New York: Harper Collins, 1996), 208.

18. Laura A. van Assendelft, *Governors, Agenda Setting, and Divided Government* (Lanham, MD: University Press of America, 1997), 81.

19. Harry Roe Hughes, *My Unexpected Journey* (Charleston, SC: History Press, 2006), 165.

20. *New York Times*, October 25, 2010.

21. Dick Thornburgh, *Where the Evidence Leads* (Pittsburgh: University of Pittsburgh Press, 2003), 110.

22. Jack D. Fleer, *North Carolina Government and Politics* (Lincoln: University of Nebraska Press, 1994), 99; Diane D. Blair, *Arkansas Politics and Government* (Lincoln: University of Nebraska Press, 1988), 248–50.

23. Nelson C. Dometrius, "The Power of the (Empty) Purse," in Herzik and Brown, *Gubernatorial Leadership and State Policy*, 100–1.

24. Rosenthal, *Governors and Legislatures*, 135–136; Tom Loftus, "The Wisconsin Budget Process," Lecture at the University of Wisconsin–Whitewater, March 17, 1986, 3.

25. McElvaine, *Mario Cuomo*, 310–11.

26. Charles Kenney and Robert L. Turner, *Dukakis: An American Odyssey*, (Boston: Houghton Mifflin, 1988), 95.

27. Daniel J. Elazar, Virginia Gray, and Wyman Spano, *Minnesota Politics and Government* (Lincoln: University of Nebraska Press, 1999), 131; van Assendelft, *Governors, Agenda Setting, and Divided Government*, 86–87.

28. Booth Gardner, "Schools for the 21st Century" in *Governors on Governing*, ed. Robert D. Behn (Lanham, MD: University Press of America, 1991), 122.

29. Maris A. Vinovskis, "Gubernatorial Leadership and American K–12 Education Reform" in *A Legacy of Innovation: Governors and Public Policy*, ed. Ethan G. Sribnick (Philadelphia: University of Pennsylvania Press, 2008), 192, 202.

30. Jon C. Teaford, "Governors and Economic Development," in Sribnick, *A Legacy of Innovation*, 107.

31. Ibid., 119.

32. Donald A. Gross, "The Policy Role of Governors" in Herzik and Brown, *Gubernatorial Leadership and State Policy*, 13.

33. National Governors Association, *Transition and the New Governor*, 64.

34. J. H. Hatfield, *Fortunate Son: George W. Bush and the Making of an American President* (New York: Soft Skull Press, 2001), 161.

35. Tom Loftus, *The Art of Legislative Politics* (Washington, D.C.: CQ Press, 1994), 125; Beard, *Growing Up Republican*, 184; Alan Ehrenhalt, "Patrick's Promises," *Governing* (November 2009): 12; George J. Marlin, *Squandered Opportunities: New York's Pataki Years* (South Bend, IN: St. Augustine's Press, 2006), 156.

36. Alan Ehrenhalt, "Butch's Battle," *Governing* (June 2009): 12.

37. Kunin, *Living a Political Life*, 363.

38. Thomas H. Kean, *The Politics of Inclusion* (New York: Free Press, 1988), 209.

39. Benjamin Prince Bagwell, *Riley: A Story of Hope* (Pickens, SC: Pickens County Publishing, 1986), 85.

40. Andrew E. Stoner, *Legacy of a Governor: The Life of Indiana's Frank O'Bannon* (Bloomington, IN: Rooftop Publishing, 2006), 253.

41. Van Assendelft, *Governors, Agenda Setting, and Divided Government*, 85.

42. Whitney, *John Engler*, 281–82.

43. Kean, *The Politics of Inclusion*, 60–61.

44. Matt Bai, "The Disrupter," *New York Times Magazine*, February 27, 2011, 35.

45. James E. McGreevey, *The Confession* (New York: HarperCollins, 2006), 413–14.

46. Richard Grimes, *Jay Rockefeller: Old Money, New Politics* (Charleston, WV: Jalamap Publications, 1984), 94–95.

47. National Governors Association meeting, Washington, D.C., February 21, 2010.

48. Ward, *New York State Government*, 61.

49. Rosenthal, *Governors and Legislatures*, 103.

50. Joe Frank Harris, *Personal Reflections on a Public Life* (Macon, GA: Mercer University Press, 1998), 101–2.

51. I am grateful to an anonymous reviewer, who clarified the distinction among mandates.

52. Kunin, *Living a Political Life*, 53.

53. Van Assendelft, *Governors, Agenda Setting, and Divided Government*, 89.

54. Ibid., 154–55, 192.

55. Bagwell, *Riley*, 128–29.

56. McElvaine, *Mario Cuomo*, 312.

57. Thornburgh, *Where the Evidence Leads*, 108–9.

58. Harris, *Personal Reflections on a Public Life*, 111–12.

59. Thornburgh, *Where the Evidence Leads*, 126–27.

60. National Governors Association, *Transition and the New Governor*, 92, 94.

61. Response from survey.

62. Henry Bellmon, *The Life and Times of Henry Bellmon* (Tulsa, OK: Council Oak Books, 1992), 202.

63. Art Weissman, *Christine Todd Whitman* (New York: Carol Publishing Group, 1996), 133–34, 205–6.

64. Bill Richardson, *Between Worlds: The Making of an American Life* (New York: Penguin Group, 2005), 323.

65. George R. Ariyoshi, *With Obligations to All* (Honolulu: Ariyoshi Foundation, 1997), 151–52.

66. Thomas E. Cronin and Robert D. Loevy, *Colorado Politics and Government* (Lincoln: University of Nebraska Press, 1993), 223.

67. Van Assendelft, *Governors, Agenda Setting, and Divided Government,* 121–22.

68. Hatfield, *Fortunate Son,* 162.

69. Carolyn Barta, *Bill Clements: Texian to His Toenails* (Austin, TX: Eakin Press, 1996), 224.

70. Rosenthal, *Governors and Legislatures,* 100, footnote 8.

71. Bagwell, *Riley,* 93.

72. Lou Cannon, *Governor Reagan* (New York: Public Affairs, 2003), 184.

73. Lamar Alexander, "What Do Governors Do?" in Behn, *Governors on Governing,* 45.

74. John Ashcroft, "Leadership: The Art of Redefining the Possible," in Behn, *Governors on Governing,* 70–71.

75. Cecil Andrus and Joel Connelly, *Cecil Andrus: Politics Western Style* (Seattle: Sasquatch Books, 1998), 103.

76. Panel on Governor Kean, Governors Project archive, Eagleton Institute of Politics, Rutgers University, April 15, 2009.

77. Thornburgh, *Where the Evidence Leads,* 197–98.

78. Charles F. Allen and Jonathan Portis, *The Comeback Kid: The Life and Career of Bill Clinton* (New York: Carol Publishing Group, 1992), 82–83; Dan Durning, "Education Reform in Arkansas: The Governor's Role in Policymaking," in Herzik and Brown, *Gubernatorial Leadership and State Policy,* 126–27.

79. Greg Lemon, *Blue Man in a Red State: Montana's Governor Brian Schweitzer and the New Western Populism* (Helena, MT: TwoDot, 2008), 98.

80. Barta, *Bill Clements,* 387–88.

81. Ibid., 252–53.

82. Hughes, *My Unexpected Journey,* 154–55.

83. Ibid., 189.

84. Thornburgh, *Where the Evidence Leads,* 111–12.

85. Ibid., 120.

86. Grimes, *Jay Rockefeller,* 185.

87. Van Assendelft, *Governors, Agenda Setting, and Divided Government,* 197.

88. Bagwell, *Riley,* 68.

89. McElvaine, *Mario Cuomo,* 341.

5

Laying the Groundwork for Their Initiatives

FOR A GOVERNOR, getting legislative support for an agenda is not simply a campaign, it is a full-time job. When the legislature is in session at the capitol, the governor is close at hand or on call. Unless special sessions occur, governors in states such as Alabama, Florida, Georgia, New Hampshire, New Mexico, South Dakota, and Virginia have to be around only for regular legislative sessions of sixty days or less. In Colorado, Delaware, Hawaii, Maryland, Minnesota, and Washington, legislatures meet in regular session for longer periods (and governors do not feel they can leave town before the legislature does). In a number of states, such as California, Illinois, Massachusetts, Michigan, New York, Ohio, and Pennsylvania, sessions are under way for half the year or more, during which governors spend much of their time ministering to the legislative branch and its members. Whether or not they like the ministerial role, it is a critical part of the policy leadership role.

Gubernatorial Involvement

In the survey conducted for this book, former governors were asked, "How would you describe your approach to the legislature, as far as getting your agenda policies adopted? Did you put your proposals out there and let the legislative process take its course, or did you manage your policy proposals through the process on a day-by-day basis?" They were asked to locate themselves on a continuum from 1 (involved throughout the process) to 7 (not involved at all), with 4 the midpoint (somewhat involved). The overall mean of their involvement is 1.91. Three out of four respondents located themselves at the 1 or 2 value on the involvement continuum. Stephen Merrill (R-NH) pointed out that since the New Hampshire legislature had 424 members, "You'd better stay involved." Merrill had more legislators than any other governor with whom to deal, but governors with much smaller legislatures also stayed involved when the session was on.

Of course, their involvement varied issue by issue and day by day. More than any other issue the budget commanded their attention. On days when members were more likely to be back in their districts, such as Mondays or Fridays, governors were afforded more down time than on the days when members were in committee meetings or on the floor. Whether the session was just starting or winding down also mattered. The rhythm for Michael Leavitt (R-UT) went as follows: "I learned to play aggressively on budget issues at the beginning and at the end of the session. I let the legislature run their process in between."[1]

Governors are involved because they have to be involved, if they want their budgets and policy agendas adopted. Even governors with little or no political experience appreciate this. If any are unsure of what they should be doing when the legislature is in town, the National Governors Association (NGA) has reminded them consistently of their duties:[2]

- Help legislators do their jobs—representing constituents, making laws, and balancing the power of the executive
- Listen to them regarding their concerns with constituency problems
- Create win-win situations
- Respect the legislature; don't get in a fight over power

Some governors take naturally to their dealings with the legislature. Zell Miller (D-GA) is a wonderful example. He understood the powers of his office extremely well, but he went further than most of his colleagues in trying to win over legislators. He had legislators and their spouses to the mansion for black-tie affairs, so that they would feel special. He walked the halls at the capitol from time to time, just to be seen. He went to committee meetings, had private talks with legislators, and pulled out just about all the stops.[3] Bill Clinton (D-AR) was another governor who enjoyed working the legislature, rubbing elbows with legislators whenever he could. He attended and testified at committee meetings, stood outside the chamber calling members off the floor, and spent time on the floor of the senate and the house, as well. Clinton always appeared to be at the spot where legislative things were happening.[4]

Most governors recognize the importance of building a relationship with the legislature and its members. Jim Hunt's (D-NC) approach was to talk to people, work with them, and find things in common. One way or another, he would always try to forge a relationship. Bob Taft (R-OH) is another governor who worked diligently along the same lines. He supported legislators' campaigns, sought input from their leaders, gave the legislature advance notice of the governor's agenda, engaged in give and take with legislative leaders, was accessible to members, demonstrated flexibility in negotiations, and invited lawmakers to bill signings. Taft made all the right moves, which helped him move his agenda.

For a governor to be involved, it is a question not only of being there and rubbing elbows, but also of knowing the issues and what needs to be done. Knowledge—both substantive and political—impresses legislators, legislative staff, and other members of the capitol community. It stands a governor in good stead. John Engler (R-MI) was a master in this respect. When managing budgets entailing eighteen or nineteen appropriation bills, Engler had complete command of the numbers and the provisions, and he knew all the tricks of the trade. On legislative measures, he had similar command of all the details. Even veteran legislators were impressed.[5] Other governors keep some distance between themselves and the legislature. Carroll Campbell (R-SC) would make recommendations to the legislature and then leave the rest to his staff. He communicated through his staff and did not spend much time cultivating relationships on a personal level. Bill Clements (R-TX) was another governor who distanced himself from the action, leaving most of it to staff. One of his aides described the governor's way as "don't bother him with the details; just go out and do it."[6] Some governors simply lack the patience that legislatures demand. Bob Casey (D-PA) faced a divided and contentious legislature. Although he was up to battle, he also felt "removed from it, impatient with all the haggling and maneuvering and accusations." Day-to-day politics in the legislature did not appeal to Casey; he preferred to spend his time on other things, and so he did.[7]

Relating to Members

Legislators want to be in the governor's good graces. The governor can make their lives happier and their careers brighter. As James D. Barber pointed out years ago in his study of members of the Connecticut general assembly, future possibilities for legislators are never well defined. If they please the governor, he or she may do right by them later on, if not earlier.[8] As Andrew Cuomo (D-NY) commented just before his election in 2010, "A governor can be a very good friend to people."[9] Most of them try to be. They reach out right away, softening up legislators for the support they, the governors, will need in the legislative encounters ahead.

By way of welcome, governors leave their door open for legislators to visit with them. Among respondents to the survey of former governors, four out of five indicated that they were very accessible to rank-and-file lawmakers of their own party. Three out of four indicated that they were very accessible to the rank and file of the other party, as well. Democratic governors were more accessible than Republican governors, but the difference was slight. When government was divided, nine out of ten governors left their doors wide open. Only a few governors would refuse access to legislators who wanted it. George Pataki (R-NY) was one of them. He preferred his relative isolation to the company of legislators.[10]

Governors don't just wait for legislators to come through the door. They reach out to legislators, because it appears to work and because it also fits their personalities. They believe in connecting personally. They seek to develop relationships one-on-one, which usually requires a lot of schmoozing. It also requires genuine talent on the parts of governors. "It's very important to get to know individuals," as George Voinovich (R-OH) put it. "I know their kids, I know their wives, I've been to their houses," summed up Mike Hayden (R-KS).

Arnold Schwarzenegger (R-CA) went out of his way in his courtship of legislators. During his first year as a celebrity governor, he invited every legislator to his office and he dropped in on them at their offices. With some, the new governor got up close and squeezed their arms to see whether their workouts were producing the right muscle development. With others, he would hand out cigars with his name on them as souvenirs.[11] One doesn't have to be a celebrity governor to charm legislators. In

New Jersey a patrician governor, Tom Kean (R-NJ), did it as well but in his own way. Kean is remembered for his ability to relate to people in the legislature and to their personal interests. If he was with Carmen Orechio (a Democratic senate president), he talked about the New York Yankees, Orechio's favorite team. If he was with John Russo (another Democratic senate president), he talked about Russo's favorite, the New York Giants football team, even though he, himself, was a Washington Redskins fan. With Alan Karcher (a Democratic speaker of the assembly), the governor discussed the latest books. "All that," related Lew Thurston, Kean's first chief of staff, "built a trust and a relationship that was really important."[12] Another active, outgoing governor, Mike Beebe (D-AR), was a very different type than his predecessor, Mike Huckabee (R-AR). The latter would hole up in his office, while Beebe worked the halls and cafeterias. "There's no telling where you'll find him in this building," said Shane Broadway, a member of the Arkansas senate. In his chats with legislators, the governor moved "right up into their faces like a baseball manager questioning a call but in an amiable way."[13]

Bob Wise (D-WV) would wander around on the second floor of the capitol, stand in the rotunda, and buttonhole legislators who were passing by. (Although as a former member, Wise as governor had the privilege of the senate floor, he felt that it was better not to use it.) Jim Hunt would take biscuits over to the North Carolina legislature every morning of the session, meeting with about twenty lawmakers on each biscuit occasion. Even Clements, who was much more hands-off than other governors, made a real effort to get together with Texas legislators. With so few Republicans to count on, Clements had to rely on Democrats. He met with committee chairmen and with more than one hundred lawmakers in small groups in the two months between his election and inauguration. He kept up the pace, working at the cultivation of legislators after he took office, inviting members into his office for drinks after 5:00 p.m. and hosting key legislators at luncheons he gave.[14]

In laying the groundwork with legislators, among the resources governors have at their disposal is their residence, the executive mansion. One of James Thompson's (R-IL) fifteen rules for getting along with the legislature, which he conveyed at an NGA meeting, was to invite members to the governor's mansion, especially at cocktail time. His gubernatorial colleagues at the meeting, upon hearing this recommendation, nodded in agreement.[15] Like Thompson, most governors put their residence to good use. In Augusta, Maine, the governor's residence is just across the street from the statehouse. The proximity helped Joe Brennan (D-ME) build relationships. When problems arose—and even in the periods between problems—the governor would invite six, seven, or eight legislators to lunch. Legislators were impressed; they liked the experience, and it paid off for the governor. In Charleston, West Virginia, the governor's mansion is within easy walking distance of the state capitol building. Gaston Caperton (D-WV) would regularly convene a meeting of legislative leaders at the mansion prior to the start of the session and often invited rank-and-file legislators over for lunch or dinner. These meetings were sometimes about specific matters, but more often they were just friendly get-togethers.[16]

Henry Bellmon (R-OK) did it the old-fashioned way, as a family undertaking at the mansion. His wife, with one helper, did the cooking, and his daughters served twelve guests at a time. "These were happy events," Bellmon writes, "and probably did much to cement relations with legislators, most of whom were Democrats and tended to be suspicious of the state's first Republican governor."[17] Parris Glendening (D-MD) wandered further from home. To build relationships with legislators, he used the state's luxury boxes at the Baltimore football and baseball stadiums and quick trips out to Chesapeake Bay on the governor's yacht (which Bob Ehrlich [R-MD] later sold).

If governors are naturally social animals, as most of them are, socializing works nicely. Their gestures are appreciated, even if the social recognition governors confer on legislators is not what it used to be. Take the beneficence of Edwin Edwards (D-LA), a master host when he held office. He had a daily shuttle of legislators to the mansion for breakfast and for lunch. "Any legislator who wanted to play," wrote a reporter, "had fun keeping up with it, being in on it." Edwards even took legislators, along with campaign contributors, with him on a trip to Europe. The trip was billed as a fundraising event, but it also served to soften up the legislators who went along. Nelson Rockefeller, as governor of New York, operated in a different style but produced similar results. He would invite legislators to his estate at Pocantico, to view his collection of sculpture on the grounds, to tour the array of paintings in the house and its galleries, and to dine and take in the exquisite scenery on the Rockefeller spread. Legislators could not help but be impressed. They naturally wanted to be invited back to Pocantico, but this depended on their staying on good terms with the governor. Though Rockefeller's invitations may not have bought any votes per se, they surely didn't hurt the governor's agenda in Albany.[18]

Some governors limit their social contact with legislators. Reagan was one of them. Legislators as a group simply did not interest him; he preferred to be removed, distant. He shunned the numerous receptions where liquor flowed and kept his hosting responsibilities to a minimum. Anyway, by the end of the day he was tired. Whenever possible, Reagan left the capitol by 5:30 p.m. and went home to a quiet dinner with his wife, Nancy. In the evening, he read or he watched *Mission: Impossible* on television.[19] After Reagan, another Republican, George Deukmejian (R-CA), also observed a strict calendar as far as rank-and-file legislators were concerned. He was not the type of governor to pull a bottle of booze out of his desk drawer or swap stories with legislators after hours.[20] Jim Edgar (R-IL) also chartered a minimal social course in Illinois. Edgar didn't drink, whereas most legislators did. "I'm not a guy they want to have dinner with, because I won't let them drink," Edgar said. He left the socializing to his staff, who were good at going out and drinking with legislators. Thornburgh had a compelling reason for not doing what he did not want to do. It was better to be removed but still informed and engaged. "If you're out drinking beer with legislators," he argued, "you risk your credibility with them." The distance may have afforded the governor additional stature, but it also fit his personality well. On his part, Jesse Ventura (I-MN) hosted a breakfast for legislators during his first year in office, so that he could get to know them better. He decided against having another breakfast the following year. Apparently, he had lost his appetite for getting to know them better.[21]

Governors do not have to be involved socially to relate well to legislators. NGA has pointed out to new governors the importance of respecting legislators' status and attending to legislators' egos.[22]

NGA further recommends that governors help legislators with their issues *before* governors ask for help with their own issues. This entails governors knowing how each member of the senate and the house operates as an individual and then anticipating what the legislator might need and might want.[23] Oklahoma's Bellmon had a very good idea of what some legislators might need and might want. Before fund-raising became a *sine qua non* of politics, Bellmon raised money for campaigns, money that had been contributed by various friends who believed it essential for the governor to have a good working relation-ship with the legislature. The funds went to the campaigns of Demo-crats and Republicans alike.[24] Other governors helped legislators get projects for their districts, gave them departmental and agency bills to sponsor so that they could claim credit, and invited them to share the platform during a gubernatorial visit to a legislative district.[25]

North Carolina's Hunt believed that he not only had to know legisla-tors personally, but he also had to know their districts. "Whenever a legislator asked me to come to his district," Hunt said, "I went." When travelling around the state, Gerald Baliles (D-VA) would always invite lawmakers—even Republican ones—to share the stage with him. Again, not every governor is willing to play that game with legislators. Clements would not put up with the pettiness of it all—"that somebody's vote would depend on getting the queen of the Tomato Festival's picture made with the governor." George Christian, a longtime political opera-tive in Texas, characterized Clements as "good at a lot of things," but not "good at politics."[26] Mike Dukakis (D-MA), during his first administra-tion, eschewed politics. He barred favors and patronage to Massachu-setts legislators, telling Democrats flatly that there would be no jobs for constituents during his tenure. Playing by his own rules, not by tradi-tional rules, Dukakis was considered aloof, pedantic, and neglectful of friends. After he was defeated in 1978 and was then returned to office in 1982, he saw things differently. Patronage became the rule, not the excep-tion, and the senate president went so far as to comment that "Dukakis has raised patronage to a fine art."[27] Dukakis was transformed. For Rea-gan, it was a matter of adjustment. At a Sacramento reception the gover-nor got into verbal sparring with Bill Bagley, an assemblyman. Bagley had little use for Reagan, and the governor reciprocated the feeling. On the ride home after the reception, Reagan gave some thought to what had happened and said to an aide: "You know, all Bill really wants is attention, and we're going to give it to him. Find some bills we can work together on and have him be the author."[28]

A lot of it boils down to respect. Legislators want respect from governors. Angus King (I-ME) went out of his way to be respectful to the Maine legislature. He felt that as an independent, he had to make a special effort. He instructed his staff at the start of his first term: "Nobody in this administration badmouths the legislature." In the Maine statehouse, the governor's office is on the second floor, whereas the legislature is on the third floor. Traditionally, governors never walked up to the third, but King broke that tradition. He went up to see them, in addition to them coming down to see him. Respect covers a broad swath, but legislators know it when they receive it and they know it even more when they don't. One of Jeb Bush's (R-FL) main adversaries in the Florida legislature was Tom Lee, a Republican senator. Even before he ascended to the senate presidency, Lee was a thorn in the governor's side. In the second year of his two-year term-limited stint as president, Lee switched to the governor's side on a number of issues. Why? Some believe that it was because Lee hoped to run statewide for a cabinet position and wanted Bush's endorsement. But Bush's biographer attributes the about-face, which found the senate president calling Bush "my governor," to a more personal factor. The two had grown closer, Lee explained, because "I think he respects me."[29]

Dealing With Legislative Leaders

Whether or not they like it, governors have to deal with legislative leaders, in particular those who command majorities in the senate and the house. The leaders of the majority party in the legislature are pivotal for the governor's policy leadership. They are elected by their legislator colleagues to represent their chamber, and especially their party caucus. To varying degrees, these leaders determine what is on their chamber's agenda. They are charged with, among other things, safeguarding the legislature's independence and coequality with the executive branch. Some of the leaders whose party controls the executive think of themselves not just as representing the legislature and their colleagues, but also as lieutenants of the governor. The leaders usually negotiate the major provisions of the budget and major policy issues, between the chambers and with the governor. Primarily because of their ability to reward, and secondarily because of their ability to punish, they can independently sway the votes of swing members on critical issues. "The key," according to Jim Hunt, "is to understand that they are the leaders, and you have to work with them."

The more powerful the leader, the more a governor will see fit to come to terms with him or her. The Illinois legislative system, especially in the house, has been leader-centric for at least the past thirty years. Mike Madigan, the Democratic house speaker, exemplifies the strong leadership tradition. He was also, in the opinion of Jim Edgar, the smartest person in Springfield. An Illinois governor had to convince not only Madigan, but also three other leaders. "But you got to have a relationship" in order to do the convincing, according to Edgar. That is because "you can't make a deal with a guy you don't trust." If a governor has a good relationship with the leaders, he or she doesn't have to spend as much time working individual member, at least, not usually. "If I got the four leaders," Edgar explained, "they'd get those guys" nearly always. Ordinarily Illinois legislators do not buck their leaders.

Strong legislative leadership also characterized Ohio in the 1970s, 1980s, and 1990s. "I inherited the most powerful speaker in the nation," as George Voinovich recalled his relationship to Vern Riffe. Voinovich had learned his lesson when he served as lieutenant governor and the speaker cut his budget. "Why?" Voinovich asked Riffe. "Partner, you didn't come up to see me," Riffe replied. As governor, Voinovich not only went up to see the speaker but, as he put it, "I genuflected before Vern."

New York is another strong leadership state, where for many years Democrats controlled the assembly, Republicans controlled the senate, and the two parties divided control of the executive. The so-called "big three" or "three men in a room" were the governor, the assembly speaker, and the senate majority leader. The system had been one of "responsible" parties, as in a parliamentary democracy, with both the majority and minority legislative parties cohesive on some overarching issues. The assembly speaker and the senate majority leader derived their strength from their party conferences (or caucuses) and negotiated the budget and other major issues with one another and with the governor. The system that had been in place in Albany for so long began breaking down in the administration of Pataki. It weakened when Eliot Spitzer (D-NY) became governor briefly in 2007 and denounced the "three men in a room" model of governing. It appears to be undergoing a resurrection with Andrew Cuomo as governor.

In some legislatures the structure of leadership is institutionally weak. There is probably no better example of this than Nebraska's legislature, which is not only unicameral but also nonpartisan. This makes the job of governor different and possibly simpler. Nebraska governors do not have to worry about a second house or about majority- and minority-party leaders. In the forty-nine-member unicameral legislature, power is highly dispersed, more so than in any other state legislature in the country. Ben Nelson (D-NE) explained that Nebraska had weak and rotating legislative leadership, with only the power to set the legislative schedule. Unlike in nearly all the other legislative chambers, the speaker does not appoint committee chairs, who instead are elected by secret ballot of committee members. In such a legislature, every one of the forty-nine members regards himself or herself as a leader. "When the legislature is in session," Nelson said, "forty-nine members look in the mirror and see the face of the governor." In what was already a strong executive system, the governor was advantaged by dealing with legislators individually rather than through the leadership of a relatively cohesive majority party. One on one with rank-and-file legislators, governors are especially well equipped to put together the votes for their programs. Working through legislative leaders, they have to bend more to the wishes of the legislature.

Governors may benefit when leadership is divided within a chamber, so that neither party has sufficient strength to challenge the executive. Divided leadership occurs when a coalition of members from both parties has control, which, although unusual, does happen from time to time. Bruce King (D-NM) in his second term faced a coalition majority in the New Mexico house. "Right away," he wrote, "I took steps to make sure I could do business with them."[30] He definitely could, by treating the members individually rather than as an organized group. Divided leadership also occurs within legislative bodies, where titular leaders have less power than some other members. Most notable in this regard was the situation in Florida during the 1970s and 1980s, when Senator Dempsey Barron reigned de facto no matter who the body elected president of the senate. Leadership may also suffer a loss of strength in states where legislators are term limited. In such chambers top leaders serve two or four years before they rotate out, making room for someone on the ladder below them. Because of term limits of six, eight, or possibly twelve years, these legislators have little experience when they ascend to leadership jobs and then have little experience doing those jobs.

While the institutional power of the leaders affects legislative-executive relationships, so does the personal standing of the individual leaders themselves. Some of them are strong by dint of their longevity in office, their personalities, or their overall orientation toward the executive branch. These factors affect how governors work with them. Tom Murphy, speaker of the Georgia house; Vern Riffe, speaker of the Ohio house; Bill Bulger, president of the Massachusetts senate; and Mike Miller, president of the Maryland senate all held top leadership for two decades or longer. Their experience enabled them to hone their skills, gain knowledge, and create power. Governors were well advised to regard these leaders cautiously.

When legislative leaders are strong, governors have little recourse but to negotiate with them rather than with the members themselves. At an extreme was Oklahoma house speaker J. D. McCarty. As described by Bellmon, McCarty was the most powerful individual in the legislature:

> Anytime he took the rostrum and pointed his thumbs upwards, the matter under consideration passed with a sizable majority. Anytime he made the opposite gesture, thumbs down, the measure failed.

As governor, Bellmon was able to try to build majorities among the forty-four members of the senate. But when it came to the house, "there was no point in dealing with anyone except J. D."[31]

Executive-legislative relationships may also depend on the leader's conception of his or her role vis-à-vis the legislature as a separate and coequal branch of government. Tom Loftus, as speaker of the Wisconsin assembly, understood the need for the legislature to demonstrate its coequality. Loftus believed that if the legislature had a justifiable opportunity to slap the governor around, it should do it. That was because the governors do not think the legislature is coequal. Moreover, the legislative coequality muscle atrophies if it is not exercised once in a while.[32] John Martin's attitude was that, as speaker, he spoke for the Maine house. He would meet early with each governor with whom he served and inform him that he would bring up problems he had with the administration in private. He warned, however, that if the governor did not respond satisfactorily, he would then attack him publicly. Martin's early-warning system, he claimed, took care of 90 percent of the disagreements between the speaker and the three governors with whom he served.[33]

New governors are routinely advised, by their colleagues and by NGA, at events and in publications, to meet regularly with legislative leaders during the course of the session.[34] On the survey, governors were asked about the schedule of their meetings with legislative leaders. Four out of five governors had regular meetings with leaders of their own party. Two out of five had regular meetings with leaders of the opposition party. Regular meetings between governors and leaders of their own party did not vary by whether or not their own party controlled the legislature. However, regular meetings with leaders of the other party were much more likely when that party controlled the legislature. For the most part, governors met separately with Democratic and Republican leaders; only one out of three met regularly with leaders of both parties together.

Bill Weld (R-MA) referred to the weekly meetings with legislative leaders as one of the most important procedures he instituted as governor. The meetings did not come naturally. Upon taking office, Weld was hardly a fan of the Massachusetts legislature. Early in his administration, however, he was advised that too much bad blood existed between the governor and the speaker, as a result of a clever remark by the witty Brahmin governor that annoyed the Irish speaker. The governor was told by advisors to get together with the speaker and break bread. On Beacon Hill in the halls of the statehouse, it is axiomatic that people who break bread together are much less likely to kill one another. A secret breakfast was arranged at the Charles Hotel in Cambridge.

"Charley [Speaker Flaherty] and I had a good breakfast, so I [Weld] said, 'Let's get together again.'" They began meeting once a week along with Bulger (the senate president). Weld believed it was important for the governor to go to the leaders, so they rotated offices for their meetings. For two out of every three meetings, the governor would walk down the hall on the third floor of the statehouse to Flaherty's or Bulger's office. These get-togethers were a great success. The governor and the leaders enjoyed themselves, but more important, they would warn one another of what was ahead: "We're going to knock your block off," "We have the votes to override your veto," and so forth. In Weld's view, the meetings were a major breakthrough in establishing good relationships and eliminating surprises.

Governors operated in the manner they found most convenient and most productive. That varied by governor and legislative leader. Baliles and the leaders met a few times a week while the Virginia legislature was in session. Elsewhere, weekly meetings were the norm. In Delaware the governor and leaders got together over lunch on Tuesdays. In Maine different governors followed different practices in their weekly meetings. Brennan breakfasted with the Democratic majority leaders, whereas every Tuesday King had eight legislative leaders to the mansion for breakfast. Frank O'Bannon (D-IN) also met weekly, as did Taft in Ohio. Wise would have a weekly luncheon at the mansion for Democratic leaders of the West Virginia legislature. In New York, Hugh Carey (D-NY) dealt personally on a regular basis only with the leaders, in what has been called "an ongoing relationship, albeit not always a happy one."[35]

Governors made adjustments in their schedules as they saw fit. For Thornburgh, it meant meeting with Pennsylvania leaders on a "regular basis," or "regularly enough to keep them on the reservation." For Edgar, it meant resorting to "shuttle diplomacy," because the four legislative leaders did not get along well together. Not much got done unless a decision had been made in advance of the meeting with all four. Also, Edgar or a member of his staff usually had to follow up in order to get the information or agreements that the administration needed. When he was governor, Kean had to scrap the practice of regular bipartisan meetings with New Jersey's legislative leaders. One reason was that he preferred to meet with individual leaders as the occasion required. More important, however, was Kean's relationship at the outset with Alan Karcher, the Democratic assembly speaker. Kean described Karcher: "Given a chance between a wise compromise and a good public scrap, he will take the scrap every time."[36]

Despite a few exceptions, governors and legislative leaders generally agree that getting together on a regular basis helps both branches. The governor can keep legislative leaders informed of programmatic plans, and legislative leaders can ask the governor questions and get the answers they need. They can clear up some of the many misunderstandings that tend to circulate in the capitol.[37] The governor can exchange ideas on issues with leaders, while also letting them know that he or she was aware of the problems that they confronted.[38] George Ariyoshi (D-HI) relied on legislative leaders even more broadly. Recognizing that legislators were in touch with their communities, and leaders were in touch with their legislators, he understood how a governor could use leadership to "get excellent cues from legislators, anticipate problems, and head them off."[39] These meetings were the occasion for the governor to ensure that his or her agenda was being treated well and making its way through the process. John Engler would meet in Michigan with the Republican leaders and push them. Once they had signed on to his initiatives, he held them to their commitments. There were times when one chamber or the other would be holding up the mutually agreed-upon agenda and there were times when dissent would arise in one of the GOP caucuses. As described by Paul Hillegonds, the house speaker at the time:

> When that happened, John showed no hesitation—no matter who the person was or how close to him—to stare at the person with a firm jaw. "I understand you have a problem with what we had all agreed to do. Do you want to tell me why?"

Usually, by the end of the meeting, Engler would have gotten his way.[40]

The bottom line is that regular face-to-face contact makes it easier for the governor and legislative leaders to reach settlements. As the survey shows, such contact makes for a better relationship between the governor and the legislature. George W. Bush (R-TX) had to work with two Democratic leaders—the speaker of the house and the lieutenant governor, who presided over the senate. Bush managed well, what with Wednesday morning breakfasts and occasional drop-bys at their offices. These private meetings were where differences were aired and settlements started to be fashioned.[41] These sessions helped Bush succeed with the Democratic legislature in Texas.

Building Relationships With Leaders

After being defeated for reelection in his Bennington district, the former speaker of the Vermont house, Ralph Wright, penned his memoirs. Included in his account is fascinating commentary on his relationships as speaker with three governors—Richard Snelling (R-VT), Madeleine Kunin (D-VT), and Howard Dean (D-VT). In a nutshell, Wright adored Snelling, had little use for Dean, and was not simpatico with Kunin. It is interesting, and a bit unusual, that Wright, a partisan Democrat, was much fonder of the Republican than of the two Democrats. For the most part, the speaker's attitude was based more on personality than on politics. The title of Wright's memoir, *All Politics Is Personal,*[42] tells his story. Maybe not "all" politics is personal, as Wright claims, but quite a lot of politics is infused with the personal.

Many governors and leaders get along well; others not so well. Over the years, governors and leaders forged good working relationships in Ohio. At first, George Voinovich and Stan Aronoff, the senate president, and Vern Riffe, the house speaker, did some sparring. But quickly the three decided to work together, and they became good friends. Dick Finan and Jo Ann Davidson, who succeeded Aronoff and Riffe, also worked well with Voinovich. With the imposition of term limits in Ohio, relationships changed. For North Carolina's Hunt, "the president pro tem was my guy." For Arne Carlson (R-MN), Dee Long as speaker would always cut him a break. Other legislative leaders were also admirable— "they didn't have horns, they didn't eat babies." Carlson found them wonderful to work with.

What accounts for good relationships that governors build with legislative leaders? Friendships that were formed when the governor was in the legislature usually carried over to the executive office. Joe Frank Harris (D-GA) and speaker Tom Murphy had served together in the Georgia legislature. Speaker Murphy had appointed Harris to the appropriations committee and supported his efforts to run for governor. The two had become personal friends along the way. Harris's attitude was, "You've got to dance with those that brung you." So when Murphy was criticized, Harris came to his defense. His aim as governor was to maintain this longtime friendship and certainly not "bite the hand that fed me."[43] Loyalty in politics may be weaker than it used to be, but it can still provide a strong bond. Tony Earl (D-WI) and Tom Loftus arrived in the Wisconsin assembly at the same time and became friends. By the time the former was governor and the latter was speaker, they "could talk without thinking the other had a hidden agenda."[44]

It helps if friendships are forged before one becomes governor. Yet, most governors work at developing friendships after they take office. Often the chemistry works. After having had such a rough time with speaker J. D. McCarty in his first term, Republican Bellmon of Oklahoma was a bit gun-shy in approaching McCarty's successor, a Democrat. After the two talked about their objectives, Jim Barker, the new speaker, revealed that Bellmon's opponent in the election had also run ads attacking him. Barker was angry at such an affront from a member of his own party and informed the governor that he had crossed party lines and voted for Bellmon in the general election. Bellmon recalled, "This was the beginning of a friendly and productive working relationship between myself and Speaker Barker."[45] A mutual enemy brought the two closer together.

Whatever a governor's personal preferences, politics may be sufficient incentive for him or her to be friendly to legislative leaders. After a shaky start, Weld shifted gears in his approach to Bulger. A Republican governor with an overwhelmingly Democratic legislature needed a bridge, and Weld and Bulger developed a solid relationship. Bulger briefly described its basis in his memoirs:

> Although each of us remained loyal to his party and to his party's philosophy, and thus differed often, ours was a symbiotic working relationship almost from the start. And it became more trusting and relaxed as we came to know each other better.[46]

Political need also inspired George W. Bush, whose policy agenda was in the hands of a Democratic legislature. Bush made it his business to bond with two Democratic leaders—Speaker James E. "Pete" Laney and Lieutenant Governor Bob Bullock. He recognized where the power resided. "The better course of action any time," Bush later acknowledged, "is to try to make alliances if they can lead to a common purpose." One of his top aides described how Bush used political skills, more akin to those of Bill Clinton than to those of his father, to personally bond with the lieutenant governor. By presenting himself as an eager and respectful pupil, Bush was able to win over the speaker as well. At their first meeting, the speaker told the new governor, "Mr. Bush, we can make you a good governor—if you let us."[47] The governor was happy to let them.

Deukmejian had to go out of his way in California to win over the Democratic speaker, Willie Brown. Their relationship began with them insulting one another in public. But Deukmejian's chief of staff recognized that Brown was certainly the key to the assembly and, to a large extent, the key to the legislature. If Deukmejian wanted to get anything done, he had to make his peace with Brown. The governor sought the advice of two former Democratic speakers, Jesse Unruh and Bob Moretti, who tutored him and his staff on what Brown thought, what he needed, and how he could be approached. The tutoring paid off, and a good working relationship between Deukmejian and Brown was forged.[48]

It helps, of course, if the governor is instrumental in the selection of the leader by the caucus or the chamber. Over thirty years ago, in responding to a survey of NGA, twenty-five of thirty-one legislative assistants of governors were of the opinion that choosing leaders was strictly an internal matter for the legislature. Yet one observer pointed out that, although governors will not endorse candidates for top leadership, it is unlikely that they remain completely neutral in most situations. NGA concluded that in many states the word gets out and governors exercise quiet influence. But the process is often so subtle that it is difficult to pinpoint.[49] This was not the case when Louisiana governors, dating at least from the epoch of Huey Long, practically organized the legislature. They appointed and also fired senate and house leaders. It was not the case in several other one-party Southern states, too, where governors chose the floor leaders in the senate or the house.

Direct intervention is much rarer nowadays. Since the legislative modernization movement that started in the late 1960s and ran for two decades, many legislators would consider such gubernatorial involvement to be an assault on their institution's independence. Nevertheless, governors have preferences and some of them work behind the scenes to get the leader they want. Their opportunities are limited, however, because more often they face entrenched leadership rather than a contest for an open seat. In other circumstances, they tend to be discrete, lest they lose and have to work with the leader whose election they opposed. Jay Rockefeller (D-WV) refused to support Donald Kopp, a veteran legislator for speaker, who had been a strong backer of Rockefeller. Rockefeller didn't think he would win the race, and he didn't want to bet on a losing horse. He had too much at risk during his first year in office. Kopp, however, won the speakership and, perhaps surprisingly, still tried to work with the new governor.[50]

Pataki's candidate for senate Republican leader was Joe Bruno. Bruno had been the first senator to endorse Pataki for governor, and the governor-elect wanted to reciprocate by replacing Warren Anderson as majority leader with him. Over the Thanksgiving weekend, New York senators were tracked down and persuaded to support Bruno. All Pataki had to say, when asked about his involvement before the caucus vote, was: "The decision is up to the 36 members of the majority. But if there is a sentiment for change, so be it."[51] When Jim McGreevey (D-NJ) took office, and the Democrats regained control of the assembly, who the new speaker would be was in doubt. The new governor, allied with state political party leaders, settled the dispute with a North Jersey–South Jersey power-sharing arrangement. McGreevey's relationships with the leaders he helped install benefitted. Reciprocally, governors gain by the removal of leaders who have been adversarial or hostile. Bellmon of Oklahoma was visited by Vondel Smith, who said he had the backing of a Republican county chairman to challenge Speaker McCarty in the primary election. Bellmon could not help but be interested. Although Smith's chances were not good, the governor supported his challenge, including raising a sizable amount of campaign money. His candidate won, and McCarty's defeat was remembered by Bellmon as "a happy moment in my political life."[52]

The establishment and maintenance of relationships is furthered if governors pay careful attention to the needs of legislative leaders and give them what they require. First, leaders want respect. Some governors have been good respect givers; they tendered it with sincerity. Dick Snelling (R-VT) would wait outside Speaker Wright's door waiting to be invited in. Wright was impressed by the governor's humility.[53] On his part, Bellmon asked McCarty's successor as speaker for permission to work in special cases with Republican legislators directly, rather than work only through the leadership.[54] This request also impressed the leadership.

Among the principal needs of legislative leaders is having their views taken into account. Most governors are adept at soliciting the opinions of others, especially top leaders. Roy Romer (D-CO) had a good relationship with Republican Bev Bledsoe, in large part because he would welcome the speaker's views, particularly on how Bledsoe wanted the process to work. On his part, the speaker would vote no on some of the governor's initiatives, but he would work with him to improve their quality. Baliles had a relationship with the president of the Virginia senate, Hunter Andrews, who he described as "my mentor and my tormentor." Andrews felt that it was his duty to render honest criticism, no matter how tough, and Baliles invited it when a problem arose. "We'd talk," said the former governor, "and we would work something out."

Soliciting the views of legislative leaders and taking them into account is important, but so is giving them the little things they need. In New Jersey the Republican senate leader, Don DiFrancesco, was unhappy with Governor Whitman, in part because members of his caucus were unhappy with her. They did not like the fact that she wouldn't schmooze or ask for their opinions. They did not like the fact that the "front office" took so long to get back to them when they asked for help for one of their constituents. According to DiFrancesco, the governor and her staff did not realize how important little things were to members of the legislature. The governor couldn't get to know that, he felt, because she didn't talk to them.[55] The senators would complain to DiFrancesco.

Other governors, by contrast, work at it. Weld was effective on all fronts of relationship building. "My job," he said, "was to figure out what was most important to each leader." If leaders had issues they wanted advanced or projects they wanted funded, the governor was at the ready. Funds for Bulger's favorites, the symphony and the library, were made available— and in the governor's budget, so that the legislature would not be criticized for spending. After Speaker Tom Finneran's chief of staff had to cancel a hunting trip he planned to take with his son, Weld invited him at a later date to go boar hunting with him. Speaker Finneran was extremely grateful for the governor's kindness.

As much as anything else, it was Weld's love of performing and his sense of humor that brought the governor and the senate president close together. At the 1991 St. Patrick's Day breakfast, hosted by Bulger, an enduring friendship started. The two shared the stage and won laughs and applause from the audience of insiders. The tall patrician and the little Irishman fit together, with each playing to type, joining in performance and laughter. In one riff, Bulger would tease the governor about his heritage and wealth, pointing out that Weld's ancestors had come over on the *Mayflower*. Weld, then, would correct him: "Actually, they weren't on the *Mayflower*. They sent the servants over on the *Mayflower* to get the cottage ready." Weld recalls the St. Patrick's Day performances and the fact that he had several speechwriters working long hours to prepare his remarks for these occasions.

Good relationships do not ensure that the legislature buys into the governor's agenda. Nor do they mean that the governor follows the legislature's lead. What friendship, respect, trust, favors, and gestures add up to is the ability of governors and leaders to engage in the give and take of negotiations that are crucial to the policymaking processes. Consider how the long-standing friendship between Harris and Murphy in Georgia helped them resolve differences. The two initially disagreed on the site for a new capitol complex. But the governor persisted in advocacy and explanation of his plan and felt that if Murphy knew and understood the options and the long-term possibilities, he would be supportive. Harris proved right; Murphy bought into the vision and helped secure the plan's adoption.[56] Murphy also started out at odds on an education bill that was a major item on the governor's agenda. After its introduction, the speaker confronted Harris in his office: "I don't know who you've been listening to, but if you think you're going to pass that bunch of trash through this General Assembly, you've got another thought [sic] coming!" That was the speaker's way of conveying to the governor that support for the bill in the house was pretty weak and members had serious questions. The governor cleared up the questions, first with the speaker, himself, and then with the house members. The speaker signed on, and with his backing, the governor achieved his "proudest moment of legislative victories," the Quality Basic Education Act of 1985.[57]

Pragmatism on the parts of both the governor and legislative leaders is a necessary component of a good working relationship. Pragmatism made executive-legislative relations remarkably successful in Ohio through a succession of governors and legislative leaders. On the executive side,

Republicans James Rhodes and George Voinovich and Democrat Richard Celeste, and on the legislative side, Republican senate leaders Stan Aronoff and Richard Finan, and the Democratic speaker, Vern Riffe, and the Republican speaker, Jo Ann Davidson, made policymaking work. On behalf of their caucuses and chambers, the legislative leaders negotiated, bargained, and managed to reach mutually agreeable settlements with one governor after another.

In another illustration of the power of pragmatism, Bill Owens and Andrew Romanoff, the Democratic speaker, recognized that the TABOR (Taxpayer Bill of Rights) initiative had made it impossible for Colorado to budget effectively. Acknowledging the seriousness of the problem, the two of them worked together to modify TABOR. In Massachusetts, if Weld needed votes in the senate, Bulger would help him with the Democratic caucus. When Bulger wanted something, Weld would try to provide it. For example, when staff members in the governor's office were pushing a plan to eliminate the Metropolitan District Commission, Bulger informed Weld that he wanted it left alone. "You forget," Weld told Bulger, "that I am the governor." "Never mind that stuff," Bulger replied, "We're the governor." Both of them laughed, and the governor agreed, assuring Bulger that "we'll strangle it [the plan] in its crib."[58]

Even with little personal chemistry between them, Reagan and legislative leaders managed to negotiate successfully in California. This was largely because they were all intent on achieving results. When Reagan and Bob Moretti first met privately, the speaker led off with: "Look governor, I don't like you particularly and I know you don't like me but we don't have to be in love to work together." Moretti saw no other way to break the impasse between the governor and the legislature, but what he found surprising was that Reagan was as genuinely interested in a productive outcome as he was. On his part, Reagan was not averse to negotiating with an adversary; he simply tried to get the best deal he could. Biographer Cannon called this meeting an "epiphany" for both Reagan and Moretti.[59]

In a number of cases, however, the governor and one or both legislative leaders simply cannot get along well together. They may be of opposing political parties or belong to the same party. More than partisanship, it is a matter of personality, temperament, history, or conflicting ambitions. Mitt Romney (R-MA) came to Beacon Hill with the mentality of a corporate executive and had little use for the Democratic legislature or its senate and house leadership. According to Robert Travaglini, the senate president at the time, the governor and his team "certainly weren't interested in talking to us."[60] Jon Corzine (D-NJ) had little sense of the legislature or how to relate to it and its leaders. To make matters worse, he had abandoned a perfectly good seat in the U.S. Senate to run for governor. Dick Codey, the senate president, who had been acting governor for about a year when Corzine made his move, felt that he deserved the Democratic nomination. But he could not stand up to the personal fortune that Corzine brought to bear. Codey backed off, but his resentment toward Corzine as governor lingered. Ann Richards (D-TX) tried to develop a relationship with her lieutenant governor, Bob Bullock, who presided over and ran the Texas senate. But over time their relationships deteriorated to the point where they no longer spoke. Indeed, Lieutenant Governor Bullock sent word to the governor and her aides that they could no longer talk to "his senators" without his permission. Although Richards and Bullock did not hit it off, the lieutenant governor was flattered and charmed by Richards's successor, George W. Bush.[61]

Even some of the worst relationships between governors and leaders, however, can work themselves out—one way or another, and after a time. One adversary may simply lose steam. McCarty was vitriolic in his repeated assaults on Bellmon in Oklahoma, but the governor kept his cool. The result on television news was a sharp contrast between Bellmon's calm appearance and the speaker's tantrums. After two years, the speaker's fire was on the wane, and not long after that it was extinguished.[62] New Jersey's Kean had a formidable adversary on his hands in Karcher. The new assembly speaker was a "partisan brawler."[63] As the governor's counsel recalled, "Alan loved to fight. He'd fight about anything."[64] With the Democrats increasing their legislative majorities in the 1983 elections, Karcher launched a blistering personal attack on Kean.[65] But after a while, both the press and the public rallied to the governor's side. Karcher had gone too far in attacking such a personable and popular governor as Kean. Eventually, the governor came out way ahead in his encounters with the legislative leader.

It took Bob Graham (D-FL) quite some time, but somehow he mended fences with the unanointed senate leader, Dempsey Barron. As a member of the Florida senate, Graham had crossed the leadership on more than one occasion. When Graham opposed Barron's bid for the senate presidency, the die was cast. Graham and his co-conspirators lost their chairmanships and were tagged as "doghouse Democrats." After Graham became governor, Barron (referred to as "the man behind the curtains in the Florida senate") declared Graham "the worst governor in the history of the world," not an enthusiastic endorsement. However, later in Graham's governorship, Barron seemed to relent. Reportedly, during a hunting trip at Barron's ranch, Barron brought forth a horse for Graham to ride. An expert rider himself, Barron figured that Graham would be afraid to mount the horse or mount it and fall off. Instead, Graham climbed on and stayed on, leaving Barron astonished. In Graham's view, "that gave us an additional bond. Helped smooth things out."[66] A governor with modest socializing skills still managed to work things out with the legendary Barron, a leader who, among other things, inspired fear. Graham's persistence paid off.

Relationships between governors and legislative leaders may change, because legislative leaders learn that they cannot prevail. Speaker Karcher learned that and abandoned his battle with Kean in New Jersey. In Illinois, Speaker Madigan refused to meet with Edgar until March of the governor's first year in office, in an effort to give him a lesson and rattle him. When Edgar vetoed a Democratic spending bill that went over budget, the speaker realized that the governor was as stubborn as he was. Then, the two developed a personal relationship based on mutual respect. Madigan had come to realize, in Edgar's recollection, "that a legislature can't win the war with a governor," not if the governor has any ability at all.

Imperfect Together

"Let's not kid ourselves," said Minnesota's Arne Carlson, "it's an adversarial relationship." Bob Wise agreed: "There are inevitable tensions and you can't smooth over everything." The constitutional separation of powers is designed to set the executive and legislative branches at odds with one another. So, even if relationships between the governor and legislative leaders are good, disputes are bound to arise.[67] Disagreements occur over the general dimensions or over the specifics of policy. As Gary Locke (D-WA) recalled, his relationship with the Washington legislature depended less on the personalities of legislators than on the issues involved. The more contentious the issue, the tougher the relationship.

Even allowing for variation by issue, overall relationships between governors and legislatures do play an important role in the policymaking process. In the survey conducted for this study, former governors were asked to characterize their relationships with the legislature during their tenure in office. Overall, 73 percent of the governors characterized their relationships as either "excellent" or "good," whereas 27 percent said that they were "fair" or "poor." Democrats were somewhat more likely than Republicans to report better relationships. Most interesting, the longer governors had served, the better they perceived their relationships with the legislature. None of the forty-five respondents who served two or more terms reported "poor" legislative relationships. Four out of five of these veterans had "excellent" or "good" relationships. It did not seem to matter whether the governor's party controlled both chambers, one chamber, or neither chamber of the legislature.

According to respondents who had "fair" or "poor" relationships, the main reason given was the controversial nature of the issues before the legislature. The runner-up was partisanship, specifically with legislative control in the hands of the other party. Also, leaders were tough to deal with and a few key legislators were tough to deal with, as reported by several respondents. Among the respondents, Ehrlich admitted to having had hard times with the Maryland legislature. Indeed, Ehrlich took some pride in having struggled with the house speaker and the senate president. Maryland, in his view, wanted something different when they elected him. "I was not elected to get along with Mike Bush and Mike Miller," he said. Nor did he.

Other governors, not included in the survey, also had troubled relationships with their legislatures. Ventura's four years featured almost continuous warfare with the Minnesota legislature. William Donald Schaefer (D-MD) had little good to say about the legislature, and his feelings were reciprocated by the Democratic-controlled senate and house. Carey and Pataki both had their problems building trust and goodwill in the New York legislature. Whitman and Corzine never succeeded in winning over the New Jersey legislature. Gary Johnson (R-NM) clashed constantly with the legislature in New Mexico.

Good relationships with the legislature depend on a variety of factors. Experience in the legislature proved helpful to most governors. A respect, and actual liking, for the legislature certainly didn't hurt. "If you don't like dealing with legislators, you put yourself in a smaller place," is the way Weld put it. Being open, direct, and sincere gives the governor a leg up. Legislators like to feel that they are getting straight information and a straight deal. A willingness to make tough decisions, and take flack for the legislature, is an asset for governors who want a good relationship.

Being confrontational, like Schaefer and Ventura, usually gets governors nowhere. George Voinovich knew from the outset that it made no sense to get mad at Ohio legislators, because that would simply be burning bridges. Showing strength usually stands governors in good stead. They can veto a large number of the legislature's enactments, as Owens did in Colorado. But it helped that he was frank with lawmakers, telling them where he stood and what he intended to do, so that they were not taken by surprise and not unduly annoyed. Romer's approach was also effective. He was open, direct, and inclusive. "They knew damned well I was the Democratic governor," he acknowledged, and they did not expect easy agreement between the two branches.

Governors who are successful with their legislatures manage to keep their egos reined in. They are comfortable sharing the stage with legislators, inviting them to consult and participate, and acknowledging their important role. "Make the legislatures partners in your progress," NGA advises new governors.[68] Many succeed in doing so. They are comfortable sharing participation, decision making, and credit, no doubt realizing that, however much credit they accord the legislature, even more will come their way. Sharing credit is probably as important as anything else a governor can do, as far as relationship building is concerned.

Reagan established a standard for the contemporary governor. He had so little ego that he did not care when a legislator won acclaim for a proposal that originated with him. His philosophy was expressed by a sign that later on would adorn his desk in the White House: "There is no limit to what a man can do or where he can go if he doesn't mind who gets the credit."[69] Bush was also willing to share credit with the Texas legislature and legislative leaders. For him, it was "an important part of the process."[70] Baliles was of the same mind: "If you don't mind sharing credit, you can get a lot accomplished." The average politician is thought to claim credit, even if credit is undeserved. But governors are not average politicians; they are confident, pragmatic, and skillful enough to confer credit on others. In the final analysis, there is always enough credit to go around, and the benefits that governors derive from generosity are worth whatever little credit they surrender.

Notes

1. Response from survey.
2. National Governors Association, *Words of Wisdom on Transition & Governing Topics* (Washington, D.C.: National Governors Association, n.d.).
3. Former aide Keith Mason's characterization, in Richard Hyatt, *Zell: The Governor Who Gave Georgia HOPE* (Macon, GA: Mercer University Press, 1997), 391.
4. Alan Rosenthal, *Governors and Legislatures: Contending Powers* (Washington, D.C.: CQ Press, 1990), 80.
5. Gleaves Whitney, *John Engler: The Man, the Leader & the Legacy* (Chelsea, MI: Sleeping Bear Press, 2002), 189–90, 232.
6. Carolyn Barta, *Bill Clements: Texian to His Toenails* (Austin, TX: Eakin Press, 1996), 231.
7. Robert P. Casey, *Fighting for Life* (Dallas: Word Publishing, 1996), 29.
8. James D. Barber, *The Lawmakers* (New Haven, CT: Yale University Press, 1965).
9. *New York Times*, October 25, 2010.
10. George J. Marlin, *Squandered Opportunities: New York's Pataki Years* (South Bend, IN: St. Augustine's Press, 2006), 71.
11. Joe Mathews, *The People's Machine: Arnold Schwarzenegger and the Rise of Blockbuster Democracy* (New York: Public Affairs, 2006), 204.
12. Panel on Governor Kean, Governors Project archive, Eagleton Institute of Politics, Rutgers University, April 15, 2009.
13. Alan Greenblatt, "The Job of a Lifetime," *Governing* (June 2009): 24–29, 30.
14. Barta, *Bill Clements*, 219–20, 252.

15. James R. Thompson, "Keynote Address on the Governor," in *The Governor and the Legislature: Eagleton's 1987 Symposium on the State of the States*, ed. Alan Rosenthal (New Brunswick, NJ: Eagleton Institute of Politics, 1988), 11.

16. Richard A. J. Bristin, et al., *West Virginia Politics and Government* (Lincoln: University of Nebraska Press, 1996), 104–5.

17. Henry Bellmon, *The Life and Times of Henry Bellmon* (Tulsa, OK: Council Oak Books, 1992), 174.

18. Rosenthal, *Governors and Legislatures*, 16.

19. Lou Cannon, *Governor Reagan* (New York: Public Affairs, 2003), 195, 232.

20. James Richardson, *Willie Brown: A Biography* (Berkeley: University of California Press, 1996), 304.

21. Dan Creed, *Governor Ventura: "The Body" Exposed* (Madison, WI: Hunter Halverson Press, 2003), 128.

22. National Governors Association, *The Many Roles of the Governor's Chief of Staff* (Washington, D.C.: National Governors Association, Office of Management Counseling & Training, 2006), 24.

23. National Governors Association, *Words of Wisdom*.

24. Bellmon, *The Life and Times of Henry Bellmon*, 169.

25. National Governors Association, *The Many Roles of the Governor's Chief of Staff*, 25.

26. Barta, *Bill Clements*, 409.

27. Rosenthal, *Governors and Legislatures*, 78.

28. Cannon, *Governor Reagan*, 230.

29. S. V. Date, *Jeb: America's Next Bush*. New York: Penguin, 2007, 7.

30. Bruce King, *Cowboy in the Roundhouse* (Santa Fe, NM: Sunstone Press, 1998), 234–35.

31. Bellmon, *The Life and Times of Henry Bellmon*, 202–3.

32. Loftus in Rosenthal, *The Governor and the Legislature*, 65.

33. Martin in Rosenthal, *The Governor and the Legislature*, 57.

34. National Governors Association, *Words of Wisdom*.

35. Daniel C. Kramer, *The Days of Wine and Roses Are Over: Governor Hugh Carey and New York State* (Lanham, MD: University Press of America, 1997), 147.

36. Rosenthal, *Governors and Legislatures*, 91–92.

37. King, *Cowboy in the Roundhouse*, 199.

38. Harry Roe Hughes, *My Unexpected Journey* (Charleston, SC: History Press, 2006), 147.

39. George R. Ariyoshi, *With Obligations to All* (Honolulu: Ariyoshi Foundation, 1997), 152–53.

40. Whitney, *John Engler*, 205–6.

41. J. H. Hatfield, *Fortunate Son: George W. Bush and the Making of an American President* (New York: Soft Skull Press, 2001), 147.

42. Ralph Wright, *All Politics Is Personal* (Manchester Center, VT: Marshall Jones Company, 1996). This book was later revised and published as *Inside the Statehouse* (Washington, D.C.: CQ Press, 2005).

43. Joe Frank Harris, *Personal Reflections on a Public Life* (Macon, GA: Mercer University Press, 1998), 88.

44. Tom Loftus, *The Art of Legislative Politics* (Washington, D.C.: CQ Press, 1994), 118.

45. Bellmon, *The Life and Times of Henry Bellmon*, 334.

46. William M. Bulger, *While the Music Lasts; My Life in Politics* (Boston: Houghton Mifflin, 1996), 270.

47. Hatfield, *Fortunate Son*, 147, 164.

48. Richardson, *Willie Brown*, 298.

49. Rosenthal, *Governors and Legislatures*, 88.

50. Richard Grimes, *Jay Rockefeller: Old Money, New Politics* (Charleston, WV: Jalamap Publications, 1984), 158–59.

51. Marlin, *Squandered Opportunities*, 61.

52. Soon after his defeat, McCarty was convicted of a felony, having failed to declare reportable income. Bellmon, *The Life and Times of Henry Bellmon*, 204–5.

53. Wright, *Inside the Statehouse*, 194.

54. Bellmon, *The Life and Times of Henry Bellmon*, 358–59.

55. Art Weissman, *Christine Todd Whitman* (New York: Carol Publishing Group, 1996), 150–51.

56. Harris, *Personal Reflections on a Public Life*, 194–95.

57. Ibid., 113.

58. Bulger, *While the Music Lasts*, 270–71.

59. Cannon, *Governor Reagan*, 356–57.

60. Jim O'Sullivan, "Man in Charge," *National Journal*, November 12, 2011, 20.

61. Jan Reid, "The Case of Ann Richards: Women in Gubernatorial Office," in *A Legacy of Leadership: Governors and American History*, ed. Clayton McClure Brooks (Philadelphia: University of Pennsylvania Press, 2008), 194.

62. Bellmon, *The Life and Times of Henry Bellmon*, 202–3.
63. Alvin S. Felzenberg, *Governor Tom Kean* (New Brunswick, NJ: Rutgers University Press, 2006), 197–98.
64. Cary Edwards, former chief counsel to Governor Kean, Panel on Governor Kean, April 15, 2009.
65. Felzenberg, *Governor Tom Kean*, 211.
66. Date, *Quiet Passion*, 99–100, 102–3, 110, 112, 116.
67. King, *Cowboy in the Roundhouse*, 197.
68. National Governors Association, *Words of Wisdom*.
69. Lou Cannon, "Preparing for the Presidency: The Political Education of Ronald Reagan," in Brooks, *A Legacy of Leadership*, 143.
70. Hatfield, *Fortunate Son*, 163.

6

Strategies and Tactics of Engagement

WHAT HAS BEEN REPORTED in earlier chapters is prologue. The constitutional and political environment, fiscal and economic conditions, the skill and experience that governors bring to office, how governors formulate their agendas and relate to the legislature—all are important, but then the most challenging work begins. Arnold Schwarzenegger (R-CA) described the work with the help of several sports metaphors. Running California is like climbing Mount Everest, or skiing an Olympic slalom course on the way down:

> It's the tightest slalom course you can find with bumps and moguls all on top of it. You have every obstacle you can think of. You jump in the middle of the air. Then do the turnaround with the gate. . . . People wipe out all the time.

To make the point, Schwarzenegger switched to weight lifting:

> You have to psych yourself up. . . . Everything's going against you. There's noise out there in the audience. There are people whistling, someone talking Russian behind you, all this stuff.[1]

Schwarzenegger governed during a difficult period and in a difficult system. Other governors probably have an easier time of it, and few are as physical in their descriptions of the challenges they face. But there is little doubt that much depends on just how governors engage in pushing their agendas.

The Types of Issues in Play

The ways in which governors engage with the legislature depend largely on the particular issues in question. They handle budgets and policy proposals differently. It matters whether or not a policy proposal requires a revenue increase, or whether a proposal is likely to divide along partisan lines. According to governors themselves, only some of the issues with which they and legislatures deal have been partisan. Take, for example, the various engagements of Jim Edgar (R-IL) during his eight years as governor. They revolved mainly around money, geography, and teachers—issues that did not divide mainly along partisan lines. Whether proposals have high visibility also has a bearing on what happens during the lawmaking process.

A number of issues are relatively easy to resolve. In these cases, the governor and the legislature agree at the outset. This may be because the legislature has participated in the formulation of the governor's agenda and differences have been worked out. It may simply be that most everybody sees eye to eye on what to do. Education, economic development, and even welfare reform are policy domains that have tended to promote executive-legislative collaboration more often than conflict. "There were a couple of joint initiatives," Edgar recalled. "They wanted to do welfare reform, we did too." The governor and legislative leaders sat down together and got it worked out. Because welfare reform also was a mutual interest of the Republican legislature and Democratic governor in Washington, Gary Locke (D-WA) had a good head start on this policy initiative. Another Locke initiative, the Promise Fellowship program for college, provided that 15 percent of high school students from low- and middle-income families would receive aid. The governor personally believed in helping both lower- and middle-income youngsters. The mix appealed to the legislature, both substantively and politically, by providing aid for low-income students, favored by Democrats, and also for middle-income students, favored by Republicans.

Right off the bat, governors identify legislative leaders who share their policy objectives. Barbara Roberts (D-OR) had a difficult time overall with the Republican legislature, but she was able to partner with the legislative majority on a number of measures. For instance, she and the chair of a house committee collaborated on setting up a trust for low- and moderate-income housing, a measure that received Republican support. William Weld (R-MA) had little difficulty agreeing with Bill Bulger, the Democratic senate president, on a number of issues, such as charter schools, the not-for-profit delivery of public services, and closing uneconomical state facilities. Weld, a Protestant, and Bulger, an Irish Catholic, also saw eye to eye on the funding of Catholic charities.

Governors also tend to agree with major legislation initiated and passed by the legislature. They follow the process, express their preferences on what should be in or left out of the legislation, and publicly or privately announce support. The legislature takes the governor's wishes into consideration as it goes about its business of initiating policy. Finally, governors sign the measures into law when they arrive at their desks. For the most part, governors go along with the legislature because they are in agreement, or at least not in disagreement.

On those issues for which agreement between the governor and the legislature does not come easily, the strategies and tactics governors employ in the legislative process can spell the difference between gubernatorial success and failure. More frequently, however, the difference is between an outcome more to the governor's liking and one less to the governor's liking.

Strategic considerations are rarely absent from a governor's thinking. What gets proposed, when, and how? First, act quickly. According to Bob Wise (D-WV), the best time for a governor to advance an agenda is in the first legislative session after taking office. The plan of Gerald Baliles (D-VA) was to start out dramatically with a $12 billion transportation package, funded in part by a tax increase. It would have to be done in his first year, because legislative elections came in the second year, the presidential election in the third, and the gubernatorial in the fourth. Schwarzenegger got similar advice. Get a spending cap quickly, to get control of the budget and reduce pressure for tax increases. It is better, the new governor of California was told, to take on the hard fights early, even at the cost of some popularity in the polls. The example put forward to Schwarzenegger was John Engler (R-MI), who revised the state's educational finance system at the outset of his first term, resulting in only 19 percent of the voters saying that they were willing to reelect him. Yet, Engler managed to serve three terms.[2] Jim Florio (D-NJ) needed to raise taxes and wanted to ban assault weapons. He and a Democratic legislature enacted the administration's tax and gun initiatives within the first six months. Enough people didn't forget, and Florio lost a close race for reelection.

Theoretically, governors can pursue one of two overarching strategies. They can play an inside game, depending for results on their persuasive and negotiating abilities with legislative leaders and rank-and-file legislators. Ned McWherter (D-TN) is an exemplar of this strategic approach. He would always go first and foremost to the legislature, building support within the institution with which he was both comfortable and effective.[3]

Alternatively, governors can play an outside game, going over the head of the legislature to the public. In practice, governors may start off with an inside strategy, but if that doesn't succeed, they can resort to an outside strategy. Typically, however, governors pursue both strategies throughout the course of their administrations, albeit not on each and every issue. John Carlin (D-KS) distinguished among issues as follows. On issues of a complex, regulatory nature the key targets were legislators and opinion leaders and not the public. He recognized there were too many issues to go public on all of them, so he was selective. In his judgment, it was realistic to place only two or three issues on the public agenda during a given legislative session.[4]

On many major issues, a combined strategy is not unusual. "The work began when we announced an initiative," is how Dick Thornburgh (R-PA) put it. Then, the administration put on "a full-court press," both in the legislature and in the public. At an early point, before provisions of the initiative had been worked out, the Thornburgh administration's public relations efforts were launched. The public relations team had to wait for the substance to be put in place. For other governors, too, the inside and outside approaches have to go hand in hand. Bruce Babbitt (D-AZ), who concentrated on a few initiatives each year, explained that he "used everything at my disposal—initiative, referendum, the bully pulpit, the press, browbeating, trade-offs, threats, rewards—to get what I needed."[5]

On the survey for this book, governors were asked about their general approach—whether they worked with the legislature (an inside game) or went to the public to build pressure on the legislature (an outside game). On a scale of 1 (inside game) to 7 (outside game), with 4 (a balance), the mean score of the sixty-nine respondents was 3.62, slightly more toward the "inside" than the "outside" but close to the middle point. Four former governors—Bruce Sundlun (D-RI), Judy Martz (R-MT), Bill Clements (R-TX), and Albert Quie (R-MN)—relied almost wholly on an inside strategy. Mike Huckabee (R-AR) and Stephen Merrill (R-NH), by contrast, relied almost wholly on an outside strategy. Nevertheless, 60 percent of the respondents took the middle ground, reporting that they employed a balanced inside-outside strategy.

Building Support and Exerting Pressure *on* the Legislature

Governors have the bully pulpit (what Lamar Alexander [D-TN] called the "noisy pulpit"), and nearly all of them use it to one degree or another. Tom Kean (R-NJ) believed strongly that "the most important power the governor has is the power of communicating." If that isn't done properly, a governor will lose his power quickly.[6] That is why the National Governors Association (NGA) advises new governors to make immediate use of the bully pulpit—not only on priority issues, but also on other matters and particularly to articulate themes of the administration.[7]

For some governors the campaign doesn't end with the election. They continue on the hustings but with different objectives in mind. Dick Snelling (R-VT) believed in going to the people:

If, by campaigning you mean that you are articulating your goals, if by campaigning you meant that you're telling people what you want to do, if by campaigning you mean that you're asking people for their support and help, what's wrong with doing that every day, 7 days a week, 12 months of the year, 48 months in every four years?[8]

Bob Graham (D-FL) was like Snelling. For him, campaigning was a learning experience as well as a way to impress upon the people of Florida that the governor was very much in touch with them and their problems. Starting when he was a member of the legislature, Graham would periodically leave the capitol for a "work day." "I have taught high school civics in Carol City, sold Burger King hamburgers in Fort Lauderdale, worked as a computer operator in Jacksonville, served as a policeman in Panama City. . . ."[9]

For most governors, however, postelection campaigning is not reflex action. It is part educational and part political. "A lot of times you have to sell a big idea," said Jim Hunt (D-NC). One of his chief roles was that of educator. Baliles was also bullish on ideas. In his view, agenda items had to be placed in a context. He appealed to both the public and the politicos in terms of how Virginia had to prepare itself for a competitive environment, with an emphasis on infrastructure. He felt that it was his role "to help people understand the need to transform themselves to the new dominion from the old dominion." Baliles also understood that by creating public understanding, he could reach the political class who held his agenda's fate in its hands. The ultimate goal, of course, was to build understanding and support in the legislature. Governors, however, do not always succeed in this type of educational-political endeavor. Jon Corzine (D-NJ), for example, made use of the bully pulpit on a twenty-one-county tour around New Jersey to reduce the state debt and pay for transportation improvements through a complex scheme of monetizing public assets. Despite Corzine's efforts, the public was skeptical and the legislature followed suit. The plan fell flat.

Not many contemporary governors hole up in their offices, except when the legislature is in town and they have to be on hand. At other times they are getting around the state listening, learning, and communicating, projecting message and image alike. Cecil Andrus (D-ID) recounted that he would hold public meetings and spend time in every county seat of Idaho's forty-four counties. As governor of New Mexico, Bruce King (D-NM) held office hours around the state for people who couldn't easily drive to Santa Fe.[10] "Capitol for a Day" in towns across Oklahoma was the method used by Henry Bellmon (R-OK).[11] Frank Keating (R-OK) took his entire cabinet on tour, giving people access similar to that which they had with their legislators. For New Jersey's Kean it was somewhat different. He started appearing on a series of radio call-in shows. He also hosted a radio program once a month, broadcast from New York City but linked to a network of eight New Jersey stations. He had monthly cable TV shows with members of his cabinet, and he also chaired town meetings across the state.[12]

The purpose of these efforts is not only to get the public on board, but also to recruit support from key groups in the state. In his first year, Baliles focused his transportation campaign by going by helicopter to places in Virginia where transportation projects were on hold because no money was available. "You need to let your legislators know," the governor told his audiences. In his second year, he targeted business to gain support for a program to protect Chesapeake Bay. Mike Hayden (R-KS) was more focused in his campaign on water issues. The public had even less of a grasp of water issues than highway issues, so Hayden traveled around the state to meet with city managers and health groups.

It would be hard to find a governor who had a better relationship with business than Hunt in North Carolina. During his campaign for lieutenant governor, he had visited all 100 counties in the state, and he had developed local business support just about everywhere. During his first two terms as governor, he built a powerful relationship with business leaders, several of whom suggested that he create a business council. He did so, and he met quarterly with the council in private for an exchange of information and views. The CEOs on the council made their research departments available to the governor for studies of transportation policy and workforce development, among other things. They also formed the cadre of advocates for Hunt's education and economic development initiatives. At the local level, Hunt would activate business groups and they would work his bills, visiting legislators in their districts when they went back home from the capitol. The tight relationship between the Democratic governor and business leaders, most of whom were Republican, paid off handsomely. Fifteen CEOs testified in favor of the governor's education agenda.

Whether or not they pursue an outside strategy, governors have to placate the media, especially the capitol press corps. Some enjoy that part of their job. Weld thought an important (and enjoyable) part of his job was "feeding the beast," as he put it. That meant dealing with the press. Many administrations devote a great deal of energy to cultivating the media, among other things to get their policy messages to the public when the occasion arises. Graham, for one, was able to charm the capitol press corps in Tallahassee by appearing in the annual skits in which reporters poked fun at Florida politicians. The governor sang and danced his way through the show. The press corps appreciated his talents as a performer, and that probably helped them appreciate his performance as governor. "Graham cultivated the press like petunias," is the way one reporter characterized his method. "He knew when to break out the sunshine and openness, when it was time for feeding, even the rarest knowledge of all, when not to lay on the fertilizer too thickly."[13]

Whatever difficulties they encounter in dealing with the "beast," governors need the media in order to reach the public. They certainly will get more attention from the media than the legislature will get. Edgar recognized his advantage here. He attributed his victory in the budget battle his first year to being able to convince the public that he, and not the legislature, was right in asserting that you can't spend money you don't have. For him, and for many of his gubernatorial colleagues, it is especially worthwhile to work hard to "get our spin because we know the politicians and the legislators, they read those papers." Legislators pay attention to what is said in the press, because they think that their constituents are reading the same thing. So, gubernatorial initiatives with the media buttress their policy initiatives.

If a governor sees little or no chance of winning in the legislature, going over the head of the legislature to the public may be the strategy de jour. That was the way Mitt Romney (R-MA) viewed the situation. With the legislature overwhelmingly Democratic, the choice as his administration saw it was to either go to the public or simply capitulate. The governor appealed directly to the public on several issues, and he managed to get what he wanted. Most governors on most issues are too cautious to resort to such confrontation. Thornburgh rarely went over the head of the legislature. He preferred to bring legislators along gradually, rather than embarrass them publicly. "If you embarrass them," he cautioned, "they'll tear off a piece of you." For him, such a strategy was "a last resort, not a first resort." Moreover, if they went to the public and still didn't prevail, they might wind up in even worse shape. As a legislative leader in New Jersey put it, "If you go to the public, you better win; otherwise you'll lose your pants in the legislature."[14]

Still, the risks may be worth taking. If a powerful interest group has succeeded in blocking an executive proposal, going to the public may be the only viable option. And it may not antagonize the legislature. Carlin spent three years trying to achieve passage of a severance tax on mineral production in Kansas. His efforts were for naught, because of the strong oil and gas lobby in the state. The governor figured that to get the tax through the legislature, he needed public pressure, pressure that could come from the realization that a tax was needed for financing state services such as education and highways. Carlin went public in 1980, but he succeeded in getting the severance tax enacted only in 1983, after winning reelection.[15] A governor may want to prove something to himself or to the legislature, and going public appears to be the way to do it. Bob Wise (D-VW) calculated his strategy before deciding to go to the public. He had been in Congress and essentially away from West Virginia for eighteen years. Although he had served in the legislature much earlier, he had no connections left. He had to develop relationships and earn the respect of the legislature. "There is a testing process that goes on," he said. He decided to meet the test by going to the people and campaigning for his agenda during his first legislative session. "I didn't have time to get everyone together around the campfire," he explained.

As far as the outside strategy is concerned, there is nothing quite as extreme as what can be called "the total legislative bypass," that is, going to the ballot with an initiative proposition. Governors frequently oppose these so-called citizen initiatives. Mike Dukakis (D-MA) opposed Proposition 2½ in Massachusetts. Jeb Bush (R-FL) fought against initiatives that mandated a high-speed rail system, created a statewide governing board for higher education, and limited class size.[16] Similarly, Ronald Reagan (R-CA) waged an all-out campaign against Proposition 9, which would have restricted property taxes and assessments.[17] Ballot initiatives are proposed by citizens or, more likely, by interest groups of one kind or another. Governors also shape or back ballot initiatives. It is a method by which they can marginalize the legislature in the lawmaking process, roll the dice with the public, and have a good chance of prevailing. Moreover, a gubernatorial initiative campaign puts pressure on the legislature to reach an accommodation rather than bet on something as uncertain as a statewide referendum. Locke, for example, was one of a number of governors of the twenty-four states where initiatives are authorized by constitution or statute. When a reduction in class size proposal failed in the legislature, Locke decided to support it as a ballot proposition. Despite opposition in the legislature, the initiative was approved overwhelmingly by Washington's voters. Locke won big.

On the survey, governors were asked how often they led or participated in a campaign to adopt an initiative by ballot, thus bypassing the legislature. About one out of five governors said that they had led or participated in an initiative campaign while they were in office. Several had resorted to the initiative only once, but others had resorted to it more frequently than three times (these tended to be governors who had been in office eight years or longer).

California is certainly the motherland of the initiative. Governors there have made greater use of it than governors anywhere else. It is worth looking at Schwarzenegger and the initiative, as reported by Joe Mathews in his thorough exploration, *The People's Machine: Arnold Schwarzenegger and the Rise of Blockbuster Democracy*. Other California governors before Schwarzenegger had led initiative campaigns, but none had resorted to it as much as he did. Even before his candidacy for governor, Schwarzenegger spearheaded a campaign for an education initiative. Its success was his biggest accomplishment before he won in the recall election of Gray Davis (D-CA). By his second day in office, Schwarzenegger was committing himself to two or three ballot initiatives and perhaps more. Schwarzenegger combined the outside game of initiatives with the inside game of backroom dealing. When the governor could not negotiate successfully in the legislature, he played his outside card. He would shift back and forth, infuriating the president pro tem, John Burton, who stormed out of the governor's office after a contentious discussion over workers' compensation. "Go take it to the people," he yelled, "I don't fucking care. Take it to your fucking people."[18]

On workers' compensation the governor played the inside-outside game to the hilt, building a fire of public pressure on the legislature so that he could get a compromise that he liked. Ironically, the reinforcement he received from the populist public made him reluctant to compromise with the Democrats in the legislature. Meanwhile, the senate president pro tem was on the inside, feeling pressure from the initiative campaign that the governor was leading. Burton felt that he would have to give in or do worse on the ballot:

> I was fighting to make something that I didn't like palatable, like when someone gives you a shit sandwich, and so you put the ketchup on it, you put the mustard on it, you put on the Worcestershire and a couple of onions.[19]

Schwarzenegger thought of the engagement as: "It's kind of the carrot-and-stick method. I like the idea of using the stick." By threatening an initiative, Schwarzenegger succeeded in the legislature. He forced the Democrats to vote for his compromise. "We are voting on this with a gun to our heads," said a Democratic senator. But the pending initiative would have been much worse.[20]

The problem with Schwarzenegger's victory, according to Mathews, was that it "left him with an outsized view of his own power and raised his own expectations for the future."[21] This house of cards collapsed not long after his great success. In 2005 he called for several reforms, but they got little traction in the legislature. He called for a special statewide election in November and proposed four initiatives for the ballot. All of the governor's initiatives were defeated—by teachers, nurses, firefighters, and public employees.[22] The ballot had proved to be a two-edged sword for the governor.

Going over the head of the legislature is the exception, not the rule. More often governors are not at war with the legislature. They are instead trying to help their policy proposals by laying the groundwork for the consensus building that goes on inside the legislature. Many governors establish a theme, package an issue so that people understand it, and then go to the public with their message. Weld's strategy in Massachusetts, for example, was not to get the public to demand that the legislature pass welfare reform. Rather it was to build public support for welfare reform, which in turn would help legislators adopt his proposals. Jim McGreevey (D-NJ) had an uphill battle to get a millionaire's tax passed by the New Jersey legislature. Democratic legislative leaders were especially reluctant to raise taxes of any kind. They remembered that after Florio forced a tax package on the legislature in the early 1990s, the Democrats lost control of the legislature for ten years. Even after they recaptured the legislature, the tax experience remained etched in their minds. McGreevey insisted on his tax proposal, however, and decided to sell the plan directly to the voters. The governor undertook a vigorous campaign. "We went county to county, visiting two or three senior centers every day, sitting in people's living rooms, church basements, and VFW halls," McGreevey described the effort.[23] Later on, Chris Christie (R-NJ) operated similarly, traveling the state for the fiscal and pension measures, local property tax legislation, and education reforms that he heaped on the legislature.

Especially if additional funding is required, governors are inclined to appeal to the people, along with appealing to the legislature. Highway funding typically involves tax increases. In Kansas, as well as elsewhere, that is what legislators are afraid of. One of Hayden's three principal agenda items was funding for the state's highway system. He started pushing this initiative in 1987 but failed to pass it in a special session of the legislature. Hayden realized that he had to build public support or at least soften public opposition. One of the questions the governor faced was how to frame an issue campaign. Highway professionals did not want to list projects in any plan, because they knew that conditions change, costs change, and priorities change. Yet, Hayden believed that it was better to let the professionals decide what and where. So the governor tried to sell his plan to the citizens of Kansas on the general grounds that it was good public policy and would enhance safety on the roads. The appeal, however, did not resonate with Kansans. Framed the way it was, the governor's appeal, according to his reflection, did not touch their lives. After another failure in the legislature, Hayden brought senate and house leaders and economic development leaders together to travel the state, hold hearings, and sell the governor's plan. This time specific projects were listed in the plan. People took kindly to the plan when they saw that there was something in it for their communities. Legislators warmed up to the plan when they saw that there was something in it for their districts. Meanwhile, legislators were hearing the same from folks back home. The old style of politics, with pork spread around for the public as well as the legislature, worked. Hayden's highway plan passed the legislature in 1989.

Bob Casey (D-PA) also had to go to the public to gain support for a drug initiative that would require more than $100 million in funding. One of the governor's priorities was a program to combat drugs and drug-related crime in the state. Casey, along with the state attorney general, state police commissioner, and other members of the cabinet, conducted public hearings across the state. High school students, police officers, recovered drug addicts, medical professionals, and family members of addicts all told their stories to a statewide television audience. Back in Harrisburg the governor issued a report and submitted a comprehensive program for the legislature to consider. Casey got the program and most of the funding he wanted. He considered it "a significant victory," and one that demonstrated the governor's capacity to set the terms of public debate, move public opinion, and have a divided legislature respond in a positive way.[24]

As noted earlier, a large majority of the nation's governors have education as a priority. Many of them employ outside as well as inside strategies. Bill Clinton (D-AR) waged an epic campaign, in which he is described as having taken up the torch for "the single most dramatic cause of his political career in Arkansas." He appointed an education standards committee, which was busy doing its work while he crossed the state of Arkansas asking people to support his program of educational reform, even though it entailed a tax increase. At the same time, Clinton worked with the interim committees of the legislature, preparing for the next legislative session. The governor's full-court press succeeded. He got his education reform package through the legislature in 1983. He credited a $130,000 public relations campaign with gaining the support necessary for victory. Betsy Wright, who was Clinton's chief of staff at the time, provided an account of the campaign, which was under way well before legislators arrived in Little Rock for their session. She wrote about the television, radio, and newspaper advertisements; the direct mail; the letters written by constituents to legislators; and the rallies across the state. All were designed "to snowball into the beginning of the legislative session so that by the time those legislators convened, each of them had a constituency in their district begging them to raise taxes for education." However well orchestrated the campaign, getting a majority in the legislature for the tax increase was no easy feat.[25]

One of the most significant educational reform achievements by a contemporary governor was that of Dick Riley (D-SC). In South Carolina, as in Arkansas, and at about the same time, going to the people was both thorough and effective. According to Riley, "just through the sheer force of leadership, governors can focus the attention of the people on an issue, explain what it is, and then move the state toward an equitable solution."[26] Here, too, the governor's education program necessitated a tax increase. The challenge was to sell the public on the need for major educational reforms, on the one hand, and the need to pay for these reforms, on the other. Riley's team took on the job as it would take on a political campaign. It commissioned a poll and then set up a detailed operation. The governor and others held a series of forums in every part of the state. These were essentially pep rallies for better schools led by the governor. Meanwhile two state committees were established—a business partnership committee and a committee on financing excellence in public education. "The result," according to one account, "was grassroots involvement, mixed with expertise from across the state."[27] All of this culminated with Riley's going on statewide television to explain the fifty-three proposals to improve education and to announce that another penny on the sales tax was required.[28] Going into the legislative session, there was little opposition to the education proposals, but opposition to the tax increase was strong. Riley explained what happened: "Because of the grassroots support we had gathered, together with the influence of the business leaders we had won over to our cause, we were able to turn around the legislative opposition and win passage of what was to be called the Education Improvement Act of 1984 and the tax increase to fund it."[29] The governor's ability to enlist the business community and go to the people had paid off.

This discussion of issue campaigns suggests that one important component is a commission, task force, committee, or the like. Such an agency can have three purposes: first, to specify the elements of a governor's policy thrust; second, to build a coalition among groups whose representatives serve on the agency; and third, to pave the way for the governor's agenda with both the public and the legislature. These commissions, task forces, and committees can be critical. That is why governors make use of them. In Arkansas, Clinton established a standards committee, with his wife, Hillary, chairing it. Her appointment raised the committee's visibility and the political stakes involved.[30] Its report in 1983 was greeted with media and public approval. It had the backing of the state department of education and the state board of education and won unanimous endorsement from the legislative joint interim committee on education.[31] Riley established a business partnership committee and a technical committee on financing, to accompany his grassroots campaign. According to a Riley aide, "The result was grassroots involvement, mixed with expertise across the state."[32]

Governors may use task forces and committees more as part of an inside strategy than an outside one. Baliles employed special commissions on transportation, education, agriculture, child care, and prison over-crowding to help produce legislative consensus in Virginia. The blue-ribbon commission on transportation, for example, included former governors and business leaders. Baliles agreed to support whatever it recommended. When the report was completed, it was delivered by state police to the door of every member of the legislature and then dealt with in a special session devoted to transportation. Carlin put education on the public agenda in Kansas, but some of his initiatives did not necessitate a grassroots approval. Issues such as an internship program for new teachers or the mechanics of competency testing did not have to be treated in a public forum. They were addressed through meetings with education leaders, college faculty members, and public school administrators and faculty. In situations such as these, Carlin pointed out, going public state-wide would be inappropriate. As governor, for instance, he had to deal with the effects of railroad deregulation. The issue was complex and most people were not directly affected by it. In this case, he needed answers to the problem but not a statewide campaign to gain support for a legislative program.[33]

Building Support and Exerting Pressure *in* the Legislature

Except in the case of an initiative campaign, which bypasses the legislature, there can be no outside game without a corresponding inside game. Public support, expert opinion, and interest-group backing all have to be translated into legislative votes. Clinton campaigned in order to mobilize public support for increased taxes and stricter school standards. Clinton conferred concurrently with interested and relevant groups and with practically every one of the 135 members of the Arkansas legislature.[34] Riley's grassroots campaign worked beautifully, but the final say was that of the South Carolina legislature, where a number of proposals—not only the governor's—competed for enactment. In what has been referred to as a "bloody battle" in the legislature, Riley did his part, inviting senators and representatives into his office for one-on-one discussions of the importance of his proposal. One legislator said that he felt like he was being "taken into the woodshed."[35]

To one degree or another, governors who pursue an inside strategy engage in a variety of activities designed either to persuade the legislature to enact an item on the governor's agenda or to defend against a legislative initiative or decision with which the governor disagrees. These activities include coalition building, strategizing, consensus building, negotiating, and compromising—the legislative process in a nutshell. Although these activities overlap and occur throughout the legislative proceedings and in no particular order, I examine them here, one by one.

Coalition building. All governors try to build coalitions within the legislature. As an independent, Angus King (I-ME) could not count on starting off with most members of either the Democratic or Republican caucus. He had to put together majorities one issue at a time. Governors also try to build coalitions among groups outside the legislature. Dukakis was skilled at this, at least in his second and third administrations. He was particularly ingenious in keeping a broad coalition together, convincing the various members that they shared common ground. The administration had a short-list of top priorities. If a member of the coalition had as a priority an item ranked fifth, it was in that group's interests to push priorities one through four so that the preferred priority five rose to the top.[36]

Tom Kean was another natural at coalition building. Like many of his gubernatorial colleagues, Kean was extremely effective in enlisting help from statewide interest groups, all of which impressed the New Jersey legislature. He brought employers on board for his high-technology items, parents for school reform, and big-city mayors for his budget and bonding proposals.[37] The first time he proposed an infrastructure bank, it was defeated in the legislature. Kean modified the measure and put together a powerful coalition of labor and business. The governor persuaded the two groups that they shared goals: business leaders wanted better roads and labor leaders wanted new jobs.[38] Although governors do manage to win support and put together coalitions behind their proposals, some interest groups may oppose much of what they advocate. Those opposing groups use direct and indirect lobbying to win over legislators to their side and against the governor. Teacher groups have been the 800-pound gorilla at the state level. In some places they have been implacable enemies of the governor. The Michigan Education

Association (MEA), for instance, could not stomach Engler and engaged in open warfare against the governor, whom it portrayed as a villain. This posture prevented the association from negotiating settlements on education issues, because any compromise would have been seen as a sign of weakness.[39]

Teacher associations often lead the opposition that governors encounter when advocating for their agenda of education reform. Organized teachers can be counted on to oppose budget cuts for schools, voucher schemes, charter schools, pension curtailments, testing programs, and student performance as a means of assessing teacher performance. Clinton's education initiatives ran into opposition from the Arkansas Education Association (AEA). Teachers were concerned about competency testing and fought the provision in the legislature. Clinton retaliated. If the association defeated the teacher testing bill, he would withdraw his own proposed one-cent sales tax increase. The governor prevailed but not without an acrimonious struggle.[40] In Maryland, teachers actively opposed Bob Ehrlich's (R-MD) charter school initiative. In Oklahoma, although teachers agreed to public school choice and charter schools, they objected to Keating's four-year requirements of math, science, and English. Finally, in New York, the United Federation of Teachers opposed and defeated George Pataki's (R-NY) proposed legislation to increase the number of charter schools.[41]

Governors run into trouble with interest groups that question their funding allocations. In Pennsylvania, for example, state funding for education increased in Thornburgh's 1980–1981 budget but not enough for the Pennsylvania State Education Association. The teachers wanted more money for education, which would have necessitated tax hikes. After the nationally influential report *A Nation at Risk,* Thornburgh produced an *Agenda for Excellence* in Pennsylvania. But his plan to have "the dollars follow the child" was countered by the teachers association's insistence on equitable funding for districts. The teachers, moreover, objected to the governor's proposal to measure school performance. On both issues, Thornburgh had to give way.[42] Teachers associations have to be reckoned with, as do many other groups. Trial lawyers, the insurance industry, business, labor, doctors, and nurses, among others, all can place obstacles in the way of a governor's policies and budgets.

Strategizing. A strategic sense is a valuable skill for a governor to have. To move a policy or budget to enactment, governors need to strategize continuously. Perhaps the critical strategic question pertains to the degree of gubernatorial involvement in pressing the legislature. Typically, governors tend to go all out. But on occasion they decide it is better to hang back and let leadership come from elsewhere. Romney, facing an overwhelmingly Democratic legislature in Massachusetts, had as the major item on his agenda health care reform. His administration consulted widely and built support for a plan the governor submitted to the legislature, prompting senate and house Democrats to fashion plans of their own. Thereupon Romney stepped away from the process and the negotiations that transpired, fearing that more aggressive leadership on his part would backfire.[43] His strategy proved to be successful.

Many decisions have to be made during the time that a measure is in committee, in caucus, on the floor, in the other chamber, in conference committee, or between stations. Probably one of the best strategists to hold gubernatorial office was Engler. He was skilled at using what is known as "the hairy arm," a diversion put out front to capture the focus of attention while a few people quietly worked out the details of legislation that the governor really wanted. Engler was also adept at a stealth technique, referred to as "killing them with kindness." If there was some bill he didn't want, Engler would add so much to it that it would collapse of its own weight. Then, there was the "irresistible amendment," when there was opposition to something Engler wanted passed. He would have an amendment proposed that legislators might have disliked but wouldn't dare vote against.[44] As governor Engler was always several steps ahead of everyone else. "He knew the end game and how to get there," wrote a former aide, "while others were still trying to figure out what the issue was." Indeed, he was considered to be a near genius when it came to strategy. One issue in 1996 involved retirement funding for state workers, technically, "defined contributions." It was a priority. His way to get the votes was to offer early retirement in one bill and link it to defined contributions. "Early retirement will be the horse that pulls the defined contributions cost along," he strategized. He went further, proposing defined contributions not only for state employees, but also for teachers.

I can never beat MEA [Michigan Education Association] on this one, but I'll draw all the fire there. I'll get all the guns blazing at the teachers' pension system and have it get through the state employees' system.[45]

The greatest coup of Engler's three terms in office involved a tremendous struggle over education finance in 1993. The governor had gone to the ballot twice to get a change in the way schools in Michigan were funded. He lost both times. Then, as he recollected, "The heavens opened up and gave us the opportunity to repeal property taxes." Democrats in the legislature offered an amendment to eliminate the property taxes that paid for public schools. Engler concluded that the Democrats were bluffing. He figured that if the Republicans opposed the amendment, Democrats going into the 1994 elections could claim that the Republicans opposed cutting property taxes. Engler decided to call their bluff and brought Republican leaders together. "Tell them to pass it," the governor said, "Tell them I'll sign it." He recalls that on this issue, the two branches of Michigan government "were working without a net." The legislature overwhelmingly voted to abolish the property tax, but without having anything to put in its place. The governor had gambled that there would be an impetus now to write tax reform legislation that was needed to replace the old system.[46]

Choosing the right time is an important part of strategizing. "You've got to set priorities and you've got to figure out your timing," is how Edgar put it. Clinton was a master of timing, particularly when it came to his education reform package. By presenting his initiative to a special session, rather than a regular session, of the Arkansas legislature, he increased his chances of success. The governor used a special session not only because he could determine its focus, but also because citizen legislators, especially during a special session, want to return as quickly as possible to their employment. They are disposed to accede to a governor's requests.[47] In most states the governor is the one with the authority to call the legislature into special session, and the governor is the one who sets the agenda for the special session. Thus, he or she can focus the legislature on a specified issue and not on myriad others. For example, Bellmon called the Oklahoma legislature into special session in 1990 to deal exclusively with education, whereas the regular session would focus on fiscal problems of the state.[48]

Strategic thinking is involved in practically everything a governor does vis-à-vis the legislature. A strategic rule for Andrus was to "always act as if I held a strong hand."[49] For Oklahoma's Keating, a strategic rule was to "go after low-hanging fruit." During the 1990s welfare reform hung low for many governors, with President Clinton advocating it in Washington and a number of other states taking it on. Moreover, Democrats in the legislature were not opposed in principle. These factors made it possible to achieve such reform.

Consensus building. According to his biographer, Alvin Felzenberg, "Kean's greatest strength as a leader was his capacity to motivate others." Kean was a cheerleader for the cause he advocated, and like a good coach, he would prod the group in the direction he wanted it to go. "He also worked to create cohesion among whatever group he was part of," wrote Felzenberg, "establishing a sense of common purpose, building a feeling of camaraderie."[50] Governors strive to bring insiders together to build support for policies on their agenda. They energize those who are already behind their proposals. But the real trick is to win over potential opponents by building consensus that appeals to them. Confrontational in his first term as governor, Dukakis later emphasized consensus building. Illustrating this approach is the consensus building that surrounded passage of a right-to-know law (which would make public the chemicals a company was using in its processes). To bring labor and industry together, Dukakis's staff conducted negotiations with both sides until a middle ground was near at hand. Then the governor invited business and labor leaders to meet with him separately at his home. Dukakis addressed the business leaders:

> Here is the principle you've stood for: that your employees ought to be protected from harmful chemicals, right? Can we all agree on the principle?

No one expressed disagreement. How could they? "Good," the governor said, "let's let the staff work out the details." Somehow, Dukakis secured tacit approval for a compromise from business. The next night he repeated the process with labor.[51] Jim Hunt was tenacious in pursuing his agenda in North Carolina, but he also had a sense of where legislators were coming from. He was willing to compromise in order to build consensus. One newspaper described his approach as follows: "Hunt's political style smoothes over differences, offers a little something for everyone, takes the middle and least offensive course whenever possible."[52]

Negotiations between the senate and the house, and with the governor, occur on some of the most significant issues of a legislative session. It helps if governors are skillful mediators, helping the two chambers resolve their differences. West Virginia's Wise found it extremely useful to position himself in the middle when battles between the senate and the house, or even between senate and house chairmen, broke out. His mediation would benefit his agenda. Riley would also serve as a go-between to "help" senate and house conferees settle their differences and arrive at a decision.[53]

Negotiating. "I was reasonable," was the self-assessment of Keating of Oklahoma. That made negotiations possible. Most other governors also are reasonable when it comes to negotiating in order to reach settlements. Indeed, negotiating is a large part of the job of leadership in policymaking. Of course, many of the negotiations between the governor and the legislature take place at the staff level. But just how this is done varies from governor to governor. In New Jersey, for instance, Florio did it one way and Christine Whitman (R-NJ) did it another. When Florio was governor, legislators would negotiate with his chief of staff, who could do a deal on behalf of the governor. When Whitman was governor, any of three coequal top staffers would negotiate with legislators, but the governor had to approve the details of any agreements.[54] Schwarzenegger also used several staff members to relate to California legislators. Multiple channels, Schwarzenegger believed, allowed him to see all the options.[55] In other states as well, and especially the larger ones, staff negotiates first and governors and legislative leaders get involved when most differences have been narrowed or worked out.

Trading can involve the priorities of governors, on the one hand, and those of the legislative leadership, on the other. Each party to negotiations has a laundry list, and each attempts to agree on items of mutual interest, trade off on others, and dispense with the rest. Trading can also take place at a more mundane level, with legislators willing to give their votes to the governor in return for appointments and special projects.[56] There is always plenty to trade, especially since legislation is crafted with this in mind. For example, Parris Glendening (D-MD) knew when to give and how to give. He would have administration bills crafted with "throwaways," which could be used and then given up in bargaining with the Maryland legislature. The gun bills he proposed are a good example of how he used "throwaways," managing to get 50 percent of what he wanted. He could settle for that.

Trading in order to secure legislators' votes makes some governors squeamish. They don't want to do it and don't even want their staff to do it. Bruce King was one who felt that each piece of legislation should stand on its own. He was not one to get involved in "you scratch my back and I'll scratch yours" to get something passed.[57] Kean refused trades in order to get a piece of legislation through the New Jersey legislature. In his memoirs, Kean wrote about a senator who told him that he might change his mind and vote for the governor's budget, if his friend got the judgeship he was seeking. Another senator had an uncle who needed a job. The governor turned down both, because he "would not trade jobs for votes."[58] Bob Graham also took an absolutist position in this respect. In trying to prevent an override of a Graham veto, Charlie Reed, the governor's chief of staff, promised a senator funding for some bridge repairs in return for his vote. After winning by one vote, Graham asked Reed how he had accomplished it. Reed told him about the money for the bridge. "Oh, we don't do that," said Graham. "Well, would you rather lose?" Reed asked. "Don't ever do that again," Graham ordered.[59]

Generally speaking, most governors appreciate that they have to give in order to get. Take Mike Beebe (D-AR), who is called a master at getting what he wants. "We're willing to let him get what he wants," said the house majority leader, "as long as we get some funding for the projects we want."[60] Jim Hodges (D-SC) had to work with Republican majorities in the legislature. He realized that "there is always something legislators want in the budget." He was flexible, as were the legislative leaders, because "everyone wants to get things done." Although Maryland's Glendening did not trade one bill for another, he did use the budget as a tool for getting what he wanted. When the legislature cut the governor's budget,[61] the reductions went into a reserve fund that the governor could reallocate in a supplemental budget. If an item that was cut was important to him,

Glendening would put it in the supplemental. Otherwise, he held the money in reserve. When a legislator came in asking for help on a local project, Glendening said he would be glad to consider it if the legislator helped on one of the bills where the governor needed a vote.

Governors understand the importance of local projects in the lawmaking process. For Edgar, money for a park or the fire department back home was not his priority, but it was a legislator's. "So, I never worried too much about giving them something as long as it wasn't outlandish, and it had to be legal, too." Bellmon was not entirely comfortable with what in Oklahoma were called "special projects." But he adapted. Lights for local baseball fields; paving local streets; and support for watermelon festivals, rattlesnake hunts, and Indian cultural events were all tools that legislative leaders needed if they were to deliver the votes necessary to pass a tax package or other major bills.[62] Thornburgh was not a trader by inclination, but he also adapted. Moreover, he knew that the legislative leaders in Pennsylvania wanted small stuff. They would settle for minor adjustments and projects. "They did not have mainly substantive issues," and they left policy to the governor. That was a small price to pay. Oklahoma's Keating also could defend trading off, but he "would never give away something important." Few governors have had and have used the storehouse of pork as have governors of Louisiana. They have exercised more control over patronage than governors in other states. They have a huge say in determining which legislative districts get money for bridges, roads, sewers, and health clinics. In addition, they have rural development grants that can be doled out to lawmakers.[63] All of this has worked to their benefit.

If legislators are thinking of increasing their pay, governors are in a position to make a deal. In return for a governor's support, signature, or plain acquiescence, legislators are willing to give a lot. Although he had always supported higher pay for public officials as a matter of principle, when a pay raise was proposed by and for Pennsylvania legislators, Thornburgh saw an opportunity. "So I played hard to get, and presented my own wish list to the legislative leaders as the price for my support," he wrote. The legislature delivered on every item and the governor abided by his part of the bargain.[64] As governor of New York, Mario Cuomo wanted the legislature in 1987 to pass a strong ethics law. The legislature was reluctant, but the governor would not agree to a pay raise legislators wanted until they approved an ethics bill that he found acceptable. The ethics bill that the legislature passed did not give Cuomo everything he wanted, but it gave him enough for him to declare victory.[65]

Compromising. Except for an intransigent few, governors expect to compromise and show a willingness to do so right off the bat. Realistically, if they want to accomplish something, they do not have much choice. The governors' survey included a question about how much governors had to compromise to get their agenda through the legislature. Not many of them—5 percent—had to compromise "a good deal." But another 51 percent had to compromise "somewhat," whereas 45 percent had to compromise "very little." Interestingly, by the time governors are in their third term, they have to compromise "very little," according to survey responses.

If participants are willing to give somewhat, compromises are not that difficult to fashion. Sometimes they occur after the fact, rather than before it. Pataki stood firm, but his welfare reform package was defeated in the 1996 session of the New York legislature. The next year Pataki agreed to drop important provisions and add some important exemptions.[66] He had to compromise and did. Ehrlich also compromised to get charter schools legislation passed in Maryland. Roberts had little difficulty compromising with the Oregon legislature on her workforce development initiative. Her initiative had one component; what the legislature wanted had another component. The two headed in the same general direction, making compromise manageable.

Compromises are a normal feature of the budget process, where differences between dollar amounts and line items can be split by the governor and the legislature. Angus King had various squabbles with the Maine legislature during his eight years in office. The worst occurred in his final year, when state expenditures were exceeding state revenues and the budget had to be balanced. At the same time, according to King, the legislative leaders were getting tired of the governor and of his successes. They wanted to beat him at something. The Republican senate and Democratic house leaders united and challenged the governor's program for distributing laptop computers in the public schools, a program that was not popular with the public. Nevertheless, King managed to achieve a compromise. Laptops were funded only for the seventh and eighth grades, and not through high school, as the governor had proposed. With everything going against him,

King still managed to salvage a compromise. In New Jersey, Republican Christie and the Democratic legislature agreed to pension reform, a budget, and a cap on property taxes in 2010. Even Christie, who during his first months in office exhibited a confrontational, bare-knuckled approach to the legislature, decided to compromise rather than insist on his plan for a constitutional amendment to limit property tax increases to 2.5 percent per year. At a special session of the legislature that he called, Christie struck a humorous note: "Some of you came into this chamber today expecting that I would offer you a take-it-or-leave-it proposition." But he backed off, and welcomed further discussion—acknowledging that even he needed the legislature to get anything done.[67]

It may be "like pulling teeth" to get an agreement, as Bob Taft (R-OH) said about his proposal on educational standards. But an extra $25 million and an extended timeline helped alleviate concerns of Ohio's teachers. Oklahoma's Keating tried to make changes in education policy, but it proved difficult because the teachers union opposed parts of his plan, while agreeing to others. The compromise was that the governor settled for three years of science, math, and English instead of the four years he originally wanted. He also went after tort reform, but the alliance of trial attorneys and Democratic legislators resisted strenuously. Keating had to settle for a compromise that limited damages.

No budgets are enacted without compromises between the governor and the legislature (more specifically, the governor, the senate, and the house). Survey respondents were asked about the type of changes the legislature made in the budget submitted by the governor. No respondents replied "no changes at all." But only a few, 6 percent, reported "major changes," whereas 46 percent said "moderate changes" and another 47 percent said "minor changes." Among the changes, 54 percent involved "mainly expenditures" and 38 percent involved "both revenues and expenditures." Only 4 percent of the changes pertained to "mainly revenues." Governors accept such changes as the way business has to be done with a separate and coequal branch of government.

It used to be that, when the budget was in a deficit mode under divided government, if one party wanted expenditure cuts and another wanted revenue increases, the middle position would be equal parts of each until balance was reached. Take Kean's budget in New Jersey as an example of a

Republican governor's and a Democratic legislature's ability to settle. The governor agreed to a one-cent increase in the sales tax in order to balance the budget without further spending cuts. But the legislature wanted an increase in the income tax. The package agreed to was a sales-tax increase and an increase of the top rate in the income tax. "It's not what I wanted or what anybody wanted," Kean said upon signing the act into law.[68]

There are few better examples of the importance of compromise between a governor and the legislature than the health insurance package in Massachusetts. It demonstrates how the lawmaking process can reach significant settlements even when it starts out with significant differences and when the governor and the legislature are of opposite parties and not on the best of terms. The story is worth retelling here.[69] Under the law that was enacted (after four months of negotiations to reach agreement), every resident of Massachusetts would be required to have health insurance. After signing the bill into law, Governor Romney said simply: "We found a way to bridge the partisan divide, and to find a coincidence of interests among the various stakeholders in the health care community." He qualified his praise for the accomplishment by adding, "It doesn't mean that everything in the bill is exactly how I'd like it." Practically everyone applauded—the advocates united under Health Care for All, the health care providers, and the business community.

Yet it was no easy matter to get from the divergent proposals advanced by the governor, the house speaker, and the senate president at the outset to substantial agreement on the end product. "Substantial agreement" rather than "complete agreement" best describes the settlement. Romney vetoed the provision requiring employers to pay a penalty if they didn't offer insurance to employees, expecting that the legislature was certain to override.[70] At the end, too, the legislative leaders agreed that the final bill was a true compromise. It was more than a "true compromise"; it was a virtual bundle of compromises. The most important and the most general compromises were those between liberals and conservatives, between Democrats and Republicans, between the house and the senate, and between the legislature and the governor. The measure brought together ideas from both the liberal and the conservative camps into an unlikely mix of seemingly incompatible concepts. One side achieved universal coverage while the other maintained the role of the private sector in furnishing most of the coverage.

When asked if the bipartisan, executive-legislative accomplishment was conservative or liberal, Governor Romney answered: "It's liberal in the sense that we're getting our citizens health insurance. It's conservative in that we're not getting a government takeover." The right-wing Heritage Foundation helped craft the bill that the governor proposed. The left-wing New America Foundation was among a number of liberal groups that found that they could support the settlement. "What's remarkable to me," said Romney in celebrating passage of the law, "is that such a disparate group of people could come together on a workable consensus." Sharing the platform with Massachusetts senator Ted Kennedy, who had been instrumental in the bill's passage, Romney quipped that his son said that the two of them supporting the same piece of legislation would help slow global warming. That would be because hell had frozen over. Kennedy, who spoke immediately after the governor, quoted his own son: "When Kennedy and Romney support a piece of legislation, usually one of them hasn't read it."

Among the many compromises that had to be made along the way was that regarding an employer's fee. Business had to be convinced that employers who did not offer health insurance should pay a fee. It was a tough sell, but business finally agreed. Speaker Salvatore DiMasi and senate president Robert Travaglini both started out with a preference for a payroll tax to finance part of the package, but they settled on a $295 worker assessment on employers who did not offer health insurance on their own. The various groups affected by this measure had to give up something, but each got a piece of what it wanted. Business succeeded in eliminating the payroll tax, which was in the house bill, but it had to agree to a fee instead. Health care providers got to sell a subsidized insurance plan to new subscribers, but the costs had to be kept low without the policies being stripped down. Hospitals and physicians got increases in Medicaid rates for medical services, even though they insisted that it would still not be enough to cover their costs. Also, payments were tied to performance measures starting in fiscal year 2008. The hospitals in Boston and Cambridge did exceedingly well, thanks mainly to the support they received from the senate. People earning low incomes wound up with state subsidies for the private coverage they were required to purchase.

Tools of Engagement

In the 1960s Richard E. Neustadt published one of the century's most influential books in the field of political science, *Presidential Power*. Simply stated, the power of the American presidency, according to Neustadt, is the informal power to persuade. Persuasion is not the only power of the president, nor is it the only power of the governor. But it is certainly one of the important ones, and it is a power that practically every governor employs. The exception should clarify (if not prove) the importance of persuasion for governors. In his first administration, Dukakis "was determined to remake government in his own image, righteous and severe, cleansed of the bargaining and trading that customarily lubricated the political process." Because of his approach, Dukakis, according to Barney Frank, then a member of the Massachusetts legislature, quickly became irrelevant as a political force on Beacon Hill:

> Michael has reduced the power of the governor to the formal legal powers. He can submit. He can veto. He can appoint. But he cannot influence.[71]

Yet it is the governor's power to influence, to persuade, that counts so heavily, especially as the lawmaking process runs its course.

Governors work hard to persuade, and they do so in a manner that suits their own personalities. One is more in-your-face, whereas another is more laid back. One emphasizes the merits; another, the politics; and still another, the personal factors needed to win over a legislator. There are governors who administer persuasion in the gentlest of forms, so that legislators are left wondering just what was wanted. Kean was averse to arm twisting, horse trading, or heavy handedness of any kind. "My idea," he said, "is to reason with them, to explain that a program is right and that it meets the needs of the state."[72] A legislator would ask, "Tom, what do you want me to do?" The governor's response, "Well, do what you think is best."[73] Another legislator described Kean's power of persuasion on the budget. Several issues divided the governor and the Republican legislative leadership. Kean invited the leaders to the mansion to discuss the issues, and the legislators came loaded for bear. By the time the meeting was over, however, they were all satisfied and they all voted for the budget. The legislators couldn't figure out how the governor accomplished what he did. "He listened patiently. He answered the questions. We had a wide reaching discussion." Kean was a persuasive individual with a low-key, yet highly effective style.[74]

For the most part, governors make the case on its merits rather than by making promises to legislators whose votes they need. Governors are used to having to help round up the last few votes to get one of their priorities over the top. In interviews, former governors do not appear comfortable relating how they nail down their votes and what they have to promise in return. Some governors deal one-on-one with legislators, others leave the horse trading to their staffs. But by one means or another they get what they need. A lot of this comes down to the personal relationships governors already have with legislators. Glendening recounted how he managed to get a gun-control bill through the Maryland senate and house. Mike Miller, the senate president, was no friend of the bill, in part because the Beretta firearms company was located in his district. Moreover, Miller and Joe Vallario, the chair of the house judiciary committee, were friends of the Beretta CEO. Glendening had the votes in the house but only after a number of provisions were watered down. The bill then was sent to the senate judiciary, known as a killer committee and chaired by Walter Baker. (Glendening had started to meet with Baker at the beginning of the legislative session, because he wanted a friendly chairman.) But Baker put the gun bill in his desk drawer, indicating that he did not intend to take action on it.

Glendening pleaded with Baker to take up the gun bill, but the judiciary chair replied, "It's already in the drawer." The governor insisted on making a case: "How many guns do you have in your house?" Baker counted the number on his fingers, his fingers of both hands. The governor persisted, "Walter, how many guns did you ever buy at one time?" "I think three," Baker replied, "but they were hunting rifles." Glendening saw his chance: "You can buy twenty-five guns in Cecil County and sell them in Baltimore. What do you think of that?" Baker appeared shocked: "That's not true, is it? I didn't know that." He said he would look into the issue and soon reached some agreements with the governor. Finally, he consented to take the bill out of the drawer and allow a vote in committee, which he did. The bill was reported out. Then, Glendening persuaded the senate president to allow a vote on the floor.

But the senate bill differed from the house bill, and Miller as senate president insisted that no changes be made in the senate version when it was sent back to the house for concurrence. Glendening had to rely on Vallario, who chaired house judiciary. Here, friendship seemed to carry the day. The governor appealed to the chairman, reminding him of their long-standing relationship, including the fact that Vallario's daughter had worked in the office of the Prince Georges county executive, when Glendening held that position. "I need your help," the governor appealed. He won over Vallario, who did not accept any amendments.

In Michigan every year-end legislative session culminated in a few hours when the governor and his staff bargained over a number of thorny issues. John Engler operated more aggressively than other governors. He would sit in his office and receive a parade of persuadable legislators whom his aides had identified. The governor, according to an aide, "pleaded, handed out favors, and, when necessary, threatened." The threatening was usually implicit, but "those who sat across from Engler when he wanted something did not need to be reminded of whose signature was required at the bottom of every bill and who could fix a constituent problem or create a political one with a single phone call."[75] A legislator's anticipation spoke as loudly as the governor's words.

Few governors articulate threats, although a threat may be implicit. Simply put, if a particular legislator does not help the governor, the governor cannot be expected to help that particular legislator. Legislators have a good idea of what a governor can and will do. On occasion, however, the threat is explicit. Even Kean once lost his bearing and laid down the gauntlet. He had as a priority a measure to authorize the state to take over failing schools. When several Republican senators resisted his arguments, the governor indicated that he would find it "very difficult" to campaign with Republican senators who voted against the takeover bill. Kean later recanted.[76] Other governors carry through on their threats. Ben Nelson (D-NE) put it this way: "I had a couple of rogues I had to deal with, and I did." He helped to get one of them defeated in his bid to be reelected, and "that sent a message." In Oklahoma, Republican Keating sponsored a right-to-work law (that is, a law requiring an open shop, with no compulsory union), which Democratic legislators fought. The governor went into the districts of Democratic opponents and campaigned against them, not without success. Finally, Democratic legislative leaders who were tired of having their members battered by the governor, put right-to-work on the ballot. It passed, affording Keating a major victory.

Governors don't take no for an answer. They keep at it. Jim Hunt called legislators day and night, repeatedly: "If they got a call after 10 p.m., they knew it was from me." Jay Rockefeller (D-WV), as the president of the West Virginia senate remembered, "was determined by hook or by crook, that he was going to change my mind." He got little encouragement, but the governor wouldn't give up. "He always kept trying to convince you that his ideas had merit," said the legislator. He succeeded in wearing down the resistance of at least a few of the doubtful members.[77] "One thing about being governor is that you have staying power," observed Kean. "If you persist—if you keep coming back at it—you can eventually prevail."[78]

Playing Defense

One chief of staff for a governor divided all the issues confronting a governor into two categories: offensive and defensive. The former are the items on the governor's agenda; the latter are those with which the governor is forced to cope.[79] Every governor, as Ben Nelson pointed out, plays both offense and defense and, like Nelson, most play the former more than the latter. Thus far, we have focused on the policy initiatives and budgets presented by governors, and how they get put together and steered through the legislature. But governors, as policymaking leaders in their states, must attend to what the legislature sends their way as well as to what they send to the legislature. The legislature also initiates. It initiates major bills, in addition to hundreds or even thousands of less major ones. All of them—major or minor—require the governor's signature, or at the very least his tacit consent, if they are to become law. As Cannon pointed out in his biography of Reagan, "what a governor opposes can be as important as what he initiates."[80] The legislature, moreover, examines the governor's budget and can add, reduce, or eliminate funding or can make other alterations in programs and operations. When the legislature has done its work, the governor has a critical role to play in giving or withholding assent to its budgetary revisions.

Major policy initiatives, however, are the governor's job. Former governors were asked on the survey, "What proportion of the major policy issues debated in the legislature were your initiatives as opposed to initiatives proposed by the legislature?" Of the respondents, 74 percent reported that two-thirds or more were their own initiatives and another 15 percent reported that about half were their own initiatives. Only 10 percent claimed initiatives for only one-third of the major policy issues, and just 2 percent claimed less than one-third of all initiatives. Democratic governors were responsible for a somewhat higher proportion of initiatives than Republicans. As many as 91 percent of those governors who had been in office eight years or longer reported being responsible for two-thirds or more of major initiatives. Not all the major policy proposals were initiated by the governor, but the large proportion were.

On some occasions, of course, the legislature took the lead while the governor remained on the sidelines. Edgar remembered that the most significant legislative initiative during his eight years in office was utility reform. The Illinois senate had been working on the issue for four years. During Corzine's administration, the New Jersey legislature undertook leadership on property tax reform, meeting in special session to do so. The governor and his staff were kept informed and were involved, but the package of bills that resulted from study and deliberation were undeniably the legislature's initiative, not the governor's.

Governors who have served in the legislature, particularly those who have held institutional positions of leadership, do not begrudge the legislature its own initiatives. Arne Carlson (R-MN) acknowledged that Minnesota lawmakers came up with "great ideas"; he welcomed their initiatives. Colorado's Owens, a former legislator, admitted that he would sign bills that he didn't like, because "as governor you have to show respect for the process that brought a bill to you." Wise invited West Virginia's legislative leaders over to listen to their proposals, rather than have them listen exclusively to his. He had no difficulty agreeing to several of them, such as a program for preschool. Jim Hodges followed suit in South Carolina. He made his priorities clear up front. He also informed legislative leaders as to whether the legislature's initiatives were acceptable to him. During Hodges's last two years in office, Republicans in the legislature would have important bills that they wanted and the governor felt he had little choice in the matter.

If the legislature is moving in a direction that the governor doesn't like, he or she will enter into negotiations to ensure that the legislature sends over a bill that is acceptable. Bruce King could not support a gasoline tax that the New Mexico legislature favored, because the revenues were going to be used to prop up the education budget. The governor felt that tax revenues raised from highways should have been used for transportation needs. However, King did not want to come into conflict with a Democratic legislature, so he finally agreed to sign the bill after the legislature agreed to put a penny of the six-penny gas increase into the road fund.[81] The Pennsylvania legislature advocated a pharmaceutical-assistance-for-the-elderly program. Thornburgh favored the idea, but he opposed its form because it could bankrupt the state's lottery fund. The two sides came together on a copay provision that overcame the governor's opposition.[82]

Because of their constitutional veto powers, governors have the last word, or practically the last word. The veto is the ultimate defensive weapon. It permits the governor to definitively say no, if he or she disagrees with a measure; and it gives the governor leverage to persuade legislators not to pursue a particular course, a course that would encounter the governor's veto. John Ashcroft (R-MO) offered a beach-ball game as a metaphor for the governor's veto power:

Unlike the individual who launches the beach ball at the sporting event . . . I am sure that I will get the ball back. If it has taken a shape that I do not believe appropriate, I can burst the ball; that's what a veto is! In my view, a veto is the deciding vote.[83]

In editorializing on Owens's vetoes in Colorado during the 2005 session, the *Denver Post* used a metaphor drawn from another game, in referring to the governor as "a baseball guy who appreciates the benefits of having the last turn at bat."[84] The veto, the line-item veto, and the conditional veto are powerful weapons in the hands of a governor. These weapons strengthen a governor's capacity to control the nature and shape of legislation that he or she signs into law. Perhaps even more important, they allow a governor to eliminate or reduce budget items inserted by the legislature. Finally, the veto strengthens the governor's hand in negotiations over both policies and budgets.

NGA regards the veto as a means of ensuring executive control.[85] Governors use the veto, and particularly the line-item veto, to control the budgets that legislatures send over to them. Whereas governors formulate most of the budgets, legislatures make changes through their appropriations, budget, ways and means, and finance committees (depending on the state and chamber). With the line-item veto at their disposal, governors can choose which changes they will accept and which they will reject. Former governors were asked on the survey about the frequency with which they used the line-item veto on legislative budget items. Although 21 percent of the states represented by the respondents did not have a line-item veto, 50 percent of the total respondents said they used it "some" or "much" of the time, and the remaining 29 percent said "rarely" or "never." The line-item veto clearly was a valuable tool for many governors. Those who wanted to keep spending down, like Owens of Colorado and Wise of West Virginia, found that the line-item veto was their most useful tool. It gave governors a big advantage over the legislature, according to Hodges.

Thornburgh used the line-item veto on those occasions when the legislature funded spending programs but offered no revenues to pay the costs. He pointed to a billion-dollar economic development program, called PennPride, which the legislature passed in 1982, in the midst of a recession. The Democrats, according to the governor, wanted to maneuver him into taking the initiative to raise taxes for the program. Thornburgh signaled the Republican-controlled senate to approve the house budget, even with a billion-dollar imbalance. He then responded with line-item vetoes that included the legislature's own funding requests for the fiscal year. The Democrats returned with a much-scaled-down budget and temporary tax increases to fund it, all of which the governor signed into law.[86]

Mark Sanford (R-SC) was used to having his vetoes overridden by the South Carolina legislature, but he persevered nonetheless. In 2008 he not only vetoed items in a budget he believed was wasteful, but he also threatened to sue legislators for failing to meet their responsibility to pass a budget.[87] Like Sanford, other governors have had their line-item vetoes overridden by their legislatures. Victor Atiyeh (D-OR) and Mike Huckabee are among them. Yet, for most governors, overrides of their line-item vetoes were rare. When former governors were asked on the survey about the frequency of overrides, only 8 percent said that they occurred "much" or "some" of the time. Another 18 percent said "rarely," and 52 percent said "never." In the states of the remaining 23 percent of the respondents, the governor did not have the line-item veto power.

Although governors can always veto the entire budget bill, it is rarely done. Compared to the line-item veto, the general veto is too blunt an instrument. In response to the survey, 80 percent said that they never vetoed the entire budget, whereas 7 percent said they rarely did it, and only 9 percent reported doing it some of the time. However, when governors lack the line-item veto, as in a number of states, their only options are to veto the entire budget, accede to legislative changes, or negotiate a settlement with which they can live.

At each session, legislatures pass a number of bills other than the budget, which are sponsored by departments and agencies, interest groups, or constituents. In some states the enactments are relatively few, in the low hundreds, as in Alaska, Indiana, Iowa, Kentucky, Minnesota, Nebraska, New Mexico, Vermont, Washington, and Wyoming. In some states the enactments are relatively many, in the high hundreds or over a thousand, as in Arkansas, Louisiana, New York, Rhode Island, Texas, and Virginia. In practically all the states the number of enactments would be higher were it not for the governor's veto. On the survey, former governors were asked how often they vetoed legislation (not including budget bills). Only 1 percent said they never made use of the veto, and 38 percent said they rarely made use of it. Half of them—51 percent—vetoed bills some of the time, and another 8 percent vetoed them much of the time. Republican governors were more inclined to veto than were Democrats.[88]

Governors veto bills for many reasons. They may be concerned about the fiscal impact of a measure. During his second term as governor Frank O'Bannon (D-IN) faced diminished state resources, but the legislature continued to pass spending bills. O'Bannon vetoed thirteen bills in the 2001 session and another fourteen in the 2003 session.[89] Governors also may want to send a message to the legislature about what the priorities ought to be, and vetoes help do that. They may take exception to the policy thrust of a measure or to its details. In Colorado, Owens vetoed about one out of five bills that crossed his desk; and in Washington, Locke in his early years set a record by vetoing fully or partially one out of three bills that came his way. One of Ehrlich's priorities in Maryland was medical malpractice reform, but in a special session the legislature passed its own bill, not the governor's. Ehrlich decided that it did not come close enough to what he wanted, so he vetoed it. One bill appeared to be too much of a backroom compromise for Benjamin Cayetano (D-HI). It provided for an increase in the minimum wage on the one hand and a tax credit for hotel renovation and new construction on the other. The governor thought that an increase in the minimum wage was long overdue, but the tax credit was simply a gift to the hotel industry and landowners. "I had little choice but to veto the bill," he wrote. Increasing the minimum wage would have to wait.[90]

In those states with an amendatory, partial, or conditional veto, governors are in a good position to have policy changed to their satisfaction. Tommy Thompson (R-WI) used a partial veto almost 300 times to change words or sentences in a bill and, in effect, change enacted policy on his own.[91] In Illinois, Edgar was also able to rewrite legislation. In Washington, both the Democratic governor and the Republican legislature favored welfare reform in principle, but they disagreed on specifics. The legislature passed a bill with prescriptive measures that Locke opposed. He was able to veto them and come out with essentially what he wanted.

As long as the governor stands by with the veto, legislators can be less responsible about what they enact. They can respond to popular or interest group pressures or the appeals of a few constituencies, leaving it to the governor to come to the rescue. The Illinois governor's amendatory veto, according to Edgar, allowed legislators, "who are kind of sloppy by nature," to be even sloppier because they knew the governor would clean it up. Edgar recounted his experience with the veto:

> I don't know how many times I'd have legislators run into my office and say, "We just passed a bill up there and we need you to amendatory veto it." I said, "Whose bill was it?" "It was mine." "Why didn't you change it up there?" "It would have caused a lot of trouble and we just think it's easier for you to do it."

Occasionally it is politically useful for legislators to take credit for the passage of a bill, while asking the governor to veto it because the legislator realizes that it is bad legislation, poor public policy.

In Indiana a veto can be overridden by a simple majority in both houses. But in the overwhelming majority of states, an override requires an extraordinary majority, usually two-thirds. This practically ensures that the governor has the last word. It is unusual for governors to have their vetoes overridden. Responding to the survey, 87 percent of the former governors reported that their vetoes of policy were rarely or never overridden. Only 8 percent said that their vetoes were overridden some of the time, and 4 percent said much of the time. Republicans Ehrlich, Huckabee, and Lincoln Almond (R-RI), all with Democratic legislatures, suffered the most overrides. Other governors have also had their difficulties in this regard. Scott Matheson (D-UT) was overridden on a regular basis by the Republican legislature. Even when the governor and legislature are under the control of the same party, the relationship may be tense. In 1990 Wallace Wilkinson (D-KY) vetoed twenty-one bills in a regular session, having thirteen of his vetoes overridden by the Democratic legislature. More than half of the overridden vetoes expanded legislative power.[92]

There are exceptions, but for the most part governors prevail. Owens had all his vetoes sustained in Colorado, even on bills sponsored by his fellow Republicans. In Oklahoma the Democratic legislature wanted to break Republican Keating's first veto as governor. But the Democrats failed as Republican legislators united in support of their governor. Keating vetoed the most bills in the state's history, with none overturned. After a while, the Minnesota legislature got the idea, said Arne Carlson, that there was no sense in passing bills if the governor was going to veto them. In Arizona, Republicans controlled the house for all eight years of Bruce Babbitt's (D-AZ) tenure and the senate for most of his terms. But the Republican margin was not large enough to override. The situation permitted Babbitt to rely heavily on his veto power, setting an Arizona record of 114 vetoes. Once Republicans realized that the governor could use the veto with effect, they agreed to negotiate at an early point in the process. Thus, Babbitt and the Democrats could bargain with Republican legislative majorities and get a respectable amount of what they wanted.[93]

With the veto at their beck and call, governors are tough bargainers. Food stamps were one of Locke's initiatives in Washington. The measure did not seem to be going anywhere, but the legislature had passed a welfare reform bill that the governor was ready to sign. However, he threatened to veto the bill unless the legislature gave him a food stamp plan in return. The legislature realized that the governor was determined and was willing to walk away from welfare reform, if he didn't get food stamps as well. The governor got what he wanted, and both measures were signed into law.

Notes

1. Mark Leibovich, "Who Can Possibly Govern California?" *New York Times Magazine,* July 5, 2009, 49.
2. Joe Mathews, *The People's Machine: Arnold Schwarzenegger and the Rise of Blockbuster Democracy* (New York: Public Affairs, 2006), 210.
3. Laura A. van Assendelft, *Governors, Agenda Setting, and Divided Government* (Lanham, MD: University Press of America, 1997), 123.
4. John Carlin, "The Governor as Administrator, Leader, and Communicator," in *Governors on Governing*, ed. Robert D. Behn (Lanham, MD: University Press of America, 1991), 82–83.
5. Alan Rosenthal, *Governors and Legislatures: Contending Powers* (Washington, D.C.: CQ Press, 1990), 104, note 15.
6. Kean in Barbara G. Salmore and Stephen A. Salmore, *New Jersey Politics and Government*, 3rd ed. (New Brunswick, NJ: Rivergate Books, 2008), 163.
7. National Governors Association, *Transition and the New Governor: A Planning Guide* (Washington, D.C.: National Governors Association, 1998), 27.
8. Snelling in Alan Rosenthal, ed., *The Governor and the Legislature: Eagleton's 1987 Symposium on the State of the States* (New Brunswick, NJ: Eagleton Institute of Politics, 1988), 37.
9. Bob Graham, "A Magical Vision and Other Ingredients of Leadership," in Behn, *Governors on Governing*, 59.
10. Bruce King, *Cowboy in the Roundhouse* (Santa Fe, NM: Sunstone Press, 1998), 207.

11. Henry Bellmon, *The Life and Times of Henry Bellmon* (Tulsa, OK: Council Oak Books, 1992), 178.

12. Thomas H. Kean, *The Politics of Inclusion* (New York: Free Press, 1988), 113–14.

13. Rosenthal, *The Governor and the Legislature*, 25–26.

14. Jim O'Sullivan, "Man in Charge," *National Journal*, November 12, 2011, 19; Rosenthal, *The Governor and the Legislature*, 110.

15. Carlin, "The Governor as Administrator, Leader, and Communicator," 83–84.

16. S. V. Date, *Quiet Passion: A Biography of Senator Bob Graham* (New York: Penguin, 2004), 148–49.

17. Lou Cannon, *Governor Reagan* (New York: Public Affairs, 2003), 324.

18. Mathews, *The People's Machine*, 239, 247, 249.

19. Ibid., 247–48.

20. Ibid., 254, 256.

21. Ibid., 256.

22. Louise Krasniewicz and Michael Blitz, *Arnold Schwarzenegger: A Biography* (Westport, CT: Greenwood Press, 2006), 134–35.

23. James E. McGreevey, *The Confession* (New York: HarperCollins, 2006), 492–93.

24. Robert P. Casey, *Fighting for Life* (Dallas: Word Publishing, 1996), 144.

25. Charles F. Allen, and Jonathan Portis, *The Comeback Kid: The Life and Career of Bill Clinton* (New York: Carol Publishing Group, 1992), 86–87, 98–99.

26. Richard W. Riley, "Overcoming Restrictions on Gubernatorial Authority: The Unique Problem of Some Governors," in Behn, *Governors on Governing*, 35.

27. Benjamin Prince Bagwell, *Riley: A Story of Hope* (Pickens, SC: Pickens County Publishing, 1986), 70.

28. Ibid., 69–73.

29. Riley, "Overcoming Restrictions on Gubernatorial Authority: The Unique Problem of Some Governors," 36.

30. Dan Durning, "Education Reform in Arkansas: The Governor's Role in Policymaking," in *Gubernatorial Leadership and State Policy*, edited by Eric B. Herzik and Brent W. Brown (Westport, CT: Greenwood Press, 1991), 126.

31. Allen and Portis, *The Comeback Kid*, 88–89.

32. Bagwell, *Riley*, 70.

33. Carlin, "The Governor as Administrator, Leader, and Communicator," 83–84.

34. Durning, "Education Reform in Arkansas," 127.

35. Bagwell, *Riley*, 74–75.

36. Richard Gaines and Michael Segal, *Dukakis and the Reform Impulse* (Boston: Quinlan Press, 1987), 228.

37. Alvin S. Felzenberg, *Governor Tom Kean* (New Brunswick, NJ: Rutgers University Press, 2006), 330–31.

38. Kean, *The Politics of Inclusion*, 101–2.

39. Al Short, a Michigan Education Association official, in Gleaves Whitney, *John Engler: The Man, the Leader & the Legacy* (Chelsea, MI: Sleeping Bear Press, 2002), 257.

40. Allen and Portis, *The Comeback Kid*, 92–93.

41. George J. Marlin, *Squandered Opportunities: New York's Pataki Years* (South Bend, IN: St. Augustine's Press, 2006), 120–21.

42. Dick Thornburgh, *Where the Evidence Leads* (Pittsburgh: University of Pittsburgh Press, 2003), 154–55.

43. Ryan Lizza, "Romney's Dilemma," *New Yorker*, June 6, 2011, 41.

44. Dennis Schormack, as quoted in Whitney, *John Engler*, 205.

45. Quoted in Whitney, *John Engler*, 279.

46. Ibid., 224–27.

47. Durning, "Education Reform in Arkansas," 136–37.

48. Bellmon, *The Life and Times of Henry Bellmon*, 353–54.

49. Cecil Andrus and Joel Connelly, *Cecil Andrus: Politics Western Style* (Seattle: Sasquatch Books, 1998), 21.

50. Felzenberg, *Governor Tom Kean*, 445.

51. Gaines and Segal, *Dukakis and the Reform Impulse*, 225–26.

52. Quoted in Jack D. Fleer, *North Carolina Government and Politics* (Lincoln: University of Nebraska Press, 1994), 103–4.

53. Bagwell, *Riley*, 94.

54. Art Weissman, *Christine Todd Whitman* (New York: Carol Publishing Group, 1996), 152–53.

55. Mathews, *The People's Machine*, 205.

56. Rosenthal, *Governors and Legislatures*, 78–79.

57. King, *Cowboy in the Roundhouse*, 160–61.

58. Kean, *The Politics of Inclusion*, 88.

59. Date, *Quiet Passion*, 116.

60. Alan Greenblatt, "The Job of a Lifetime," *Governing* (June 2009), 25.

61. The Maryland legislature can only cut; it cannot increase items nor can it switch funds for one item to another.

62. Bellmon, *The Life and Times of Henry Bellmon*, 339–40.

63. Tyler Bridges, *Bad Bet on the Bayou* (New York: Farrar, Strauss and Giroux, 2001), 64.

64. Thornburgh, *Where the Evidence Leads*, 192.

65. Robert S. McElvaine, *Mario Cuomo: A Biography* (New York: Scribner's, 1988), 376.

66. Marlin, *Squandered Opportunities*, 151–52.

67. *New York Times*, July 2, 2010, A21.

68. Felzenberg, *Governor Tom Kean*, 208–9.

69. Taken essentially from Alan Rosenthal, *Engines of Democracy* (Washington, D.C.: CQ Press, 2009), 397–99.

70. See Lizza, "Romney's Dilemma," 41.

71. Gaines and Segal, *Dukakis and the Reform Impulse*, 131.

72. Felzenberg, *Governor Tom Kean*, 203.

73. Donald Di Francesco, on Panel on Governor Kean, Governors Project archive, Eagleton Institute of Politics, Rutgers University, April 15, 2009.

74. Lisa Randall, on Panel on Governor Kean, Governors Project archive, Eagleton Institute of Politics, Rutgers University, April 15, 2009.

75. Whitney, *John Engler*, 402.

76. Felzenberg, *Governor Tom Kean*, 251–52.

77. Richard Grimes, *Jay Rockefeller: Old Money, New Politics* (Charleston, WV: Jalamap Publications, 1984), 215–16.

78. Felzenberg, *Governor Tom Kean*, 279.

79. National Governors Association, *The Many Roles of the Governor's Chief of Staff* (Washington, D.C.: National Governors Association, Office of Management Counseling & Training, 2006).

80. Cannon, *Governor Reagan*, 364.

81. King, *Cowboy in the Roundhouse*, 330–31.

82. Thornburgh, *Where the Evidence Leads*, 152.

83. John Ashcroft, "Leadership: The Art of Redefining the Possible," in Behn, *Governors on Governing*, 71.

84. "Gov. Owens Wields a Busy, Fair Veto Pen," *Denver Post*, June 4, 2005.

85. National Governors Association, *Transition and the New Governor*, 95.

86. Thornburgh, *Where the Evidence Leads*, 145.

87. Josh Goodman, "A Government Adrift," *Governing* (August 2008): 39.

88. One governor exhibited especial showmanship when vetoing bills. Brian Schweitzer (D-MT) used a branding iron to burn his veto message into a number of Republican bills, while adding the caveat that "at an actual branding party, there's some castration, but we're not doing any of that today." Quoted in the *Billings Gazette*, as reported in *State Net Capitol Journal*, April 18, 2011.

89. Andrew E. Stoner, *Legacy of a Governor: The Life of Indiana's Frank O'Bannon* (Bloomington, IN: Rooftop Publishing, 2006), 310–12.

90. Benjamin J. Cayetano, *Ben: A Memoir From Street Kid to Governor* (Honolulu: Watermark Publishing, 2009), 505.

91. Tom Loftus, *The Art of Legislative Politics* (Washington, D.C.: CQ Press, 1994), 72.

92. Penny M. Miller, *Kentucky Politics and Government* (Lincoln: University of Nebraska Press, 1994), 129.

93. David R. Berman, *Arizona Politics and Government* (Lincoln: University of Nebraska Press, 1998), 117.

7

Succeeding as Policy Leaders

CONSTITUTIONALLY AND POLITICALLY, governors are central to policy-making in their states. They formulate the main policy agendas, they shape the budgets, and they manage the campaigns inside and outside the legislature to have their proposals enacted into law. Policymaking leadership is a job on which they spend much, if not most, of their time and much, if not most, of their energy, and it is the job that typically makes or breaks their administration. How well do they perform this gubernatorial job? How successful are they as policymaking leaders?

How Successful Are They

Up until now, I have made the claim that most governors succeed as policymaking leaders. But I have not yet provided solid support for that assertion. Here I shall provide evidence based mainly on reports from governors themselves.

When asked on the survey to characterize their success on policy issues, 46.6 percent of the governors responded that the legislature enacted nearly "all" of what they asked for and another 42.5 percent said the legislature enacted "most" of what they asked for. The remaining 11 percent got only "some" of what they proposed.[1] Even allowing for some exaggeration, governors are quite successful. Not many do as well as Ned McWherter (D-TN). In his eight years, he claimed a 100 percent batting average (but he only advanced five major initiatives).[2]

In his first year as governor, Gerald Baliles (D-VA) sent 108 bills to the legislature, 107 of which passed. "When I finished, I was satisfied," said Baliles, commenting on a 95 percent batting average. His accomplishments included a transportation initiative, funding for family and mental health services, and proposals for child care and environmental protection. Looking back on her six-year record, Madeleine Kunin (D-VT) claimed a 90 percent success rate and the achievement of a great deal of what she had promised. That included a dozen environmental bills, kindergarten funding, a rise in the minimum wage, and mandatory automobile insurance. Ben Nelson (D-NE) had to settle for an 80 percent average, as did John Waihee (D-HI). Terry Branstad's (R-IA) success rate was 85 percent. Bill Owens (R-CO) could not recall any legislative defeats during his eight years as Colorado's governor. His leading policy accomplishments were a school choice plan; a highway and rail transportation project; and the reduction of income taxes and taxes on capital gains, interest, and dividends. In addition, he steered a bill through the legislature that repealed a system under which the state automatically withheld union dues from employee paychecks.

Governors succeeded across the policy spectrum. According to their responses to the survey, the large majority got most or all of what they wanted from the legislature in each of the specified policy domains. Sixty-seven of the seventy-five responding governors initiated major policy in the field of education, and 75 percent of them claimed to have gotten most or all of what they wanted. Southern governors, especially, focused on education reform, mainly because their states ranked low on indicators of educational achievement and they had a lot of ground to make up. South Carolina's Education Improvement Act of 1984 was one of the major efforts in this field. It was Dick Riley's (D-SC) signal achievement as governor. Comprehensive education reform had also been accomplished in California and Florida in the 1970s. Yet governors in the 1980s and 1990s, and into the first decade of the twenty-first century, continued to reorient education in these states. In South Carolina, as well as other places, successive governors had left some mark on education.

Education was the core focus and most prized achievement of many governors. For John Ashcroft (R-MO), it was "the single most important contribution of my governorship."[3] Nothing equaled the importance of education for Bob Graham (D-FL), who was also very concerned about the prison system and crime. When it came to state funds, according to Graham's budget director, "It was not just that the prison system was pitted against education. *Everything* was pitted against education."[4] Henry

Bellmon (R-OK) called the signing of HB1017 in 1990, which was designed to improve Oklahoma's schools, "the highlight of my political career."[5] Bill Clinton (D-AR) demonstrated great political skill in a thirty-eight-day special session of the Arkansas legislature, where he prevailed on a huge education reform package.[6] Tom Kean (R-NJ), Roy Romer (D-CO), Zell Miller (D-GA), Dick Thornburgh (R-PA), Jim Hunt (D-NC), Jim Hodges (D-SC), and Baliles all were successful in passing legislation and appropriating funds to elementary, secondary, and higher education in their states.

The economy and economic development is the second favorite policy area of governors. Their record of success has been equal to that in education, with 74 percent of them having gotten most or all of what they hoped to get from the legislature. The economy and economic development covers the broadest possible range of policies. Just examine Bill Richardson's (D-NM) attainments in this area. He pushed through a cut in taxes that he thought were inhibiting economic growth. He also got tax credits for new technology companies and for those companies that provided high-wage jobs. He put controls on spending, while investing in the state's transportation and economic infrastructure. And he instituted reforms in education in order to prepare students for employment in the new economy.[7] Economic development was an important part of Thornburgh's agenda as well. He tried to create a better business climate in Pennsylvania, which was a high-tax state. He took great pride in Pennsylvania's resurgent economy during his watch, which had been called at the time "the best single state economic development program in the country."[8] Economic development can also be more narrowly conceived, as by Arne Carlson (R-MN), who won "a big victory" by changing the workers' compensation system in order to keep Minnesota business from leaving Minnesota and heading to North or South Dakota.

In the third most popular area of policy initiation, that of the environment and energy, 82 percent of the governors claimed success. Florida's Graham allocated hundreds of millions of dollars for the purchase of environmentally sensitive lands and for acquiring undeveloped beachfront for the state park system.[9] Jim McGreevey (D-NJ took credit for passage of the Highlands Act in New Jersey, which he referred to as "the single most sweeping environmental law in a generation." That was the capstone of his administration, which McGreevey remembers as "by far the most significant policy initiative I had ever undertaken."[10]

The highest success rate for governors was in the domain of welfare. During the late 1980s and through the 1990s, welfare reform was at the top of state agendas. Tommy Thompson (R-WI) received great credit for his innovative policies in this field, but other governors had their own successes in reshaping their states' welfare systems. John Engler (R-MI) virtually eliminated the existing structure of welfare in Michigan. Pennsylvania, with 5 percent of the national population, had 20 percent of those on general assistance when Thornburgh became governor. He put forward a plan to reduce welfare caseloads and move welfare recipients into jobs. Backed by Republicans and opposed by Democrats, "Thornfare," as the initiative was labeled by its opponents, was watered down in the legislature, but the administration still got about two-thirds of what it wanted. "We bit off more than we could chew," Thornburgh concluded. But it could still be considered a gubernatorial win.[11]

Gubernatorial success rates were lowest in the domain of health. But even here, 67 percent believed that they had wins rather than ties or losses. Mike Dukakis (D-MA) managed to obtain employer mandated health coverage, the first step toward universal coverage in Massachusetts, and Lawton Chiles (D-FL) attained a managed care system in Florida.[12] Mitt Romney (R-MA) had a big win in Massachusetts, albeit one that he shared with the legislature.

Rarely is gubernatorial success total. Even the most legislatively effective governors cannot escape losing on a provision or two. They settle for less but still walk away declaring victory. Governors usually lose on more than a provision or two. They fail on some of their important initiatives. Romney had as one of his objectives removing Bill Bulger, the former senate president, from his post as president of the University of Massachusetts. He pushed legislation that would have reorganized the university and incidentally abolished Bulger's position. The plan went nowhere in the legislature (but Romney applied constant pressure on the university trustees and Bulger finally retired). Both Jim Edgar (R-IL) and Engler suffered important policy losses. Edgar did not enact the tax reforms he wanted nor did he get a third Chicago airport authorized. In looking back, he didn't see what he could have done differently. In any case, he recalled, one of the nice things is that "when you go out a winner, you don't have many regrets." Despite his mastery of the process, Engler came away with a split decision after clashing with the Michigan teachers association.

George W. Bush (R-TX) proved to be a master of the politics of the possible in Texas. Not everything was possible. Bush lost on property tax reform and on school vouchers. The welfare reform provisions passed by the Texas legislature were not nearly what he wanted. He got much closer to what he wanted on civil court procedures, because the legislature was as pro-business as the governor.[13] Jeb Bush (R-FL) dominated the Florida legislature during his two terms, but he too could not always get what he wanted. The legislature blocked his attempt to deregulate electricity production and the change he had made in the board of regents was undone by a constitutional amendment. Still, "these setbacks were the exceptions that proved the rule. Generally what Jeb wanted, Jeb got, both in terms of actual policy objectives as well as the expansion of his own power."[14] Thornburgh's legislative agenda fared well in Pennsylvania, but he was unable to convince the legislature to pass his initiative for the merit selection of judges. Nor was he able to privatize the state's liquor monopoly. He recommended establishing maximum and minimum sentences and abolishing parole for newly convicted felons, but the legislature did not act on either proposal.[15]

Another successful governor, North Carolina's Hunt, also had to live with policy failures. He didn't get mandatory sentencing, the elimination of a sales tax limit on luxury vehicles, or the appointment instead of the election of judges.[16] George Voinovich (R-OH) had a winning run, but several of his proposals were voted down by the legislature, including the repeal of a soft-drinks tax and reform of the workers' compensation system. In Washington, Gary Locke (D-WA) lost on several proposals to reorganize state government. "The legislature just had different ideas as to how it should be done," he explained.

Gubernatorial failure probably happens most frequently on revenue initiatives. For example, Bob Casey (D-PA) wrote in his memoirs, "I should also own up to at least one major failure." It was tax reform, aimed at making Pennsylvania's school finance system less dependent on the property tax.[17] Frank Keating (R-OK) wanted to shift some of the income tax burden to a sales tax on services, but he couldn't get it through the legislature. Because of the passage of an initiative that severely limited state revenues, Barbara Roberts (D-OR) was behind the eight ball from the outset. She needed to raise revenue desperately. She called a special session of the legislature to enact her tax plan and put it on the ballot. She won in the senate, but in the house she lost 31–28. Losing that tax plan was "a huge political loss" for her, with the defeat setting the tone for the second legislative session of her administration.

"He will not be associated with legislative accomplishments," is the way a member of Jon Corzine's (D-NJ) administration summarized the governor's first and only term. Indeed, Corzine's gubernatorial administration is likely to be remembered for his DOA (dead on arrival) plan to "monetize" the New Jersey Turnpike and other state highways, with the proceeds going toward the retirement of half of the state's burgeoning debt. Corzine traveled around the state discussing an arrangement to set up a public benefit corporation that would sell up to $38 billion in bonds, backed by toll increases of 50 percent or more. He couldn't generate much public support, and his plan received hardly any legislative support. It never got off the ground.[18]

Just as not every governor gets everything he or she goes after, virtually every governor gets something. No one is shut out, and everyone can rightfully claim policy victories. Even governors who have had the shortest tenures, the most difficult times, or major losses can boast of some achievements. Sarah Palin (R-AK) did not even complete her term of office and appeared to be at war with a large contingent in the legislature. Yet, in her first year and a half she had two impressive accomplishments. Setting aside her social conservatism, she focused on putting together coalitions to reach her objectives. She won bipartisan support in the legislature for her oil-profits tax proposal, turning the revenues into a rebate check for every resident of the state. She also got the legislature to agree to a natural gas pipeline.[19] Jesse Ventura (I-MN) had longer to compile a record, but his relations with the Minnesota legislature were tumultuous. His pet idea for state reform, a unicameral legislature, went nowhere, but he did get the tax rebates he wanted and his first budget passed pretty much intact.[20] Like Ventura, Hawaii's Benjamin Cayetano (D-HI) didn't prosper legislatively. However, after six years of work on the health care fund, he finally got legislation passed. In his autobiography, Cayetano noted that no legislators showed up at the bill signing.[21]

As far as policy leadership goes, there may be big winners but there are no big losers among the nation's contemporary governors. Arnold Schwarzenegger (R-CA) illustrates this point wonderfully. He had to govern in a most difficult environment: with a state structural budget deficit that was worsened by the recession that began in 2008; a legislature controlled by the Democratic Party; a two-thirds vote requirement to pass a budget; and the initiative process, which further hamstrung the executive and legislature (but also provided an alternative process for governors who couldn't sell the legislature on their proposals). For several years, Schwarzenegger skillfully used his celebrity status to combine inside and outside games. His strategy was to push initiative proposals to create leverage so that he could cut deals with the Democratic legislature.

He achieved impressive victories at the ballot box with Propositions 57 and 58. In the legislature he managed to reduce the tax on autos, pass a budget without a tax increase, and reform workers' compensation. On the 2004 ballot, the governor took a position on fourteen initiatives and was on the winning side on twelve of them. Stymied in the legislature, Schwarzenegger put even more reliance on the initiative. During 2005, which he dubbed a "year of reform," he devoted his policy leadership to four measures—Proposition 74, lengthening the apprentice period for teachers to get tenure and making it easier to discharge teachers who weren't performing; Proposition 75, requiring the consent of members before unions could use their dues for political purposes; Proposition 76, limiting state spending; and Proposition 77, establishing an independent panel to draw the state's districts. Unlike in the legislative process, once an initiative was on the ballot there was no possibility of compromise. The governor would either win big or lose big. Schwarzenegger did the latter. According to the chronicler of "blockbuster democracy" in the state, "This was the greatest defeat by a California governor since all of Hiram Johnson's propositions went down in the 1915 special election."[22]

Chastened, but unbowed, the governor persisted in supporting initiatives, albeit less insistently and dramatically than before. He made gains here, persuading voters to approve of nonpartisan primaries in which the top two candidates, regardless of party, would compete in the general election. He also pressed successfully for an initiative that finally took legislative redistricting out of the hands of the legislature and entrusted the task to a nonpartisan, nonpolitical panel of citizens. On the legislative front the governor made headway on prison reform, water conservation, and pensions.[23] One of his biggest achievements was passage of a budget, which gave the governor some changes that he wanted, including a roll-back in pension benefits that had been negotiated with public employee unions and a doubling of the revenue committed to the state's rainy-day fund, if approved by the electorate. The governor could claim at least a measure of success but by no means victory. In California, it would appear, victory on the budget was practically out of the question.

The requirement that a budget has to be passed by a super majority existed only in California and two other states and made reaching a final agreement more difficult. Budgets are usually difficult to put together and pass, even by majorities. As the principal architects of their states' budgets, governors have to work hard to steer them through the legislature. The budget and policy are intertwined. Indeed, as the National Governors Association has pointed out, "It is impossible to separate the policy goals from the budget process."[24] Many of a governor's major initiatives require spending—for education, economic development, the environment, or other worthwhile purposes. That requires funding through the budget and, perhaps, new or expanded sources of revenue.

When asked what they considered to be their main policy priorities during their time in office, 60.3 percent of the governors surveyed indicated the area of budget and fiscal policy. Republican governors were more inclined than their Democratic counterparts to make budget and fiscal policy a priority—by 72.2 percent to 48.6 percent. Like Pennsylvania's Thornburgh, they believed in the precept that the first order of business is "to get the fiscal situation straightened out."[25] This commonly entails cutting or holding the line on spending and cutting, or at least not raising, taxes.

Governors manage to dominate the budget process, although they have to work at it to do so. In this domain a governor's skills are put to the test. Riley served as governor of South Carolina, where the chief executive had limited formal budget power. Still, he prevailed in the budget process. In his view, it depended on gubernatorial leadership. If leadership in setting priorities is effective, Riley wrote, "an executive can influence the budget, and through it, the policy of the state. . . . [G]ood budget management is dependent on strong leadership."[26] "We had good luck with the budget," summed up Bob Taft (R-OH). Mike Hayden (R-KS) represented his success as typical of governors. The legislature agreed to virtually everything he had in his budget—99.5 percent. That was normal, for in his estimation governors generally get a 90 percent return. Angus King (I-ME) recalled some budget fights, but all of them around the margins; he received 85 to 90 percent of what he went after. John Sununu (R-NH) recalled his budgetary success when he was in office. The $2 billion biennial budget submitted by the executive was passed with about $3 million in changes—as small an amount as anybody could remember.[27]

As former governors see it, they were quite successful in achieving their objectives in the budget process. Overall, 50 percent of the respondents to the survey reported that their legislatures gave them nearly all of what they asked for. Another 47 percent reported getting most of what they asked for. Only 3 percent said that they got only a little. As might be expected, governors who recalled doing well in getting their policy initiatives enacted also recalled doing well in getting their budgets passed. The relationship between policy success and budget success is strong and statistically significant.[28]

In responding to the survey, governors may not have considered revenue measures to be part of their formal budget responsibilities. It is in the domain of revenues and taxes that governors have met the most resistance, had to give substantial ground, and have suffered defeats. As one might imagine, it has been much easier for governors to reduce taxes than to raise them. When Weld took the helm in Massachusetts, the first big issue he took on was a repeal of the sales tax on services. The Democratic leaders of the legislature opposed repeal. But the rank and file, under pressure from their constituencies, deserted their leaders and supported the governor. Weld's prized achievement over the course of two administrations was twenty-one tax cuts without any tax increases. Christine Whitman (R-NJ) promised in her election campaign to reduce New Jersey's income tax by 30 percent. She succeeded, with Democratic as well as Republican support in the legislature.[29] Colorado's Owens also took pride in successfully reducing taxes on income, capital gains, interest, and dividends. North Carolina's Hunt had little problem reducing the sales tax on food.

Although the legislature is not without budgetary impact, its impacts are usually at the margins. In budgets, however, the margins can be important. Thornburgh dominated the process in Pennsylvania. But when he proposed an extension of the sales tax to fund his transportation program, the legislature substituted a two-cents-per-gallon gasoline tax increase.[30] New Jersey's legislature had rarely made budgetary waves, content to focus on a few pet programs and so-called Christmas tree items for members. When Corzine in his first budget sought to raise the sales tax by one penny, the assembly resisted, fearing a taxpayer revolt. The senate was more acquiescent, but the legislature and governor stalemated and part of state government had to be shut down. Corzine won the battle eventually, but not without the legislature winning a big concession. Half the penny sales tax increase would be dedicated to property tax relief.

When governors reflect on their policymaking leadership, their policy priorities, along with revenues to fund them, get top billing. They think of the good measures they got through the legislature, not the bad ones they kept from becoming law. For them, success comes from playing offense and getting much or some of what they asked the legislature to give them. Policymaking leadership, however, also involves playing defense, that is, preventing the legislature from making law that runs contrary to the governor's wishes. As Lou Cannon pointed out in his book on Ronald Reagan, whereas most evaluations concentrate on a governor's constructive accomplishments, "what a governor opposes can be as important as what he initiates."[31]

The ultimate weapon here is the veto, which every governor enjoys today. The veto not only allows a governor to definitively say no, if he or she disagrees with the legislature's policy or appropriation. It also affords him or her leverage to persuade legislators not to pursue a particular course, lest their efforts lead to a veto. As a practical matter, the veto power gives the governor the last word. That is because an extraordinary majority in each chamber is required to override a veto. Relatively few are overridden by the legislature. Gary Johnson (R-NM), for example, vetoed 750 bills during his eight years in office. Only two of them were overridden. The survey of former governors substantiates this: 87 percent reported that their vetoes of substantive bills had never or rarely been overridden and 70 percent reported that their line-item vetoes of budget items had never or rarely been overridden (with 23 percent of the respondents in states where the governor did not have the line-item veto power). In part because of their veto power, governors appeared to perform as well on defense as they did on offense. When questioned in the survey as to whether the legislature succeeded in enacting any policy initiatives that they opposed, only 8 percent responded that the legislature had done so on a number, and 28 percent on a few, of its initiatives. But 64 percent responded that the legislature had not succeeded in enacting any initiatives the governor opposed.

What Makes Them Successful

How governors "get what they want out of the legislative process" is the subject of a recent book by Thad Kousser and Justin Phillips that found that governors got most or some of what they asked for on over half their initiatives. Their success, the authors summed up, is attributable to their use of the veto, rewards and punishments to lawmakers, the ideology of the legislature, their time in office, and their overall approval ratings.[32] Earlier research by Margaret Ferguson found that gubernatorial success depended on features of the legislature, political party strength, the economic well being of the state, and the tenure and experience of the governors themselves.[33]

My own research, although of a different nature from that of Kousser and Phillips and Ferguson, found that the success governors achieve is shaped by a number of factors related to the powers and resources at their disposal, the situations that they encounter upon taking office, the nature of the legislature, the initiatives they propose, and the experience, orientations, and leadership behavior of the governors themselves. Of central importance here are the issues governors take on—the budgets they formulate and the policies they propose. Most governors succeed legislatively, but some governors do fail. Their failure seems to be attributable to one or several of the following factors: the economic and fiscal situations they encounter, the dysfunctional political systems in which they function, a partisan majority in opposition in the legislature, and an erratic or confrontational leadership style on the part of the governors themselves.

Having the Upper Hand

Governors succeed because they are constitutionally and institutionally advantaged as soon as they take office.[34] Not every governor is the constitutional, statutory, and political equal of every other governor. Some, like those in New York, New Jersey, Louisiana, and Maryland, are more advantaged than their counterparts in Colorado, Indiana, and Texas. But the differences are minimal compared to the enormous differences between the power of governors and that of legislatures. To illustrate the point, we explored the relationship between an index of gubernatorial power in the states and the policy and budget success of governors, as reported in the responses to our survey. A statistically significant relationship between the two did not appear, suggesting that differences in constitutional, statutory, and political powers among governors in various states were not significant as far as policy success was concerned. The point is that their institutional advantages over the legislature loom much larger than do differences in their formal and informal powers state by state.

In every state, the governor has the advantage of unity. He or she is a single figure elected statewide and with a statewide constituency. The legislature is a series of multiples—two houses, two parties, and anywhere from 60 to 424 members.[35]

The oneness of governors facilitates their policy initiation and their budget formulation. Governors are expected by the legislature itself to establish the agenda for the lawmaking enterprise. Speaker Steve Lewis of Oklahoma expressed the view of other legislative leaders when he commented that a major tax bill became law because several people did what they were supposed to. "The governor set the agenda as he is supposed to do," said Lewis.[36] That view is echoed by Tom Loftus, who wrote in his memoirs that the job of the governor was to propose, while the job of the legislature was to dispose, with the legislature typically passing what the governor had initiated.[37] Gubernatorial oneness also advantages governors in their efforts to persuade legislatures to adopt their initiatives. Whether working an inside game or an outside one, governors are the focal point for legislators, the media, and the public. They frame the issues, and they direct the policy campaigns.

Even in states with relatively strong legislatures, the institutional differences between the two branches are substantial. David Jennings, a former house speaker in Minnesota, acknowledged that the legislature was not the place to develop bold new initiatives. "Legislators react to what the governor and others propose be done, and eventually develop a plan that may or may not resemble what's been proposed—but, however it ends up, it is a reflection of the governor's proposal."[38] Thus, governors whose formal powers are comparatively weak, such as Riley in South Carolina, can be remarkably successful as policy leaders. It matters less that the South Carolina governor has been weak compared to governors elsewhere than that a skillful South Carolina governor can persuade the legislature to accept much of what he or she wants.

A strong legislature may present a greater challenge than a weaker one. So the extent of legislative professionalization may matter, as does whether or not a legislature is term limited. Professionalization strengthens a legislature, at least in terms of capacity.[39] Still, in examining the survey responses of the seventy-five former governors, I found no statistically significant relationship between the professionalism of legislatures and gubernatorial policy or budget success. Political scientists who have studied the effects of term limits agree that their major impact is to strengthen the power of governors vis-à-vis legislatures.[40] Although this is undoubtedly the case, in the present study I was not able to compare gubernatorial policy and budget success in term-limited and non-term-limited states.[41] More than anything else, a dysfunctional governmental structure may impede a governor's policy leadership. California's ballot initiatives have imposed constraints on governors and legislatures alike, and the state's requirement for a two-thirds vote to pass a budget in the legislature has made it extremely difficult for governors to succeed in fiscal policymaking. Lou Cannon, a chronicler of California politics and politicians, summed up: "The state's last two governors, Democrat Gray Davis and Republican Arnold Schwarzenegger, with much help from clueless legislators, have made a compelling case that California is ungovernable."[42] Under circumstances such as those existing in California, a governor is forced to play a very different game—as Schwarzenegger and predecessor governors did when they led their own initiative campaigns in order to achieve policy objectives that couldn't be won in the legislature.

Playing the Cards They Are Dealt

Governors succeed because they are adaptable. They do not have much control over the political or economic conditions that face them as they take the oath of office. They have to govern, whatever the conditions. But governors operate differently depending on a variety of factors, the two principal ones being partisan control of the legislature and the economic and fiscal position of the state.

The preferred situation for governors is to face legislatures controlled by their own party (also known as unified government). Divided government, in which the other party controls one or both houses of the legislature, is less desirable. Political science research has produced mixed findings on the effects of divided government on gubernatorial agendas. In her statistical analysis of gubernatorial success, Ferguson found that divided government hampered a governor's legislative success. Kousser, in his examination of California, concluded that divided government was primarily responsible for policy gridlock there. By contrast, in her qualitative research on four southern governors, van Assendelft found no strong connection between divided government and gubernatorial success with the legislature.[43]

The conclusion of the present study is that divided government makes a difference to gubernatorial success. Governors do better—but only somewhat better—when their party also has majorities in the two houses of the legislature. A statistically significant relationship exists between the policy and budget success of governors and whether government is unified or divided. In terms of policy, when government was unified, 63 percent of governors achieved nearly all of what they wanted, but when government was divided, only 34 percent achieved the same. In terms of budgets, when government was unified, 69 percent achieved nearly all of what they wanted, but when government was divided, only 37 percent achieved the same.[44] The relationships between policy success and divided government and budget success and divided government are both strong and statistically significant. Governors clearly benefit when their party has the majority in the legislature.

A governor is more apt to run into a buzz saw when the opposition has command. That's what happened to Bob Holden (D-MO). The Republicans had taken over the senate and managed with a minority to exercise control of the house as well. "Republican leaders were in a no-compromise mode," Holden said. "They smelled blood." Compromise was beyond the governor's reach, so Holden "let the chips fall where they may—and they fell." This governor made a full-scale attempt but, by his own admission, he failed to leave behind the desired legacy of policy achievement.

Other governors tend to fare better, even with a strong opposition party in the legislature. Republican Bob Ehrlich had an uphill battle in Maryland from the very start. What made his job winning over the Democratic legislature so tough were differences in party and ideology and clashes over power. Nonetheless, he got his proposal for charter schools through the first year in office, because the legislature's attitude was to give the new governor something he wanted. Thereafter, he had to fight strenuously and had little to show for his efforts. During the first two years as governor of South Carolina, Democrat Hodges had a Democratic senate and a Republican house, each controlled by narrow margins. During the second two years, Republicans had solid majorities in both chambers. The situation was contentious, but Hodges still achieved several things that he wanted. On some educational issues, he even got bipartisan support; on others, he didn't.

Although divided government is an impediment, the fact is that even the governors who are somewhat less successful than others still get much of what they ask for in their budgets and policy proposals. They are able to do so because they make adjustments at the outset to account for the other party's legislative domination. Jeanne Shaheen (D-NH), who faced a Republican legislature, explained on behalf of those who shared such circumstances, "As governors, we're used to being bipartisan."[45] That is, governors know how to work with the other party when they have to. Indicative of their ability to do so is the fact that their relationship with the legislature does not depend on which party has the majority. When asked in the survey about their overall relationships, governors in divided-government situations were just as likely to have had positive relationships as governors in unified-government situations. They just had to make an extra effort to get along, and they did.

Governors make friendly gestures to the other party in a variety of ways. Invariably, in situations of divided government, the executive approaches the legislature differently. A number of survey items addressed how the orientation and behavior of governors vary depending on whether government is unified or divided. Governors recognize at the outset that the legislature will be exercising somewhat more policy leadership and the governor somewhat less. They expect more major initiatives to come to their office from the legislature. Governors meet with the leaders of their own party under all circumstances, but when government is divided they also meet with leaders of the opposition. They also consult with opposition leaders more and pay attention to what they say in formulating their policies and budgets. Moreover, they are more accessible to rank-and-file members of the opposition when government is divided. Finally, they are slightly more inclined to resort to an outside game in campaigning for the agenda items they are advocating.

The other major adjustment that governors make immediately upon entering office stems from the economic and fiscal conditions of their state. There is little doubt that the money available to state government matters. It affects how governors and legislatures negotiate budgets. The tougher the financial conditions, the more likely legislatures will let the governor take the lead. When funds are available, legislatures want to play a larger role in divvying them up.[46] Money also affects the job performance ratings of governors. If an individual is unlucky enough to govern during a time of recession, he or she can expect a decline in popularity. Such a situation will sometimes cost a governor reelection. Allen Olson (R-ND) attributed his defeat at the polls to his state's negative economy.[47] Most governors have the experience of inheriting from their predecessors a deficit—whether modest or more substantial. This has no effect on their ability to succeed, as indicated by survey responses, but it certainly affects the first budget they submit. Because the budget has to be balanced, governors in these circumstances are somewhat limited in the new spending for which they can call. Their budget takes the imbalance into account. Governors adjust as they go along.

More significant than inherited deficits are the overall economic conditions. Relatively few governors during the period of study (1980–2010) had good economies during their entire tenure in office. About half of those responding to the survey had mixed economic conditions and about one out of four had poor economies all or nearly all the time they governed. Good, mixed, or poor, the state of the economy does not affect governors' success rates, according to survey findings. Even so, poor economies undoubtedly affect the shape of the budgets and policy proposals they send to the legislature. When state revenues are on the decline and when governors want to keep taxes as low as possible, they are going to ask legislatures for less that requires funding. In short, the health of their states' economies affects their budget formulations and the measures that become part of their agendas. Educational issues, for example, will remain on most agendas, but costly ones will fall by the wayside.

What governors ask for, thus, depends in part—and probably large part—on what they anticipate they can get. If money is in short supply and increases in taxes are not a preferred option, they will adjust their sights and go after what is attainable.

Having the Right Stuff

Governors succeed because, except for the unexceptional few, they are personally and professionally qualified to lead. Just getting elected to statewide office is an achievement that is indicative of their abilities, and the institutional and political power of the office furnishes them the tools with which to exercise leadership.

It may also help if they have won their offices by large margins, suggesting to the legislature that they bring with them a mandate for their policy agendas. Ferguson, thus, hypothesized that "electoral success strengthens the executive's bargaining position and should increase legislative success." But she found no confirmation for the hypothesis in her data.[48] If not votes, then popularity might account for gubernatorial legislative success. Legislators tend to show greater deference to governors whose performance ratings are high in public opinion polls. They would just as soon not oppose a popular chief executive, but they don't mind distancing themselves from an unpopular one's policy proposals. Ferguson, however, found no support for the hypothesis that gubernatorial job performance ratings correlate with their legislative success.[49] Unpopular governors still appear to manage. For example, Jim Gibbons (R-NV) not only had a Democratic legislature (and one that overrode many of his vetoes) with which to deal, but he also was unpopular with the people of Nevada. Nonetheless, he set the agenda and exercised control. "Everybody marched to his tune," is the way one close observer put it.[50] A lack of popularity may not disqualify a governor from either leadership or success.

The personal skills of governors no doubt are important for each of them. Yet there doesn't appear to be any set of characteristics that are requisite for every one of them. Out of a huge bundle of personality characteristics, which ones are essential? It may be that no single characteristic is essential. Different governors succeed with different combinations. It would appear, however, that a governor would be well served if he or she could choose a few of the characteristics that many of them share naturally. Prominent among them is self-confidence. By the time individuals are elected governor, they have a number of accomplishments under their belts. This feeds their confidence as they undertake the job of chief executive. With this confidence comes a sense of control and a sense of command but, in most instances, not arrogance. Nearly all governors seem to qualify on the self-confidence requirement. In addition, governors have a preference for consensus building while also being willing to engage in conflict when necessary. If they have a choice, they ought to be firm, but they ought to be willing to compromise, as well.

Most gubernatorial personalities seem to work for them. This is not to say that governors do not have personal failings, or failings that get them into trouble. These failings affect their careers, how they do their jobs, and to some extent the success of their agendas. But even governors who have wound up discredited for one reason or another—such as Edwin Edwards (D-LA) and John Rowland (R-CT), for example—compiled records of legislative accomplishment.

The criticism of Schwarzenegger is revealing in this regard. The California legislature, it is believed, quickly lost respect for him, because he was perceived as rudderless, weaving from one position to another, wavering, and willing to back down. Neither legislative Republicans nor legislative Democrats welcomed him as one of their own. One observer saw his fundamental flaw as doing little more than "acting as a lagging indicator of public opinion."[51] Schwarzenegger could be infuriating and may deserve some blame for having squandered the opportunity to reverse California's decline, as critics charged. But the structure and rules of state government were enormous hurdles for any governor to get over and the Democratic legislature was a huge hurdle for any Republican governor to get over. In any case, when Schwarzenegger left office in early 2011, he was not lacking in policy accomplishments.

Governors do not have to be one of the boys or girls, cozying up to and comfortable with legislators. It probably helps, but they can do nicely without this quality. Thornburgh kept his distance but had a commanding presence in the Pennsylvania legislature—establishing mutual respect rather than warmth. Parris Glendening (D-MD) generally was not well liked by legislators. Yet, he was effective. Hugh Carey (D-NY) had even less going for him in personality terms. Few New York legislators had much affection for him and a number resented his disdain. Yet, he accomplished a lot of what he set out to do, including helping to rescue New York City from a fiscal crisis of unparalleled proportions.[52] Romney's corporate executive mentality and inability to relate to the legislature did not prevent him from achieving significant accomplishments. Brian Schweitzer's (D-MT) biographer wrote that, if he were writing a report card for Schweitzer, "next to the line *Plays well with others*, I would have to scribble 'needs improvement.'" Yet, Schweitzer's biographer "would give him mostly A's and a few B's" for his achievements.[53] Quite like the men mentioned so far, some women do not seem to fit comfortably into the dominant environment of the legislature. Vermont's Kunin was not on the same wavelength as a number of the veteran male members, but she had an estimable record of accomplishment. In New Jersey, Whitman's fellow Republicans complained about her aloofness, but she achieved her major objective, a large reduction in taxes.

One of the characteristics that would seem to shape gubernatorial behavior in office is the experience they bring with them. Earlier we suggested that experience as a prosecutor, for instance, isn't the optimal preparation for a governor. Much of one's learning as a prosecutor has to be overcome, if a governor is to establish good relationships with the legislature and succeed legislatively. Bill Weld (R-MA) and Thornburgh are among a number who managed to set aside prosecutorial orientations. Their agendas did well. Chris Christie in New Jersey, as of the end of 2010, continued his prosecutorial ways. He also was doing well and had the Democratic legislature marching to his Republican drumbeat. Experience as a business leader doesn't necessarily help a governor in legislative relationships. Nonetheless, Bush in Texas and Michael Leavitt (R-UT) managed to achieve success in their legislative agendas.

Generally speaking, however, legislative experience trumps any other type of experience, although the relationships between legislative experience and policy and budget success are not statistically significant. Of course, like anything else, having legislative experience is no guarantee of success. Men and women serve in the senate or house for years without the legislature rubbing off on them. But most governors who have served in the legislature benefitted substantially. They acquired knowledge of the issues and of how state government works. Governors who are former legislators already know the members of the legislature—who they are, where they are from, and what they want. They have already made friends, a valuable resource upon which to draw when they become chief executives. Friendships are built on trust, and trust facilitates the negotiations in which governors and legislators engage.

Probably most important are the orientations toward the legislature that governors take into office. Having been one of them, these governors can empathize with legislators, even as they pursue very different roles in the governmental system. They may be more or less assertive, but they understand that it is usually up to them, and not the legislature, to provide leadership. Yet, they also appreciate that the legislature has a role to play— leading on occasion, but more often consulting, reviewing, modifying, and even rejecting. Having been legislators, governors have developed respect for legislators, legislative leadership, and the legislature as an institution. One reason a governor like Riley of South Carolina did so well in a "weak-governor" state was that he respected legislators and legislators respected him.[54] By contrast, Ventura showed no respect whatsoever for the Minnesota legislature and received none in return. Riley's agenda benefitted; Ventura's suffered.

If governors don't quite have the requisite qualifications for success, their staffs may make up for some of their deficiencies. A chief of staff, chief counsel, or legislative liaison director, however, is no substitute for a governor, but rather an extension of the governor. Governors who lack experience in the legislature are well advised to appoint staff who have served in the legislature or worked for the legislature. Even legislatively experienced governors will not go wrong appointing legislatively experienced staff. Most governors staff their legislative-liaison operations effectively. And it makes a difference. Thornburgh gave credit to his staff operation for his success. "Because of the methodology we used and the quality of people, we did pretty well," he said. Of course, Thornburgh himself had a lot to do with it.

Asking for What They Have a Chance of Getting

Governors succeed because the large majority of them are pragmatists. For the most part, they pursue what they think is achievable. They want to get their policy initiatives and their budgets enacted by the legislature. They are far more interested in getting things done than in tilting at windmills. Their policy agendas and their budgets are largely designed with political and economic realities in mind. This does not mean that governors never reach. They do, and some clearly reach farther than others. It does mean that putting together a policy agenda and a budget, to a large extent, is an exercise in political strategizing and not in wishful thinking.

As mentioned earlier, governors take into account two principal considerations in figuring out what to ask the legislature for. The first is whether their party has control of the legislature or whether government is divided, with the party opposed to them holding at least one chamber. If the governor's party is in control, it gives him or her some leeway for an agenda. When government is divided, governors make adjustments. They are likely to tailor their agenda more to the liking of the opposition. Even so, they do not do as well as when their party exercises control. The second principal consideration relates to the state of the economy and projected revenues. Budgets and policy agendas vary depending on whether times are good or bad. In the latter case, governors who are loathe to raise taxes are constrained in the items they put on their agendas. Most simply curtail their plans for spending. Thus, governors do not fail to get a good deal of what they want because of political or economic conditions; they simply declare realistically that they want less—and that is what they get.

One principle that governors follow in shaping their agendas is that of focus or concentration. Veteran governors and the National Governors Association advise newcomers to limit the number of items on their agendas. They have good reasons for doing so. An analysis of Clinton's educational reform proposals when he was governor of Arkansas "shows that a governor who focuses his powers on a particular policy proposal is difficult to stop." In part this is because a governor can bring tremendous resources to bear at any time on one or two policy battles, enhancing his or her ability to overwhelm a legislature.[55] Most governors, as has been reported here, limit the number of items on their policy agendas. According to a statistical analysis of the survey responses of former governors, whether governors propose somewhat fewer or somewhat more policy items doesn't affect their legislative success. Even those with larger agendas presumably focus on some items more than others, and those are the ones that count most to them.

A gubernatorial agenda isn't the agenda until governors have an idea it will fly. The Thornburgh administration did not announce an initiative until they were pretty sure they had a winner. The process of formulating both the policy agenda and the budget is a critical one for governors and their staffs. During this process, governors consult with legislative leaders and key legislators, especially on policy initiatives. As a result of such consultation, governors are made aware roughly of what they can and cannot get. Most governors tailor their requests to the preferences and advice they receive from these legislative consultations. Beyond such consultation is that which is done by gubernatorial staffs, which review proposals in terms of their prospects in the legislature. In addition, governors call upon blue-ribbon commissions and panels of outside experts to help construct proposals and at the same time sell them to the media, the public, and the legislature. Their formulations, therefore, are deliberative in both a policy and a political sense.

Still, governors are willing to take risks—on some issues and on some occasions. Weld might have been defeated on his various proposals for tax cuts in Massachusetts. Massachusetts Democrats were not known for cutting taxes. But the governor, thanks to his good relationships with Democratic leaders (who were themselves fiscally conservative), recorded twenty-one tax cuts without any tax increases. "This was quite a stretch for the Democratic leaders," Weld recalled, "but they knew that this was my number-one issue." He claimed credit for having "undemonized tax cuts in the eyes of Democrats." Other governors also dove in but were less successful swimming upstream. Ohio's Taft advocated for legislation requiring the safe storage of guns in homes. It was what Taft described as "a heavy lift." He didn't expect it to pass; indeed, it never got to the floor, because gun groups were too effective. Thornburgh went after some long shots. He tried to get the system of judicial selection changed, which would have required a constitutional amendment. He didn't have much hope for his proposal, and he soon abandoned it. He also attempted to get rid of the state liquor control and turn over Pennsylvania's liquor business to private enterprise, and here, too, he failed.

Most governors on most issues, however, play it relatively safe. They calculate their chances and pursue the attainable. But they try to reduce the uncertainty in the lawmaking process, while enhancing their chances of walking away with something they can claim as an accomplishment. One way of doing this is by choosing policy proposals on which there is general, if not specific, agreement. Gross described the situation:

> The legislation supported by a governor may often pass a legislature merely because a sufficient number of legislators are in fundamental agreement with the policy implications of the legislation. It seems that we often have a tendency to assume that it was the governor who used his or her influence to get the legislation passed. At the same time, such legislation may never have reached the stage of legislative action if the governor had not acted to get the item on the public agenda.[56]

Mutual agreement can happen naturally. Governors may choose to confront issues that have been around and have been problematic but that the legislature also wants to resolve. The school finance formula had been an issue in New Jersey since the 1970s when the state supreme court entered the educational thicket. Governors and legislatures since then tried to devise a formula that would satisfy political and educational needs and also satisfy the courts. The Corzine administration developed a school-aid formula that satisfied majorities of legislators in both parties and both chambers and also withstood challenge in the courts. Corzine succeeded legislatively, primarily because the legislature, for its own reasons, was on his side anyway.

"When we're right, they'll vote with us," is the way Angus King characterized his relationship with the Maine legislature. The objective of a governor, therefore, is either to persuade the legislature of the rightness of his or her agenda or, better still, to put forward an agenda that the legislature believes is right from the outset. If the two branches see eye to eye, both will have their way.

It helps if the governor's policy agenda has popular appeal. That is one reason why the gubernatorial focus on education and economic development policy makes sense. These policy domains have not been perceived as partisan and, therefore, differences between governors and legislatures have a good chance of being worked out. If agreement exists on general goals and if both sides are willing to compromise on more specific ones, a settlement can be reached on policy. As a policy domain, education sounds good to the public and to business. It is not only a priority in and of itself, but it is also a major engine of economic development. It helps too if a measure appears to be relatively noncontroversial. Edgar's major accomplishment in Illinois, as he saw it, was on an issue that was not partisan at all. It wasn't headlined in the press. But as governor, Edgar managed to get the law on adoptions changed, so that during the course of his two administrations Illinois went from the fiftieth to the first state in the number of adoptions.

Because governors are so intent on success, they keep in mind just how their record looks. That is why Romer worked at being less confrontational with the Republican legislature in Colorado, kept a clear mental picture of what he could and could not do, learned to be general rather than specific about legislative proposals, and thereby escaped looking like a loser when specific bills or issues failed in the legislature.[57] Edgar also was cognizant that a score card was being kept on his policy leadership performance. The scorecards with winners and losers were printed at the end of the Illinois legislature's session. "You always knew that was going to happen," said Edgar, "and so you always had to try to maneuver so you looked like a winner."

Laying the Groundwork

"Don't underestimate relationships in any of this," said Andrew Cuomo (D-NY) just before he was elected governor.[58] Governors believe that relationships count, and they devote a lot of time and attention to cultivating relationships with legislative leaders and rank-and-file members. Most of them are adept in relating to legislators. They keep their doors open, provide ready access, and demonstrate, as Cuomo put it, that "a governor can be a very good friend to people."[59] Gubernatorial respect for legislative leaders—of one's own party and of the other party, if the opposition controls the legislature—goes a long way. Perhaps as important to relationships are the ability and willingness of governors to consult with legislative leaders. Most of them consult on a regular basis and, at least to some extent, their consultative approach helps them to achieve their policy agendas.

Good relationships with leaders and rank and file pay off. The payoff may be marginal, but margins make a difference in a process in which they can be decisive. If they get along with legislative leaders, governors are likely to get the benefit of the doubt from them. "They cut me a lot of slack," explained Weld, who got along famously with senate president Bulger in Massachusetts. Joe Frank Harris (D-GA) benefitted similarly because of his close working relationship with speaker Tom Murphy. King attributed his success with the legislature in Maine to the strategy of cultivation he pursued. A good relationship is no guarantee, but it does make a difference, as Hayden of Kansas attested: "My relationship with the legislature helped all along, but it was no slam dunk." Schweitzer, on the other hand, found it difficult to relate to a Republican legislature in Montana, but he still accomplished a number of his priority items. He might have accomplished more, however, if his personality hadn't kept tensions higher than they might have otherwise been.[60]

Examination of the responses of former governors to the survey demonstrates a connection (but not a statistically significant one) between good relationships on the one hand and gubernatorial legislative success on the other. Governors were more successful where relationships were excellent or good than where they were only fair or poor: 51 percent of the former and only 18 percent of the latter had nearly all or most of their policy priorities enacted, 58 percent of the former and 29 percent of the latter got nearly all of the budget items they requested, and 69 percent of the former and 53 percent of the latter had no major legislative policy initiatives passed that they opposed.

Not all governors are able to manage as well with legislators, because of their own personalities or because of those of the legislative leaders who bar their way. With notable exceptions—like Eliot Spitzer (D-NY), Ventura in Minnesota, and William Donald Schaefer (D-MD)—they make a determined effort. Spitzer didn't last long enough for us to find out whether he could tame the beast. Ventura failed. Schaefer did get much of what he wanted from the legislature, but had he approached the legislature differently, he might have accomplished more, and with less turbulence. Chris Christie, who took office in 2010, may be the leading exception to the rule that relationships matter. A former prosecutor and a Republican governor facing a Democratic legislature, he has shown little respect for the legislature as an institution or for legislators as elected public officials. His style has been confrontational, not collegial. Nonetheless, during his first two years, Christie was extremely successful in getting his budget and policy proposals through the legislature.

It is helpful if governors consult with, do favors for, show respect toward, and engage in the give and take of negotiations with legislators. But they are also helped by showing determination and strength (while not being overly confrontational). In the survey, former governors were asked where they stood on who—the governor or the legislature—should exercise policy leadership. Respondents were asked to locate themselves on a seven-point continuum from total legislative policy leadership (1) to total gubernatorial policy leadership (7). Responses ranged from equal policy leadership (4) to total gubernatorial policy leadership (7). Governors who assumed greater responsibility for policy leadership were more successful than those who assumed lesser responsibility. Some 60 percent of the former and 24 percent of the latter had nearly all or most of their policy priorities enacted, 58 percent of the former and 36 percent of the latter got nearly all of the budget items they requested, and 70 percent of the former and 42 percent of the latter had no major legislative policy initiatives passed that they opposed.

Waging Budget and Policy Campaigns

In her memoirs, Kunin looked back on her six-year legislative record as governor of Vermont. She got her proposals enacted nearly all of the time and achieved a great deal of what she promised. But, she wrote, it required "constant attention and enormous effort expended working with individual legislators, committees, and outside constituencies."[61] Her involvement inside and outside the legislature was typical. Still, the greater the involvement of governors themselves, and not only their staffs, the more effective their policy leadership is likely to be.

Depending on the issue at hand, governors tend to pursue both outside and inside strategies to get the votes they need in the legislature. A few, like Tennessee's McWherter, relied almost totally on working face-to-face with legislators. But most knew when and how to generate support around the state to build support in the statehouse. What works best in this respect is for governors to appeal to the public, not to overcome a legislature that is clearly opposed, but rather to provide the legislature with a little additional pressure or the encouragement that accompanies public approval of a measure. Some governors find it difficult to make connections with the public in issue campaigns or otherwise. Most governors, however, are effective and some are extraordinarily so. Schwarzenegger, for instance, had "a seemingly supernatural ability to get more attention than any other political figure—as a result of his fame and his hyper-aggressive campaigns for even little-known or unexciting issues."[62]

Outside skills cannot substitute for inside ones, however. Governors have to be able to make points in the capitol clinches, as well as outside the ring. Michigan's Engler could negotiate anything, especially the budget. Every year he would have insiders shaking their heads in wonder. Inevitably he was able to craft deals that would pay for public schools and cut taxes, while avoiding a deficit. The prevailing view in Lansing was that Engler had "an infinite number of rabbits to pull out of his hat."[63] Unlike policy proposals, the state budget has to be resolved—usually by a specified date, although occasionally late. "In the end we all knew we had to get a budget passed," observed Hayden of Kansas. "We bickered and we horse-traded, but we got it done."

The success of governors depends, at least to some extent, on their abilities to persuade legislators. The merits of the case, as the governor presents them; the benefits the governor can bestow; and the punishments by veto, line-item veto, or other measures the governor can inflict, all weigh in. Arm-twisting, cajoling, asking for legislators' votes, and keeping at it are all relevant to effective policy leadership. Kunin needed a vote from a member of the Vermont House. It required a low-number license plate and schmoozing with someone with whom she did not have much in common.[64] So be it. Engler could twist arms with the best of them. He could be brutal, but more often he was charming and reasonable. "What's your issue? Let me explain to you why this is such important policy." He was very good at getting what he wanted.[65] Florida's Graham was known for his persistence. He kept at it until he persuaded enough legislators of his position or wore them down so that they gave in.[66]

However persuasive they might be, governors still have to compromise—at the end of the process as well as along the way. The large majority of contemporary governors would agree with Thornburgh that the "perfect shouldn't be the enemy of the good." Governors may pursue the ideal in their minds, but they settle for less in the trenches. Take Bellmon, for example. The day following his inauguration as governor of Oklahoma, he proposed the state's record tax increase in order to maintain state services and not jeopardize the economic recovery that was under way. It was obvious to the governor that the legislature would resist, and it did. His first package of tax proposals was obviously going nowhere, so Bellmon turned around and put together a second package that had a better chance of being adopted.[67] Sometimes it takes all the skill the governor has to get the necessary votes. Bob Wise (D-WV) passed his college scholarship initiative by one vote. To do that, he had to take out all the stops—mobilize public support, meet the concerns of legislators, and make a few deals.

If governors are selective in what they propose, exploit the advantages they possess, take on the responsibilities of leadership, engage with the legislature, are willing to consult and compromise, and are willing to settle for less than they want, the odds are that their budget and policy initiatives will fare well.

Notes

1. Kousser and Phillips report 47 percent of the governors' proposals as having succeeded and 12 percent as having resulted in a compromise. Thad Kousser and Justin A. Phillips, *The Hidden Power of American Governors* (Cambridge: Cambridge University Press, in process).
2. Laura A. van Assendelft, *Governors, Agenda Setting, and Divided Government* (Lanham, MD: University Press of America, 1997), 108.
3. John Ashcroft, "Leadership: The Art of Redefining the Possible" in *Governors on Governing*, ed. Robert D. Behn (Lanham, MD: University Press of America, 1991), 76–77.
4. S. V. Date, *Quiet Passion: A Biography of Senator Bob Graham* (New York: Penguin, 2004), 129.
5. Henry Bellmon, *The Life and Times of Henry Bellmon* (Tulsa, OK: Council Oak Books, 1992), 373.
6. Dan Durning, "Education Reform in Arkansas: The Governor's Role in Policymaking," in *Gubernatorial Leadership and State Policy*, ed. Eric B. Herzik and Brent W. Brown (Westport, CT: Greenwood Press, 1991), 135.
7. Bill Richardson, *Between Worlds: The Making of an American Life* (New York: Penguin Group, 2005), 307, 341.
8. Dick Thornburgh, *Where the Evidence Leads* (Pittsburgh: University of Pittsburgh Press, 2003), 146.
9. S. V. Date, *Jeb: America's Next Bush* (New York: Penguin, 2007), 126.
10. James E. McGreevey, *The Confession* (New York: HarperCollins, 2006), 53.
11. Thornburgh, *Where the Evidence Leads*, 148–49.
12. Colleen M. Grogan and Vernon K. Smith, "From Charity Care to Medicaid," in *A Legacy of Innovation: Governors and Public Policy*, ed. Ethan G. Sribnick (Philadelphia: University of Pennsylvania Press, 2008), 219–21.
13. J. H. Hatfield, *Fortunate Son: George W. Bush and the Making of an American President* (New York: Soft Skull Press, 2001), 158–61, 182, 273–74.
14. Date, *Quiet Passion*, 133.
15. Thornburgh, *Where the Evidence Leads*, 159, 163, 167.

16. Wayne Grimsley, *James B. Hunt: A North Carolina Progressive* (Jefferson, NC: McFarland, 2003), 133, 135.

17. Robert P. Casey, *Fighting for Life* (Dallas: Word Publishing, 1996), 143.

18. Discussion with Bill Castner, former counsel, and Edward McBride, former chief of staff to Governor Jon Corzine, November 11, 2009.

19. Scott Conroy and Shushannah Walshe, *Sarah From Alaska* (New York: Public Affairs, 2009), 73–77.

20. Dan Creed, *Governor Ventura: "The Body" Exposed* (Madison, WI: Hunter Halverson Press, 2003), 128.

21. Benjamin J. Cayetano, *Ben: A Memoir From Street Kid to Governor* (Honolulu: Watermark Publishing, 2009), 474, 476.

22. Joe Mathews and Mark Paul, *California Crackup* (Berkeley: University of California Press, 2010), 234–35, 269, 274–75, 309–10, 392–94.

23. Troy Senik, "Who Killed California?" *National Affairs* (Fall 2009): 64–65; Jennifer Steinhauer, "It's Lonely Outside," *New York Times*, July 11, 2010.

24. National Governors Association, *Transition and the New Governor: A Planning Guide* (Washington, D.C.: National Governors Association, 1998), 76.

25. Thornburgh, *Where the Evidence Leads*, 134.

26. Richard W. Riley, "Overcoming Restrictions on Gubernatorial Authority: The Unique Problem of Some Governors" in Behn, *Governors on Governing*, 34.

27. John H. Sununu, "Reality and Perception in Gubernatorial Management" in Behn, *Governors on Governing*, 173.

28. The two achievements are part of the same dynamic or part of the same recall by governors.

29. Art Weissman, *Christine Todd Whitman* (New York: Carol Publishing Group, 1996), 127–29, 238, 257.

30. Thornburgh, *Where the Evidence Leads*, 125–26.

31. Lou Cannon, *Governor Reagan* (New York: Public Affairs, 2003), 364.

32. Kousser and Phillips, *The Hidden Power of American Governors*.

33. Margaret Robertson Ferguson, "Chief Executive Success in the Legislative Arena," *State Politics and Policy Quarterly* 3 (Summer 2003): 159.

34. Kousser and Phillips disagree. They believe that a governor's formal power is minimal and that governors are disadvantaged in contesting policymaking power with the legislature. Kousser and Phillips, *The Hidden Power of American Governors*.

35. It may be argued that in some states governors do not enjoy the "unity" claimed for them here. Lieutenant governors, attorneys general, chief state school officers, and even utility commissioners are elected statewide. The point here is not that other political leaders have no authority independent of the governor, but rather that oneness is an advantage in the governor's leadership of the legislature.

36. Bellmon, *The Life and Times of Henry Bellmon*, 372.

37. Tom Loftus, *The Art of Legislative Politics* (Washington, D.C.: CQ Press, 1994), 67.

38. Minnesota Civic Caucus discussion, September 2, 2010.

39. Ferguson found that legislative professionalism is positively related to gubernatorial legislative success. Ferguson, "Chief Executive Success in the Legislative Arena," 171.

40. See Karl T. Kurtz, Bruce Cain, and Richard G. Niemi, eds, *Institutional Change in American Politics: The Case of Term Limits* (Ann Arbor: University of Michigan Press, 2007).

41. Too few governors have been in office since term limits went into effect in the fifteen states where they are in place.

42. *State Net Capitol Journal*, December 21, 2009.

43. Ferguson, "Chief Executive Success in the Legislative Arena," 171; Thad Kousser, "Does Partisan Polarization Lead to Policy Gridlock in California?" *California Journal of Politics & Policy* 2 (2010): 10; van Assendelft, *Governors, Agenda Setting, and Divided Government*, 58–59, 207–21.

44. Responses to the survey item on policy success were as follows: "nearly all of what I asked for," "most of what I asked for," and "some of what I asked for." No one responded "only a little of what I asked for." Responses to the survey item on budget success were as follows: "nearly all of what I asked for," "most of what I asked for," and "only a little of what I asked for."

45. Brian Friel, "The (Red) Governators," *National Journal*, June 27, 2009, 26.

46. Discussion with Rich Bagger, chief of staff to Governor Chris Christie, and Edward McBride, former chief of staff to Governor Jon Corzine, New Jersey, at Eagleton Institute of Politics, Rutgers University, November 3, 2010.

47. Response on survey.

48. Ferguson, "Chief Executive Success in the Legislative Arena," 169.

49. Ibid., 160, 169–70.

50. Discussion at National Association of State Lobbyists, 2010 meeting, Washington, D.C.

51. Quoted in Joe Mathews, *The People's Machine: Arnold Schwarzenegger and the Rise of Blockbuster Democracy* (New York: Public Affairs, 2006), 211–12.

52. Daniel C. Kramer, *The Days of Wine and Roses Are Over: Governor Hugh Carey and New York State* (Lanham, MD: University Press of America, 1997), 149.

53. Greg Lemon, *Blue Man in a Red State: Montana's Governor Brian Schweitzer and the New Western Populism* (Helena, MT: TwoDot, 2008), 146.

54. Benjamin Prince Bagwell, *Riley: A Story of Hope* (Pickens, SC: Pickens County Publishing, 1986), 117.

55. Dan Durning, "Education Reform in Arkansas: The Governor's Role in Policymaking," in Herzik and Brown, *Gubernatorial Leadership and State Policy*, 37.

56. Donald A. Gross, "The Policy Role of Governors," in Herzik and Brown, *Gubernatorial Leadership and State Policy*, 19.

57. The characterization is by a top aide to Romer, Wade Buchanan, in Thomas E. Cronin and Robert D. Loevy, *Colorado Politics and Government* (Lincoln: University of Nebraska Press, 1993), 213.

58. Quoted in *New York Times*, October 25, 2010.

59. Ibid.

60. Lemon, *Blue Man in a Red State*, 143.

61. Madeleine M. Kunin, *Living a Political Life* (New York: Vintage, 1994), 374.

62. Mathews, *The People's Machine*, 306.

63. Gleaves Whitney, *John Engler: The Man, the Leader & the Legacy* (Chelsea, MI: Sleeping Bear Press, 2002), 369.

64. Ralph Wright, *Inside the Statehouse* (Washington, D.C.: CQ Press, 2005), 181–82.

65. Whitney, *John Engler*, 204, 396.

66. Date, *Quiet Passion*, 112.

67. Bellmon, *The Life and Times of Henry Bellmon*, 338–39.

8

Legacy and Beyond

THERE COMES A TIME in the life of every governor when he or she leaves office. Most leave voluntarily, some not so voluntarily. Either way, their paths continue in one venue or another. A number remain in their states, pursuing careers or enjoying retirement. A few wander off and then return home, like Mike Hayden (R-KS) after a brief tour as assistant secretary of the Interior Department in Washington, D.C. Since coming back to Kansas, he has been in the cabinets of three governors and at one point headed the agency established under his policy leadership as governor from 1987 to 1991. As might be expected, a good number of ex-governors wind up in the nation's capital—as members of the U.S. Senate, in the president's cabinet or subcabinet, heading national organizations and associations, practicing law, and lobbying.

How They See Their Legacies

Whatever they choose to do next, ex-governors want to leave something behind for their states. We typically think of what they leave behind, what they pass on, what they bequeath to future generations as their "legacy." Governors start thinking about their legacies while they are in office. In his memoirs Cecil Andrus (D-ID) offered advice that "building for the next generation and leaving a legacy are essential to public service."[1] From the very beginning of his administration, Jim Edgar (R-IL) gave thought to the legacy he would leave behind. How he would be remembered was both a nagging concern and an incentive to do a good job. By the time his administration was in its final year, Edgar's staff began to document his record over eight years as governor.[2] The case for his legacy would start there.

The last item on the survey asked, "Looking back on your service as governor, what would you consider to be your principal legacies to the state and its people?" Not every respondent replied to this open-ended question, but most did. William Janklow (R-SD), for one, refused to advance a claim, writing that "history will determine." Charles Thone (R-NE) indicated that he would have been able to lay claim in a few policy areas, if only he had won a second term. But he was defeated and any legacy was derailed. Others were more than willing to stake out their legacies.

Arch Moore (R-WV) implied that his legacy was his entire career in politics—in the state legislature two years, in the U.S. House twelve years, and as governor eight years. Then, unfortunately, he lost a bid for a U.S. Senate seat, because he was a Republican in a Democratic state. He took pride not only in his own career, but also in that of his daughter, who was serving her eleventh year in the U.S. House. His legacy was public service.

Some of the former governors listed several legacy items, others only one or two. Some stated their legacies in general terms, others in specific terms, and some in both. Jim Blanchard (D-MI) thought of his legacy as, on the one hand, establishing the office of job training and, on the other, creating a positive attitude in Michigan toward the future. Most governors wanted to be remembered for what they accomplished in various policy domains. Education, in the eyes of many, was the principal area of endeavor and the principal area of accomplishment. "I will be remembered as the education governor," wrote Jim Hunt (D-NC), citing the Smart Start program he initiated and the improvements in staffing and teaching. Mark White (D-TX) recalled one legacy, HB72, which improved the educational system, whereas Jim Hodges (D-SC) also recalled a single legacy, First Steps, which constituted a new approach to early health and education readiness for children. The Promise Scholarship program was what Bob Wise (D-WV) singled out. John Engler (R-MI) laid claim to property tax reform and the funding of education, his most significant achievement, but he also mentioned student choice and charter school programs that injected competition into the system.

A number of governors take credit for the economic and fiscal gains their states made. Oklahoma moved from forty-fifth to thirty-eighth place in per-capita income during the administration of Frank Keating (R-OK), who believed that he had a lot to do with that advance. Inheriting a bad fiscal situation and turning it around is what several governors felt distinguished their terms. Arne Carlson (R-MN) pointed to his tough fiscal decisions, including one subsidizing Northwest Airlines to keep the company from leaving the state. For Judy Martz (R-MT), it was taking the largest budget deficit in her state's history and turning it into the largest surplus, while getting rid of a structural budgetary imbalance along the way. George Ariyoshi (D-HI) and Victor Atiyeh (R-OR) made similar claims. Several governors, including Ben Cayetano (D-HI) and Bill Weld (R-MA), wanted to be remembered for reducing taxes. John Carlin (D-KS) took pride in his willingness to raise taxes.

For Bob Ehrlich (R-MD), it was his "fiscal stewardship" of the state. On his part, Jim Florio (D-NJ) wanted to be remembered for his "adult supervision" of the budget process. The appointment of more women, African Americans, and Hispanics to leadership positions in state government comprised Bob Holden's (D-MO) claim. Better managed government was what Dick Thornburgh (R-PA), Gary Locke (D-WA), and George Voinovich (R-OH) had in mind as their legacies. According to Thornburgh, keeping taxes down and cutting public jobs, along with good management, improved the economic climate. Locke pointed to his initiative whereby state agencies were given incentives to save state funds, which, along with his administrative leadership, enabled him to "transform state government."

Although only a few governors advocated for hot-button issues, these few wanted to be remembered for their legacy accomplishments on such matters. George Allen (R-VA) took credit for requiring parents to be involved in the decisions of unwed minor daughters who were contemplating abortion. Doug Wilder (D-VA) took credit for gun-control measures, and Howard Dean (D-VT) took pride in civil unions legislation that passed on his watch.

"How much credit do you get for reaching zero, when you start out far behind?" West Virginia's Wise wondered. His real legacy was in taking on the tough issues, such as medical malpractice, the workers' compensation fund, and how much weight coal trucks could carry. "We didn't blink," he recalled. "We took on tough issues that had been there for years, but came due on my watch." Along similar lines, Mike Sullivan (D-WY) saw his legacy defensively, as that of keeping the Republican legislature from dismantling government, just as Holden saw his as protecting the funding for education and health care, which was in peril.

Integrity was an important bequest for several governors. Sullivan was one of them. He wanted to be remembered as someone who "provided an example—based on values, love of the state, and integrity—that would encourage others to participate in public service." George Nigh (D-OK) admitted to bragging but took great pride in stating that his principal legacy was that "you can and should serve with integrity." For Bruce Sundlun (D-RI), his legacy was two terms of honest government and no corruption.

Over the course of his eight years as governor, Tom Kean (R-NJ) expressed great pride in the fact that he helped to get New Jerseyans to feel better about their state. "New Jersey and you, perfect together" was a major theme of his administration. Angus King (I-ME) considered his most important accomplishment to be a change in attitude by the people of a depressed state. "Maine is on the move" were the words he used in his first inaugural. King's plan was to build optimism, which translated into confidence and encouraged economic activity, leading to further confidence. He felt that he did what he had set out to do.

How They Are Remembered

In looking back, these men and women remember what they accomplished while in office. To them, this is their legacy. They would like to be remembered by others for the same accomplishments. The question here is, how are they remembered and by whom? Does the existence of a legacy depend on the accomplishment's taking root in the public mind? Bruce King (D-NM) wanted to be regarded as being an excellent public official who had an impressive record in New Mexico and who had made a mark on history. But another governor at the time, Ned McWherter (D-TN), had a different take on how King would be viewed when he was no longer in office. "How many people come to his funeral will depend a great deal more on the weather that day than what he's done."[3] There is much truth in McWherter's comment, for politics has been referred to by insiders as "a profession in which you are forgotten soon after leaving the stage."[4]

Governors may not be remembered quite as they believe they ought to be. Edgar said that "people think that I was a good governor" and Parris Glendening (D-MD) said that people regard him as an "effective" governor. The likelihood, however, is that neither one is remembered by many people at all, and surely not for what they consider to be their policy accomplishments.[5] A political newsletter in New Jersey reported on a legacy of Jim Florio; his name was the answer to 12 across in the *New York Times Magazine* crossword puzzle.[6]

Governors certainly are not likely to be remembered by the public in states other than their own. Even during their administrations they are usually not known beyond their state's borders. Only a few governors are exceptions. Those who already had widespread recognition for achievements in other fields, such as Arnold Schwarzenegger (R-CA), will continue to be recognized, but not necessarily for the good job they did as governor. Those who achieved greater recognition after they left office, such as Ronald Reagan (R-CA), Bill Clinton (D-AR), and George W. Bush (R-TX), all of whom became president, will surely be more familiar to the American public after having lived in the White House. Even former governors like Mike Dukakis (D-MA), who lost his race for the presidency, are apt to be better known because of their national campaigns for the highest office. In these cases, they are remembered not for their gubernatorial efforts or accomplishments, but for being prominent on the national stage.

Several governors left behind a legacy of sorts, but not the one that they would have liked to have left. Rod Blagojevich (D-IL), Eliot Spitzer (D-NY), and John Rowland (R-CT) exited office under a cloud, and many citizens of their states, and even beyond, can be expected to have been left with an unfavorable view of them.

For a governor to have made a dent on public opinion outside of his or her state is a tall order. But shouldn't we expect, and don't governors themselves expect, to be remembered at home, at least when the public is asked about their overall impression of individuals who have served as governor over past years? This was a question on the Monmouth University/Gannett New Jersey Poll in January 2010 (released on February 11, 2010). The names of nine living former governors of New Jersey were read over the telephone to individuals who could then choose "favorable," "unfavorable," or "no opinion/not heard enough" as their responses. People appeared to have either a positive or a negative opinion of the most recent governors, excluding Chris Christie, the governor in office at the time of the poll. The "no opinion/not heard enough" responses were relatively low—14 percent for Jon Corzine, 24 percent for Jim McGreevey, and 27 percent for Christine Whitman. When one goes further back in time, say fifteen years, the "no opinion/not heard enough" responses increased: for Jim Florio (1990–1994), 45 percent; for Tom Kean (1982–1990), 44 percent; and for Brendan Byrne (1974–1982), 63 percent.

A thirty-four-year-old respondent would have been eighteen when Florio left office, fourteen when Kean left, and six when Byrne departed. An eighteen-year-old would have been two at Florio's departure, and not yet born when Kean and Byrne governed. The age 18–34 "no opinion/not heard enough" responses were 72 percent for Florio, 75 percent for Kean, and 81 percent for Byrne. A governor's afterlife, even in the most general sense, does not last beyond people who have lived during the governor's administration. Even with Kean—who was most popular when compared to other incumbents, and who co-chaired the U.S. 9/11 Commission and was a presidential appointee to other bodies—three out of four New Jerseyans under thirty-five years of age couldn't make a judgment.

If governors are remembered at all, it is rare to have them remembered just the way in which they would like to be remembered. Even if people recalled the name of the governor and even if a positive evaluation were triggered, with the rarest of exceptions they would not be able to associate the governor with any of the legacies to which he or she laid claim. For instance, Thornburgh's name is linked to the Three Mile Island nuclear crisis more than anything else. As long as that near-disaster is part of the public memory, Thornburgh, the governor who responded so effectively, will also be recalled. But he will not be recalled for his economic and fiscal accomplishments, for which he believes he merits credit.

This is not to say that no one at all remembers. It is to say that, state by state, those who remember are few—family and friends, members of gubernatorial administrations, political insiders, statehouse journalists, biographers, historians, political scientists, and archivists. These members of the inner circles of memory participate in keeping alive the achievements of America's governors. They work at building legacies, promoting what governors have undertaken and what they have achieved. In a few cases, such as the Rockefeller Institute in New York or the Sanford School of Public Policy in North Carolina, academic programs and research centers are established to build on the legacies of former governors. Gubernatorial archives now exist in most states. Although these repositories vary greatly in how they are organized and the quality of their collections, they do provide raw information for historians and other researchers on governors and governing. In a number of states today, former governors have an online presence by virtue of web sites that offer a record of their time in office. At my own institution, the Eagleton Institute of Politics at Rutgers University, a center on governors has recently been established. Among its initial efforts are oral histories of the Byrne and Kean administrations, with the goal of recording oral histories of the Florio and Whitman administrations, and subsequent administrations as well.[7] The National Governors Association maintains an extensive biographical database of all former governors, dating from colonial times. Also, the association commissioned two books on governors to mark its centennial.[8]

For anyone wanting a quick fix on a former governor, Wikipedia offers useful biographical summaries—but not much more. Substantial coverage is provided in autobiographies, biographies, memoirs, and other accounts—a literature on which I partially rely for this book. It is in the interest of individual governors on their way out of office to engage in such writing. They also may commission or encourage it. Yet, there would appear to be little demand for it. It is difficult to imagine that biographies about governors who are not running for president or serving as president or appealing for redemption would sell many copies or be read by many people. For example, Rutgers University Press published a biography of Tom Kean,[9] who was very popular when he left office in 1990 and who remained in public life thereafter. The book was promoted and advertised by a fund collected by Kean's friends. In five years, only 2,400 copies of the book had been sold. The work that governors have done is important, as are the efforts being made to provide a record for the public. The problem is that not much of a public seems to care.

What Difference They Made

What is more important than how governors are remembered, or forgotten, by the public is how they feel they ought to be remembered, if not by a real public, then by a theoretical posterity. In other words, what were the results of the policy accomplishments for which they wish to be acknowledged? Did governmental performance or governmental programs improve? Did policies and practices change in fundamental ways? Did these changes persist over time? Was the state better off as a consequence of their having held office?

There can be little doubt that the states and ergo their governors have contributed to public policy at the national level. There are probably no better examples than welfare reform and health care, where, respectively, Tommy Thompson (R-WI) and Mitt Romney (R-MA) had significant influence on what transpired in Washington, D.C. Nonetheless, not many governors achieved dramatic policy gains and made sizeable and lasting differences in their states, especially during the past twenty years or so. It is fair to say that their legacies are far fewer than their policy successes.

This should not be surprising, in view of the difficulties inherent in implementing policies and making them work. Inevitably, there will be slippage in the stages from enactment to funding to implementation to effect. A policy legacy cannot be realized if policies are not implemented fully or adequately. Then, the effects can be assessed only after the passage of time, and their measurement may not be possible at all. Many accomplishments, moreover, are incremental policy adjustments, tweaks here and tweaks there, to ongoing policies and policy directions. Increases in spending, for instance, fall in this category. They are absorbed. This is not to mitigate their importance, but only to question whether they merit legacy status.

In addition, successor governors have their own priorities, which are not likely to be precisely those of their predecessors. Indeed, as the survey showed, two out of five governors manage to repeal or change programs of their predecessors. Each governor wants to make his or her distinctive mark. Bill Clements (R-TX) expressed doubt about how long his programs for Texas would endure after he failed to win election to a second term. His program, designed to make the government more efficient, including reducing bureaucracy, was unlikely to survive. "I doubt that the incoming administration has the inclination—certainly they don't have the background—to continue the program," he said. "It'll drop in the cracks."[10]

Almost all governors have worked to improve education. They have succeeded in funding schools at higher levels and have changed how schools were organized or operated. But their successors have had their own education agendas. Wave after wave of education reform has been legislated. One reform melds with or supersedes a prior one. The emphasis shifts; changes evaporate or are absorbed by the system. The educational bureaucracy cannot pay equal attention to every program, but it does have to give priority to what the incumbent governor enacts as his or her own reform agenda. The old gets left behind. However much they hope to improve learning, few of the many "education governors" from the 1980–2010 generation have left footprints in the schools.

Education scholars have been trying to measure the impact of school reform for decades. It is most difficult to do. Thornburgh acknowledged the problem in his memoirs. Certain short-term indicators were positive for the programs his administration initiated. The dropout rate decreased by nearly 15 percent in a few years, and college entrance scores increased slightly as well. It wasn't much. Thornburgh's sense—but only his sense—was that without his policies things would have been worse, because of the violent crime, drug abuse, sexual promiscuity, and despair caused by broken homes during the 1980s and 1990s. These factors, according to him, "were of such magnitude that they had a tendency to override whatever marginal improvements might have been made in the classroom."[11] One might also question whether Thornburgh's initiatives, and not other factors, were actually the cause of whatever gains were made by Pennsylvania's educational system.

Not many governors attempt to change the baseline, which fundamentally alters the way people think about and approach an issue. Undeniably, Engler's initiative in Michigan that shifted the structure for financing education away from local property taxes constitutes a baseline change, one that has had an enduring impact. School finance reform is appropriately linked to Engler's leadership as governor. But what about educational change beyond how schools are financed? A former Democratic house speaker had great respect for Engler and gave him credit for a willingness to take tough stands and fight for them to the finish. But he wondered whether Engler deserved credit for reforming education. "Only time will tell if kids are really smarter and schools are truly better," he added.[12] Dick Riley (D-SC) is another governor who made the baseline type of change. His initiatives led South Carolina's policymakers to think differently about schools and education. The same could be said of Wisconsin's Thompson and his policy revolution with respect to welfare reform.

Not many governors deserve greater credit for policy achievement than Romney, whose Massachusetts health care initiative was enacted in 2006 with almost two-thirds of the public in favor. By the end of the decade, one of the major objectives of the initiative had been met: nearly all of the residents of Massachusetts were insured, and at a cost of only about 1 percent of the state budget. The state, moreover, continued to build on the achievement, trying to reduce the cost of health care by making flat (rather than fee-for-service) payments to networks for keeping patients well. Ironically, however, Romney had to distance himself from his legacy accomplishment when he ran for the 2008 Republican presidential nomination and again when he ran for the 2012 nomination.

"You spend your time on education, health, and welfare . . . you can't see the actual results, like a road or a building," Voinovich pointed out. In some cases, however, the results might be discernable, along with the governor's input. "The trick is to institutionalize changes," said Gerald Baliles (D-VA). Some policy achievements, in his view, "stick better than others." His transportation program was built on by his successors. Baliles also created a department of world trade, but in the recession of the 1990s the department was merged with another one. Although the structure was no longer the same, Baliles was gratified that the functions carried on. Some of the policy accomplishments of governors—probably those of a structural nature—are built on by their successors. If the standard is that of having been built on, then much of what governors get done has consequences, at least in the short term. Whether or not legacies rightfully can be claimed, governors do deserve credit for making a contribution.

One governor, Hugh Carey (D-NY), left a very different kind of legacy. Through policy initiatives, he kept New York City afloat during a harrowing fiscal crisis. He stepped into the breech—taking the lead on legislation that created the Municipal Assistance Corporation and the Emergency

Financial Control Board—and brought a measure of fiscal reform to the city.[13]

A number of governors associated their legacies with changes their policies made in the physical environment of their states. Byrne took special pride in having protected New Jersey's Pinelands from development, a policy achievement that he did not think would have happened without his leadership. Maryland's Ehrlich regarded the Chesapeake Restoration Act as his most dramatic accomplishment. Bob Graham (D-FL) was an education governor first and foremost, but he pointed proudly to an annual ranking of beaches in the nation, on which Florida consistently has half of the best beaches. Most of them were purchased under Graham's Save Our Coasts program.[14] Mike Hayden could also point out that the current highway system in Kansas is rated as tops in the nation. Is he correct, however, in his assumption that the rating is the effect of the highway initiatives he undertook when governor?

The more tangible the results, the likelier the legacy status. Perhaps Nelson Rockefeller's establishment of a state university system in New York is a model. Rockefeller left many buildings behind, as well as a first-rate educational system that has stood the test of time. (He also left a legacy of taxes and debt.) Other governors also have had an impact on higher education. Thornburgh played the leading role in the consolidation of the fourteen teachers' colleges in Pennsylvania into a single university system.[15]

In the eyes of governors themselves, results need not be earth shaking to qualify them for legacy status. Joe Frank Harris (D-GA) took special pride in getting a dome built on the Atlanta football stadium so that the city could win its bid for the 1996 Olympics, host the 1994 Super Bowl, and keep the Atlanta Falcons in Georgia. He also claimed responsibility for the expansion of public libraries in the state—142 new libraries in 97 of the state's counties.[16] Oklahoma's Keating chalked up a dome on the capitol building as one of his three legacies.[17] Together with his wife, Rita, Clements considered one of his major legacies to be the restoration of the governor's mansion and the capitol. That's what, it was thought, Texans would remember about him.[18]

Not every governor has the opportunity to leave behind an edifice. Voinovich recalled that as mayor of Cleveland he was vitally concerned with the physical development of the city. He got a lot built and, after leaving office, he could see the physical results of his administration. Then, he followed Jim Rhodes (R-OH) in office as governor. The problem for Voinovich was that Rhodes had already built everything; there was nothing left to build, but there was a lot to maintain. No bragging rights go with maintenance, so Voinovich had to look elsewhere for legacy.

Yes, governors succeed with their policy agendas while in office, but not much of what they achieve is acknowledged for very long, if at all. Not much of what they enact as policy has demonstrable and sustained impact. If a governor makes any footprints in the state, they can be washed away as easily as if they had been made on one of Bob Graham's sandy beaches. Benjamin Cayetano took away one lesson from his experience governing, during which he had to deal with a legislature whose views conflicted with his own. A reformer, he wanted to change Hawaii. After a twenty-five-year career, he came to the realization that "the best any politician can hope for . . . is that he helped make life a little better for people."[19] Mario Cuomo (D-NY) also fell short of making dramatic gains. An inspiring governor, he did not have achievements that came near to matching the vision he offered in his speeches. But Cuomo believed in incremental improvements, with government performing an ameliorative function, helping to see that people's lives got better little by little.[20] That seemed to be enough for him.

Perhaps *legacy* isn't the right word to apply to governors. It is less what governors leave behind than what they do while they govern. With a policy exception here and there, what governors mainly do is in some sense closer to custodial than legacy-building. Much of what they accomplish can be considered as maintenance. By referring to governors as custodians or maintenance men and women, we do not mean to diminish their accomplishments but rather to keep them in perspective. Their accomplishments are important and governors deserve credit for them. They are byproducts of the job that they have, along with the legislature, to take care of the state and serve the needs of its people during the time they are entrusted with office. The task is complex and difficult. Their budgets and their policy initiatives are part of the care they give, which in various degrees carry over after they depart. Then, their successors take on the responsibility, which requires them to work with the legislature fashioning majorities for the policy and budgetary care they deem necessary for the well-being of the state and its people.

If legacies are what governors are seeking, they may be disappointed. They usually have to settle for less. But what they settle for is still very impressive.

Will a New Generation of Governors Be Different?

A new generation of governors has ascended to power. It includes a few returning old-timers and several carry-overs. But essentially what I refer to in this study as the generation of 1980–2010 has departed. The question with which I conclude this exploration is whether a new cohort will differ in policymaking leadership from the older one. Should we expect current and future governors to be self-confident and pragmatic, strategically and tactically skillful, and legislatively adept like their predecessors?

There is little reason to believe that the abilities and orientations of those who win gubernatorial office will change much in the near future. Governors likely will continue to be experienced and accomplished when they arrive. Half of them probably will continue to be socialized in the legislature prior to becoming chief executive in their states.

The office they fill, however, may not be quite the same. I began this book with Jerry Brown's decision to run for governor in 2010, having served two terms more than a quarter of a century earlier, but ready to use his years of experience to rescue California from fiscal decline and partisanship. However, he was unprepared for what he would face this time around. Approaches that once had worked—softening up Republican legislators, offering concessions, winning a vote here and a vote there— weren't productive anymore. The new governor did reap the benefit of a change in governance, thanks to Proposition 25, which eliminated the requirement for a two-thirds vote to pass a budget. And Brown also got his budget passed on time. Yet, after less than a year in office, he admitted, "some of my old tools aren't going to work." At least they weren't effective with the Republican minority in the legislature. To get some of his tax initiatives on the ballot, he needed help. But every important matter seemed to be a party-line vote.[21]

Not only in California, but in most places, being governor today is tougher than it used to be, and it is not likely to get easier in the years ahead.[22] The record of gubernatorial accomplishment may decline as a result. Two principal factors account for the changing nature of the job. First, difficult economic and fiscal conditions demand response and severely constrain the range of policies that governors are able to pursue. Second, the increased partisanship in national and state politics makes settlements harder to reach.

Hard economic times are certainly not unknown to governors. Three out of four members of the 1980–2010 cohort of governors had to face sagging economies or budget shortfalls sometime during their administrations. But the environment is worse for governors who have just attained office. The 2008 recession and the sputtering economy, the structural imbalances in state budgets, steadily rising medical costs, a huge funding gap for the retirement benefits of government workers, and the high rate of jobless residents—all these factors place heavy burdens on those currently in power.

Given the economic challenges nearly everywhere, it would seem that governors will have to cut spending drastically or raise taxes at least somewhat, or do a combination of both. A new austerity may be a prominent feature of state environments for some time ahead. All of this means that governors will have less wiggle room. They must make the economic and fiscal situations their top priority. The states have pretty well exhausted budgetary fixes. Services have to be provided, infrastructure has to be maintained, and tax increases are more politically problematic than earlier. Voters, who expect much, will get much less. Given all these pressures, governors will have to scale back their policy objectives and, like the public they serve, will have to settle for less.

Intense partisanship in the states did not arise suddenly. Many of the 1980–2010 generation of governors operated in partisan environments, particularly in comparison to those who came before them in the 1960s and 1970s. Many had to face legislatures in which one or both houses were controlled by the other party. But most of the governors who are the focus of this study knew how to compromise with the other side and accomplished a good deal under divided government. Today the two political parties are farther apart than ten years ago and much farther apart than twenty or thirty years ago.

The polarization exists not only between Democratic and Republican office holders but also between rank-and-file Democrats and Republicans who participate in the political process. Ideology matters practically everywhere.[23] The stakes, thus, are high. In many places the competition for power is intense. Either party is able to win in the race for governor. And in over half the states, either party stands a chance of taking control of one or both houses of the legislature.

The initial response of the new generation suggests that if the governor's party controls the legislature, Republicans will address economic and fiscal issues and other issues in one way and Democrats will address them in another. During the 2011 legislative sessions, the two parties appeared sharply divided. Where Republicans controlled both branches, they were able to limit the bargaining rights of public employees, pass tougher immigration laws, and require voters to display a photo ID.[24] By contrast, the two states that increased broad-based taxes in order to close budget gaps were controlled by Democrats, as were four of the five states where gay marriage passed.

If they can rely on the votes of their own legislative parties, most Republican and Democratic governors seem disinclined to accommodate the minority party. Their concern is with getting the votes necessary within their own ranks, rather than making compromises across the aisle. We cannot be certain, but in earlier years, under conditions of unified control the minority party appeared to be consulted more and to play a greater role in the lawmaking process than it does now. Yet there are exceptions today, such as Dannel Malloy, the Democratic governor of Connecticut. Even with a Democratic legislature, Malloy included in his economic development initiative Republican proposals for cutting business regulations as well as new tax credits for business. He managed to get almost unanimous legislative support.

The current governors may be more ideological than their predecessors, but this does not necessarily mean that they are no longer pragmatic. They can achieve what they want to achieve, without having to tailor their initiatives to the liking of the minority party, as long as they have their own partisans on board. Thus, contemporary governors whose party controls both houses of the legislature will be able to get the policy results they want without crossing the aisle to do so.[25]

The real test of whether today's governors differ from yesterday's is how they relate to the legislature when government is divided. If past governors are indicative, present-day governors will cultivate legislators, tailor their agendas, and compromise when the other party has control of one or both houses. It is much too early to tell whether they will do so, but there are some indications that gubernatorial pragmatism remains the norm. For example, Nevada's Brian Sandoval and New Mexico's Susana Martinez, both Republicans, managed to accommodate Democratic legislatures. Sandoval entered the 2011 session looking like a hard-nosed conservative but exited as a practical moderate. Martinez, soon after her election, started building relationships with the legislature. Both compromised with the Democratic legislature and both were able to achieve policy gains.[26]

Democrat Andrew Cuomo had the benefit of a Democratic assembly but faced a senate narrowly controlled by Republicans in New York. Cuomo worked assiduously to court the legislature, exhibiting what one observer referred to as "non-ideological political sensibility." With few exceptions, he did not reveal the specifics of his policy proposals until he had reached a deal with the Democratic assembly and the Republican senate to approve them. He held in strictest confidence the compromises he and the legislative leaders made. "He gave everyone what they needed to give him what he wanted," said a Democratic political consultant. The governor referred to the legislature (which was known in *New York Times* editorials as "the dysfunctional New York Legislature") as the best legislative body in the nation. His doors were open to members, and legislators got to visit with Cuomo more in six months than they had visited the governor during several administrations with George Pataki (R-NY).[27] On the budget, Cuomo and the legislative leaders agreed to overall levels, but the governor let the legislature make the cuts. On gay marriage, he reached a compromise with Republican senators that protected religious organizations from lawsuits and the loss of state aid if they refused to provide their services for same-sex marriages. A one-time chief of staff to the former senate majority leader, Joe Bruno, assessed Cuomo's policy success in the 2011 session: "The governor, quite frankly, ran the table."[28] The governor's major policy achievement came still later that year, when he won almost unanimous legislative approval for an overhaul of the state's tax structure.[29]

Even under conditions of divided control, not every new governor conforms to the Cuomo, Sandoval, or Martinez type. Chris Christie does not mirror his contemporaries or his predecessors. Unlike them, he doesn't pay much attention to the care and feeding of legislators. Indeed, he has shown contempt for the legislature and its members. He seems to have gone out of his way to alienate Democratic leaders in the legislature, as well as their core constituencies. His approach, as described by one journalist, has been "unrelentingly brutal."[30] Christie has campaigned for his agenda items around the state, attacking the Democratic legislature for obstructionism. In contrast to the overwhelming majority of governors examined here, he has done almost everything possible to lose friends and make enemies. But, still, he has compromised when necessary and, in his first two years as governor, has achieved a record of considerable policy and budget success. He did it his way, not the conventional way. It remains to be seen whether Christie's aggressive approach[31] will be as effective in his second two years as it was in his first two, or whether he will become more conciliatory, less combative. As his term approached the halfway mark, it should be noted, Christie sounded somewhat different. In a speech at the Ronald Reagan Presidential Library in California, he talked about "leadership and compromise" (at about the same time that he was vetoing items in the budget for the legislature's operations).

Christie, during his brief tenure as governor, appears to be the exception. My guess is that most governors will continue to be respectful of their legislatures and willing to consult and negotiate with them. In the main, I expect them to tailor their objectives to economic and political circumstances, consult and negotiate with the legislature, and compromise in order to achieve their objectives. This approach has helped most governors succeed as policy leaders in the past, and most governors probably will stay with this approach as long as it works.

Notes

1. Cecil Andrus and Joel Connelly, *Cecil Andrus: Politics Western Style* (Seattle: Sasquatch Books, 1998), 187.
2. Discussion with Edgar at Eagleton Institute of Politics, Rutgers University, December 2010.
3. Bruce King, *Cowboy in the Roundhouse* (Santa Fe, NM: Sunstone Press, 1998), 352.
4. Adam Nagourney, "The Contender," *New York Times Magazine,* May 8, 2011, 48.
5. It is possible, however, that Edgar is thought of by a number of Illinoisans as one of the few recent governors of the state who was not indicted, convicted, or sentenced, as were a number of recent governors of Illinois.
6. *Politifax* xiii (30), January 27, 2010.
7. The interviews with former governors and members of their administrations are available online.
8. See Clayton McClure Brooks, *A Legacy of Leadership: Governors and American History* (Philadelphia: University of Pennsylvania Press, 2008); Ethan G. Sribnick, ed., *A Legacy of Innovation: Governors and Public Policy* (Philadelphia: University of Pennsylvania Press, 2008).
9. Alvin S. Felzenberg, *Governor Tom Kean* (New Brunswick, NJ: Rutgers University Press, 2006).
10. Carolyn Barta, *Bill Clements: Texian to His Toenails* (Austin: Eakin Press, 1996), 295.
11. Dick Thornburgh, *Where the Evidence Leads* (Pittsburgh: University of Pittsburgh Press, 2003), 156.
12. Gleaves Whitney, *John Engler: The Man, the Leader & the Legacy* (Chelsea, MI: Sleeping Bear Press, 2002), 378–79, 391.
13. Among Albany insiders, Carey is also remembered as the first New York governor in history to have a veto overridden by the legislature.
14. S. V. Date, *Quiet Passion: A Biography of Senator Bob Graham* (New York: Penguin, 2004), 126.
15. Thornburgh, *Where the Evidence Leads,* 156.
16. Response from survey.
17. Ibid.
18. Barta, *Bill Clements,* 403.
19. Benjamin J. Cayetano, *Ben: A Memoir From Street Kid to Governor* (Honolulu: Watermark Publishing, 2009), 548.

20. Robert S. McElvaine, *Mario Cuomo: A Biography* (New York: Scribner's, 1988), 328.

21. Adam Nagourney, "Shift in Politics Trips Up Governor in California," *New York Times,* September 21, 2011.

22. Such an assessment was made by former governors at a National Governors Association session, Washington, D.C., February 21, 2010.

23. See Alan I. Abramowitz, *The Disappearing Center* (New Haven CT, Yale University Press, 2010).

24. Ronald Brownstein and Scott Bland, "Separate Ways," *National Journal,* July 23, 2011.

25. Scott Walker in Wisconsin and John Kasich in Ohio are two Republican governors who in 2011 steamrolled the Democratic minority in the legislature but later tried to build bridges with the opposition. Walker and Kasich pushed through laws restricting bargaining rights for public employees, paying little heed to Democratic objections. After six months, Walker made an overture to Democrats with the objective of finding shared agenda items and building trust. Kasich, after Democrats began collecting signatures to put the law to a vote on a statewide referendum, also began talking of negotiations and compromise. *New York Times,* August 22, 2011.

26. Ben Smith and Byron Tau, Politico.com, August 13, 2011.

27. *New York Times,* July 7, 2011.

28. *State Net Capitol Journal,* July 4, 2011.

29. *New York Times,* December 7, 8, and 10.

30. Matt Bai, "The Disrupter," *New York Times Magazine,* February 27, 2011.

31. Ibid.; Bai characterized him as "about as slick as sandpaper."

Appendix A

Governors, 1980–2010

State			Name (Party)	Years in Office
Alabama			Forrest Hood James (D, R)	1979–1983; 1995–1999
			George Corley Wallace (D)	1983–1987 (1963–1967; 1971–1979)
			Harold Guy Hunt (R)	1987–1993
			James Elisha Folsom (D)	1993–1995
	S		Donald Eugene Siegelman (D)	1999–2003
			Bob Riley (R)	2003–2011
Alaska			Jay S. Hammond (R)	1974–1982
	S		William Jennings Sheffield (D)	1982–1986
			Steve Cowper (D)	1986–1990
			Walter J. Hickel (I)	1990–1994 (1966–1969)
			Tony Knowles (D)	1994–2002
	S		Frank H. Murkowski (R)	2002–2006
		L	Sarah Palin (R)	2006–2009
			Sean Parnell (R)	2009–
Arizona			Bruce Edward Babbitt (D)	1978–1987
			Evan Mecham (R)	1987–1988
			Rose Mofford (D)	1988–1991
			J. Fife Symington (R)	1991–1997
	S		Jane Dee Hull (R)	1997–2003
			Janet Napolitano (D)	2003–2009
			Jan Brewer (R)	2009–
Arkansas		L	William Jefferson Clinton (D)	1983–1992; 1979–1981
			Frank D. White (R)	1981–1983
			Jim Guy Tucker (D)	1992–1996
	S		Mike Huckabee (R)	1996–2007
			Mike Beebe (D)	2007–
California		L	Edmund Gerald Brown (D)	1975–1983
			George Deukmejian (R)	1983–1991
			Pete Wilson (R)	1991–1999
			Gray Davis (D)	1999–2003
		L	Arnold Schwarzenegger (R)	2003–2011
Colorado	S		Richard D. Lamm (D)	1975–1987
		I	Roy Romer (D)	1987–1999
	S	I	Bill Owens (R)	1999–2007
			Bill Ritter (D)	2007–2011
Connecticut			William A. O'Neill (D)	1980–1991

State			Name (Party)	Years in Office
	S		Lowell P. Weicker (I)	1991–1995
	S		John G. Rowland (R)	1995–2004
			M. Jodi Rell (R)	2004–2011
Delaware			Pierre Samuel Du Pont (R)	1977–1985
			Michael Newbold Castle (R)	1985–1992
			Dale Edward Wolf (R)	1992–1993
			Thomas R. Carper (D)	1993–2001
	S		Ruth Ann Minner (D)	2001–2009
			Jack Markell (D)	2009–
Florida		L	Daniel Robert Graham (D)	1979–1987
			Robert Martinez (D, R)	1987–1991
			Lawton Chiles (D)	1991–1998
		L	Jeb Bush (R)	1999–2007
			Charlie Crist (R)	2007–2011
Georgia			George Dekle Busbee (D)	1975–1983
	S	L	Joe Frank Harris (D)	1983–1991
		L	Zell Miller (D)	1991–1999
	S		Roy E. Barnes (D)	1999–2003
			Sonny Perdue (R)	2003–2011
Hawaii	S	L	George Ryoichi Ariyoshi (D)	1974–1986
			John Waihee (D)	1986–1994
	S	L	Benjamin J. Cayetano (D)	1994–2002
			Linda Lingle (R)	2002–2010
Idaho	S		John Victor Evans (D)	1977–1987
		L	Cecil Dale Andrus (D)	1987–1995 (1971–1977)
			Philip E. Batt (R)	1995–1999
			Dirk Kempthorne (R)	1999–2006
			James E. Risch (R)	2006–2007
			C. L. "Butch" Otter (R)	2007–
Illinois		L	James Robert Thompson (R)	1977–1991
	S	I	Jim Edgar (R)	1991–1999
			George H. Ryan (R)	1999–2003
			Rod R. Blagojevich (D)	2003–2009
			Pat Quinn (D)	2009–
Indiana	S		Otis Ray Bowen (R)	1973–1981
			Robert D. Orr (R)	1981–1989
			Evan Bayh (D)	1989–1997
		L	Frank O' Bannon (D)	1997–2003
			Joseph E. Kernan (D)	2003–2005
			Mitchell Daniels (R)	2005–
Iowa	S		Robert D. Ray (R)	1969–1983

(Continued)

State	S	I	L	Name (Party)	Years in Office
	S		L	Terry E. Branstad (R)	1983–1999
				Thomas J. Vilsack (D)	1999–2007
				Chet Culver (D)	2007–2011
Kansas	S			John Carlin (D)	1979–1987
		I		John Michael Hayden (R)	1987–1991
				Joan Finney (D)	1991–1995
	S			Bill Graves (R)	1995–2003
				Kathleen Sebelius (D)	2003–2009
				Mark Parkinson (D)	2009–2011
Kentucky				John Y. Brown (D)	1979–1983
				Martha Layne Collins (D)	1983–1987
				Wallace G. Wilkinson (D)	1987–1991
				Brereton C. Jones (D)	1991–1995
				Paul E. Patton (D)	1995–2003
				Ernie Fletcher (R)	2003–2007
				Stephen L. Beshear (D)	2007–2011
Louisiana			L	Edwin Washington Edwards (D)	1972–1980; 1984–1988; 1992–1996
				David C. Treen (D)	1980–1984
				Buddy Elson Roemer (D, R)	1988–1992
				Mike Foster (R)	1996–2004
				Kathleen Babineaux Blanco (D)	2004–2008
				Bobby Jindal (R)	2008–
Maine		I		Joseph Edward Brennan (D)	1979–1987
				John Rettie McKernan (R)	1987–1995
	S	I		Angus S. King (I)	1995–2003
				John E. Baldacci (D)	2003–2011
Maryland	S		L	Harry Roe Hughes (D)	1979–1987
			L	William Donald Schaefer (D)	1987–1995
	S	I		Parris N. Glendening (D)	1995–2003
	S	I		Robert L. Ehrlich (R)	2003–2007
				Martin O' Malley (D)	2007–
Massachusetts				Edward Joseph King (D)	1979–1983
	S		L	Michael Stanley Dukakis (D)	1983–1991 (1975–1979)
		I		William Floyd Weld (R)	1991–1997
				Argeo Paul Cellucci (R)	1997–2001
				Jane Maria Swift (R)	2001–2003
				Mitt Romney (R)	2003–2007
				Deval Patrick (D)	2007–
Michigan				William Grawn Milliken (R)	1969–1983
	S			James Johnston Blanchard (D)	1983–1991
	S	I	L	John Engler (R)	1991–2003

State				Name (Party)	Years in Office
				Jennifer M. Granholm (D)	2003–2011
Minnesota	S			Albert Harold Quie (R)	1979–1983
				Rudolph George Perpich (D)	1983–1991 (1976–1979)
		I		Arne Helge Carlson (R)	1991–1999
			L	Jesse Ventura (I)	1999–2003
				Tim Pawlenty (R)	2003–2011
Mississippi	S			William Forrest Winter (D)	1980–1984
				William A. Allain (D)	1984–1988
				Raymond Edwin Mabus (D)	1988–1992
			L	Daniel Kirkwood Fordice (R)	1992–2000
				David Ronald "Ronnie" Musgrove (D)	2000–2004
				Haley Barbour (R)	2004–
Missouri				Joseph P. Teasdale (D)	1977–1981
				Christopher S. Bond (R)	1981–1985 (1973–1977)
			L	John Ashcroft (R)	1985–1993
				Mel Eugene Carnahan (D)	1993–2000
				Roger B. Wilson (D)	2000–2001
	S	I		Robert L. Holden (D)	2001–2005
				Matt Blunt (R)	2005–2009
				Jeremiah W. (Jay) Nixon (D)	2009–
Montana				Thomas Lee Judge (D)	1973–1981
	S			Ted Schwinden (D)	1981–1989
				Stan Stephens (R)	1989–1993
				Marc Racicot (R)	1993–2001
	S			Judy Martz (R)	2001–2005
			L	Brian Schweitzer (D)	2005–
Nebraska	S			Charles Thone (R)	1979–1983
				Joseph Robert (Bob) Kerrey (D)	1983–1987
				Kay A. Orr (R)	1987–1991
		I		E. Benjamin Nelson (D)	1991–1999
				Mike Johanns (R)	1999–2005
				Dave Heineman (R)	2005–
Nevada				Robert Frank List (R)	1979–1983
	S			Richard H. Bryan (D)	1983–1989
	S			Bob Miller (D)	1989–1999
				Kenny Guinn (R)	1999–2007
				Jim Gibbons (R)	2007–2011
New Hampshire				Hugh J. Gallen (D)	1979–1982
	S		L	John H. Sununu (R)	1983–1989
				Judd Gregg (R)	1989–1993
	S			Stephen Merrill (R)	1993–1997

(Continued)

State			Name (Party)	Years in Office
			Jeanne Shaheen (D)	1997–2003
			Craig Benson (R)	2003–2005
			John Lynch (D)	2005–
New Jersey	S		Brendan Thomas Byrne (D)	1974–1982
	S	L	Thomas H. Kean (R)	1982–1990
	S		Jim Florio (D)	1990–1994
	S	L	Christine Todd Whitman (R)	1994–2001
		L	James E. McGreevey (D)	2002–2004
			Richard J. Codey (D)	2004–2006
			Jon Corzine (D)	2006–2010
New Mexico		L	Bruce King (D)	1979–1983; 1991–1995 (1971–1975)
			Toney Anaya (D)	1983–1987
	S		Garrey E. Carruthers (R)	1987–1991
			Gary E. Johnson (R)	1995–2003
		L	Bill Richardson (D)	2003–2011
New York		L	Hugh Leo Carey (D)	1975–1983
		L	Mario Matthew Cuomo (D)	1983–1995
		L	George E. Pataki (R)	1995–2007
		L	Eliot Spitzer (D)	2007–2008
			David A. Paterson (D)	2008–2011
North Carolina	I	L	James B. Hunt (D)	1977–1985; 1993–2001
	S		James G. Martin (R)	1985–1993
			Michael F. Easley (D)	2001–2009
			Bev Perdue (D)	2009–
North Dakota	S		Arthur Albert Link (D)	1973–1981
	S		Allen Ingvar Olson (R)	1981–1985
	S		George Albert Sinner (D)	1985–1992
	S		Edward Thomas Schafer (R)	1992–2000
			John Hoeven (R)	2000–2010
Ohio			James Allen Rhodes (R)	1975–1983 (1963–1971)
	S	L	Richard F. Celeste (D)	1983–1991
	I	L	George V. Voinovich (R)	1991–1998
	S	I	Bob Taft (R)	1999–2007
			Ted Strickland (D)	2007–2011
Oklahoma	S		George Patterson Nigh (D)	1979–1987 (1963)
		L	Henry Louis Bellmon (R)	1987–1991 (1963–1967)
			David Lee Walters (D)	1991–1995
	S	I	Francis Anthony Keating (R)	1995–2003
			Brad Henry (D)	2003–2011
Oregon	S	L	Victor G. Atiyeh (R)	1979–1987
			Neil Goldschmidt (D)	1987–1991

State	S	I	L	Name (Party)	Years in Office
		I		Barbara Roberts (D)	1991–1995
				John A. Kitzhaber (D)	1995–2003
				Ted Kulongoski (D)	2003–2011
Pennsylvania	S	I	L	Dick Thornburgh (R)	1979–1987
			L	Robert P. Casey Sr. (D)	1987–1995
	S			Tom Ridge (R)	1995–2001
				Mark Schweiker (R)	2001–2003
				Edward G. Rendell (D)	2003–2011
Rhode Island				J. Joseph Garrahy (D)	1977–1985
				Edward D. DiPrete (R)	1985–1991
	S			Bruce G. Sundlun (D)	1991–1995
	S			Lincoln Almond (R)	1995–2003
				Don Carcieri (R)	2003–2011
South Carolina	S		L	Richard Wilson Riley (D)	1979–1987
			L	Carroll A. Campbell (R)	1987–1995
	S			David M. Beasley (R)	1995–1999
	S	I		Jim Hodges (D)	1999–2003
				Mark Sanford (R)	2003–2011
South Dakota	S			William J. Janklow (R)	1979–1987; 1995–2003
				George S. Mickleson (R)	1987–1993
				Walter D. Miller (R)	1993–1995
				Mike Rounds (R)	2003–2011
Tennessee			L	Lamar Alexander (R)	1979–1987
			L	Ned Ray McWherter (D)	1987–1995
	S			Don Sundquist (R)	1995–2003
				Phil Bredesen (D)	2003–2011
Texas	S		L	William P. Clements Jr. (R)	1979–1983; 1987–1991
	S			Mark White (D)	1983–1987
			L	Dorothy Ann Willis Richards (D)	1991–1995
			L	George W. Bush (R)	1995–2000
				Rick Perry (R)	2000–
Utah				Scott M. Matheson (D)	1977–1985
				Norman Howard Bangerter (R)	1985–1993
	S			Michael Okerlund Leavitt (R)	1993–2003
				Olene Smith Walker (R)	2003–2005
				Jon Huntsman (R)	2005–2009
				Gary Richard Herbert (R)	2009–
Vermont				Richard A. Snelling (R)	1977–1985; 1991
	S		L	Madeleine M. Kunin (D)	1985–1991
	S			Howard Dean (D)	1991–2003
				Jim Douglas (R)	2003–2011

(Continued)

State			Name (Party)	Years in Office
Virginia			John Nichols Dalton (R)	1978–1982
			Charles Spittal Robb (D)	1982–1986
		I	Gerald L. Baliles (D)	1986–1990
	S	L	L. Douglas Wilder (D)	1990–1994
	S		George Allen (R)	1994–1998
			James S. Gilmore (R)	1998–2002
			Mark R. Warner (D)	2002–2006
			Tim Kaine (D)	2006–2010
Washington			Dixy Lee Ray (D)	1977–1981
	S		John Dennis Spellman (R)	1981–1985
	S	L	Booth Gardner (D)	1985–1993
	S		Michael Lowry (D)	1993–1997
		I	Gary Locke (D)	1997–2005
			Chris Gregoire (D)	2005–
West Virginia		L	John Davison Rockefeller (D)	1977–1985
	S		Arch A. Moore (R)	1985–1989 (1969–1977)
			Gaston Caperton (D)	1989–1997
			Cecil H. Underwood (R)	1997–2001 (1957–1961)
		I	Bob Wise (D)	2001–2005
			Joe Manchin III (D)	2005–2010
Wisconsin			Lee Sherman Dreyfus (R)	1979–1983
	S		Anthony S. Earl (D)	1983–1987
			Tommy G. Thompson (R)	1987–2001
			Scott McCallum (R)	2001–2003
			Jim Doyle (D)	2003–2011
Wyoming			Edward Herschler (D)	1975–1987
	S		Michael J. Sullivan (D)	1987–1995
			Jim Geringer (R)	1995–2003
			Dave Freudenthal (D)	2003–2011

Note. S = governor was surveyed; I = governor was interviewed; L = literature on governor was used. Dates in parentheses represent terms of office preceding the 1980–2010 range.

References

Ahlberg, Clark D., and Daniel P. Moynihan. "Changing Governors—and Policies." In Beyle and Williams, *The American Governor in Behavioral Perspective*, 95–104.

Alexander, Lamar. "What Do Governors Do?" In Behn, *Governors on Governing*, 40–47.

Allen, Charles F., and Jonathan Portis. *The Comeback Kid: The Life and Career of Bill Clinton*. New York: Carol Publishing Group, 1992.

Andrus, Cecil, and Joel Connelly. *Cecil Andrus: Politics Western Style*. Seattle: Sasquatch Books, 1998.

Ariyoshi, George R. *With Obligations to All*. Honolulu: Ariyoshi Foundation, 1997.

Ashcroft, John. "Leadership: The Art of Redefining the Possible." In Behn, *Governors on Governing*, 66–77.

Atiyeh, Victor G. "The Role of Business Management Techniques in State Government." In Behn, *Governors on Governing*, 106–14.

Bagwell, Benjamin Prince. *Riley: A Story of Hope*. Pickens, SC: Pickens County Publishing, 1986.

Baker, Donald P. *Wilder: Hold Fast to Dreams*. Cabin John, MD: Seven Lockers Press, 1989.

Bai, Matt. "State of Distress." *New York Times Magazine,* October 25, 2009, 38–45, 86, 87.

————. "The Disrupter." *New York Times Magazine,* February 27, 2011, 32–39.

Balogh, Brian. "Introduction: Directing Democracy." In Sribnick, *A Legacy of Innovation,* 1–21.

Balz, Dan. "California Governor's Race: Jerry Brown Steps Back in at a Time of Crisis." *Washington Post*, February 10, 2010.

Barber, James D. *The Lawmakers*. New Haven, CT: Yale University Press, 1965.

Barnes, James A. "Governors at High Noon." *National Journal,* May 2, 2009, 52–53.

Barta, Carolyn. *Bill Clements: Texian to His Toenails*. Austin, TX: Eakin Press, 1996.

Beard, Patricia. *Growing Up Republican*. New York: Harper Collins, 1996.

Behn, Robert D. *Governors on Governing*. Lanham, MD: University Press of America, 1991.

Bellmon, Henry. *The Life and Times of Henry Bellmon*. Tulsa, OK: Council Oak Books, 1992.

Benjamin, Gerald, and T. Norman Hurd, eds. *Making Experience Count: Managing Modern New York in the Carey Era*. Albany, NY: Nelson A. Rockefeller Institute of Government, 1985.

Berman, David R. *Arizona Politics and Government*. Lincoln: University of Nebraska Press, 1998.

Bernick, Lee, and Charles W. Wiggins. "Executive Legislative Relations: The Governor's Role as Chief Legislator." In Herzik and Brown, *Gubernatorial Leadership and State Policy*, 73–91.

Beyle, Thad L. "Governors' Views on Being Governor." *State Government* 52 (Summer 1979): 103–9.

————. "The Institutionalized Powers of the Governorship." *Comparative State Politics Newsletter* 9 (1988): 29.

————. *Governors and Hard Times*. Washington, D.C.: CQ Press, 1992.

————. "The Evolution of the Gubernatorial Office: United States Governors over the Twentieth Century." In Brooks, *A Legacy of Leadership*, 202–18.

Beyle, Thad L., and Lynn Muchmore. *Being Governor: Views From the Office*. Durham, NC: Duke University Press, 1983.

Beyle, Thad L., and J. Oliver Williams, eds. *The American Governor in Behavioral Perspective*. New York: Harper & Row, 1972.

Blair, Diane D. *Arkansas Politics and Government*. Lincoln: University of Nebraska Press, 1988.

Boyer, Peter J. "The Right Aims at Texas." *Newsweek*, June 6, 2011, 32.

Branstad, Terry E. "Restructuring and Downsizing the Iowa State Government." In Behn, *Governors on Governing*, 144–45.

Bridges, Tyler. *Bad Bet on the Bayou*. New York: Farrar, Strauss and Giroux, 2001.

Bristin, Richard A. J., et al. *West Virginia Politics and Government*. Lincoln: University of Nebraska Press, 1996.

Brooks, Clayton McClure. *A Legacy of Leadership: Governors and American History*. Philadelphia: University of Pennsylvania Press, 2008.

Brownstein, Ronald, and Scott Bland. "Separate Ways." *National Journal*, July 23, 2011, 16–23.

Bulger, William M. *While the Music Lasts; My Life in Politics*. Boston: Houghton Mifflin, 1996.

Cannon, Lou. *Governor Reagan*. New York: Public Affairs, 2003.

_____. "Preparing for the Presidency: The Political Education of Ronald Reagan." In Brooks, *A Legacy of Leadership*, 137–55.

Carlin, John. "The Governor as Administrator, Leader, and Communicator." In Behn, *Governors on Governing*, 78–95.

Casey, Robert P. *Fighting for Life*. Dallas: Word Publishing, 1996.

Cayetano, Benjamin J. *Ben: A Memoir From Street Kid to Governor*. Honolulu: Watermark Publishing, 2009.

Celeste, Richard F. "The Governor as CEO." In Behn, *Governors on Governing*, 96–105.

Clynch, Edward J., and Thomas P. Lauth, eds. *Governors, Legislatures, and Budgets*. New York: Greenwood Press, 1991.

Conroy, Scott, and Shushannah Walshe. *Sarah From Alaska*. New York: Public Affairs, 2009.

Cox, Raymond, III. "The Management Role of the Governor." In Herzik and Brown, *Gubernatorial Leadership and State Policy*, 55–71.

Creed, Dan. *Governor Ventura: "The Body" Exposed*. Madison, WI: Hunter Halverson Press, 2003.

Cronin, Thomas E., and Robert D. Loevy. *Colorado Politics and Government*. Lincoln: University of Nebraska Press, 1993.

Date, S. V. *Quiet Passion: A Biography of Senator Bob Graham*. New York: Penguin, 2004.

_____. *Jeb: America's Next Bush*. New York: Penguin, 2007.

Diggs, Don W., and Leonard E. Goodall. *Nevada Politics and Government*. Lincoln: University of Nebraska Press, 1996.

Dometrius, Nelson C. "The Efficacy of a Governor's Formal Powers." *State Government* 52 (Summer 1979): 121–25.

_____. "The Power of the (Empty) Purse." In Herzik and Brown, *Gubernatorial Leadership and State Policy*, 94–104.

Durning, Dan. "Education Reform in Arkansas: The Governor's Role in Policymaking." In Herzik and Brown, *Gubernatorial Leadership and State Policy*, 121–39.

Ehrenhalt, Alan. "Woodrow Wilson and the Modern American Governorship." Paper prepared for the Woodrow Wilson School's Colloquium in Public and International Affairs, *Woodrow Wilson in the Nation's Service*. Princeton University, April 28, 2006.

_____. "Butch's Battle." *Governing* (June 2009): 11–12.

_____. "Patrick's Promises." *Governing* (November 2009): 11–12.

Elazar, Daniel J., Virginia Gray, and Wyman Spano. *Minnesota Politics and Government*. Lincoln: University of Nebraska Press, 1999.

Feldman, Daniel L., and Gerald Benjamin. *Tales From the Sausage Factory: Making Laws in New York State.* Albany: State University of New York Press, 2010.

Felzenberg, Alvin S. *Governor Tom Kean.* New Brunswick, NJ: Rutgers University Press, 2006.

Ferguson, Margaret Robertson. "Chief Executive Success in the Legislative Arena." *State Politics and Policy Quarterly* 3 (Summer 2003): 158–82.

Fleer, Jack D. *North Carolina Government and Politics.* Lincoln: University of Nebraska Press, 1994.

Forsythe, Dall W. *Memos to the Governor: An Introduction to State Budgeting,* 2nd ed. Washington, D.C.: Georgetown University Press, 2004.

Friel, Brian. "The (Red) Governators." *National Journal,* June 27, 2009, 18–29.

Gaines, Richard, and Michael Segal. *Dukakis and the Reform Impulse.* Boston: Quinlan Press, 1987.

Gardner, Booth. "Schools for the 21st Century." In Behn, *Governors on Governing,* 118–29.

Goodman, Josh. "A Government Adrift." *Governing* (August 2008): 36–40.

Graham, Bob. "A Magical Vision and Other Ingredients of Leadership." In Behn, *Governors on Governing,* 57–64.

Green, Joshua. "The Tragedy of Sarah Palin." *Atlantic,* June 2011, 56–65.

Greenblatt, Alan. "The Job of a Lifetime." *Governing* (June 2009): 24–29, 30.

Grimes, Richard. *Jay Rockefeller: Old Money, New Politics.* Charleston, WV: Jalamap Publications, 1984.

Grimsley, Wayne. *James B. Hunt: A North Carolina Progressive.* Jefferson, NC: McFarland, 2003.

Grogan, Colleen M., and Vernon K. Smith. "From Charity Care to Medicaid." In Sribnick, *A Legacy of Innovation,* 204–30.

Gross, Donald A. "The Policy Role of Governors." In Herzik and Brown, *Gubernatorial Leadership and State Policy,* 1–24.

Gurwitt, Rob. "The Ordeal of David Paterson." *Governing* (March 2009): 26–33.

Gutman, Amy, and Dennis Thompson. "The Mindsets of Political Compromise." *Perspectives on Politics* 8 (December 2010): 1125–43.

Hallett, Joe. "The Voinovich Years 1991–1998." *Plain Dealer,* January 3, 1999.

Harris, Joe Frank. *Personal Reflections on a Public Life.* Macon, GA: Mercer University Press, 1998.

Haskins, Ron. "Governors and the Development of American Social Policy." In Sribnick, *A Legacy of Innovation,* 76–103.

Hatfield, J. H. *Fortunate Son: George W. Bush and the Making of an American President*. New York: Soft Skull Press, 2001.

Herzik, Eric B. "Policy Agendas and Gubernatorial Leadership." In Herzik and Brown, *Gubernatorial Leadership and State Policy*, 25–37.

Herzik, Eric B., and Brent W. Brown, eds. *Gubernatorial Leadership and State Policy*. Westport, CT: Greenwood Press, 1991.

Honeycutt, Leo. *Edwin Edwards: Governor of Louisiana*. Baton Rouge, LA: Lisburn Press, 2009.

Hughes, Harry Roe. *My Unexpected Journey*. Charleston, SC: History Press, 2006.

Hyatt, Richard. *Zell: The Governor Who Gave Georgia HOPE*. Macon, GA: Mercer University Press, 1997.

Jewell, Malcolm E. "The Governor as a Legislative Leader." In Beyle & Williams, *The American Governor in Behavioral Perspective*, 127–40.

Kasdin, Stuart. "California's Once and Future Budget Crisis." *California Journal of Politics & Policy* 2:2 (2010): article 7.

Kean, Thomas H. *The Politics of Inclusion*. New York: Free Press, 1988.

Kenney, Charles, and Robert L. Turner. *Dukakis: An American Odyssey*. Boston: Houghton Mifflin, 1988.

Keyserling, Harriet. *Against the Tide: One Woman's Political Struggle*. Columbia: South Carolina Press, 1998.

King, Bruce. *Cowboy in the Roundhouse*. Santa Fe, NM: Sunstone Press, 1998.

Kousser, Thad. "Does Partisan Polarization Lead to Policy Gridlock in California?" *California Journal of Politics & Policy* 2:2 (2010): article 4.

Kousser, Thad, and Justin A. Phillips. *The Hidden Power of American Governors*. Cambridge: Cambridge University Press, in process.

_____. "The Roots of Executive Power." Unpublished paper, dated May 25, 2010.

Kramer, Daniel C. *The Days of Wine and Roses Are Over: Governor Hugh Carey and New York State*. Lanham, MD: University Press of America, 1997.

Krasniewicz, Louise, and Michael Blitz. *Arnold Schwarzenegger: A Biography*. Westport, CT: Greenwood Press, 2006.

Kunin, Madeleine M. *Living a Political Life*. New York: Vintage, 1994.

_____. "The Rewards of Public Service." In Behn, *Governors on Governing*, 48–55.

Kurtz, Karl T., Bruce Cain, and Richard G. Niemi, eds. *Institutional Change in American Politics: The Case of Term Limits*. Ann Arbor: University of Michigan Press, 2007.

Leibovich, Mark. "Who Can Possibly Govern California?" *New York Times Magazine,* July 5, 2009, 28–33, 44, 46, 49.

Lemon, Greg. *Blue Man in a Red State: Montana's Governor Brian Schweitzer and the New Western Populism.* Helena, MT: TwoDot, 2008.

Liebschutz, Sarah F. *New York Politics and Government,* 93–108. Lincoln: University of Nebraska Press, 1998.

Lizza, Ryan. "Romney's Dilemma." *New Yorker,* June 6, 2011, 38–43.

Loftus, Tom. *The Art of Legislative Politics.* Washington, D.C.: CQ Press, 1994.

Long, Norton. "After the Voting Is Over." In Beyle and Williams, *The American Governor in Behavioral Perspective,* 76–94.

Marlin, George J. *Squandered Opportunities: New York's Pataki Years.* South Bend, IN: St. Augustine's Press, 2006.

Masters, Brooke A. *Spoiling for a Fight: The Rise of Eliot Spitzer.* New York: Henry Holt, 2006.

Mathews, Joe. *The People's Machine: Arnold Schwarzenegger and the Rise of Blockbuster Democracy.* New York: Public Affairs, 2006.

Mathews, Joe, and Mark Paul. *California Crackup.* Berkeley: University of California Press, 2010.

McBeath, Gerald A., and Thomas A. Morehouse. *Alaska Politics and Government.* Lincoln: University of Nebraska Press, 1994.

McElvaine, Robert S. *Mario Cuomo: A Biography.* New York: Scribner's, 1988.

McGreevey, James E. *The Confession.* New York: HarperCollins, 2006.

Mehrotra, Ajay K., and David Shreve. "To Lay and Collect." In Sribnick, *A Legacy of Innovation,* 48–95.

Mendell, David. "What About Me?" *New Yorker,* July 26, 2010, 40–47.

Miller, Penny M. *Kentucky Politics and Government.* Lincoln: University of Nebraska Press, 1994.

Morgan, David R., Robert E. England, and George G. Humphreys. *Oklahoma Politics and Policies.* Lincoln: University of Nebraska Press, 1991.

Nagourney, Adam. "The Contender." *New York Times Magazine,* May 8, 2011, 46–51.

National Governors Association. *Governing the American States: A Handbook for New Governors.* Washington, D.C.: National Governors Association, Center for Policy Research, 1978.

_____. *Transition and the New Governor: A Planning Guide.* Washington, D.C.: National Governors Association, 1998.

_____. *The Many Roles of the Governor's Chief of Staff.* Washington, D.C.: National Governors Association, Office of Management Counseling & Training, 2006.

_____. *Words of Wisdom On Transition & Governing Topics.* Washington, D.C.: National Governors Association, n.d.

Nyhan, David. *The Duke.* New York: Warner books, 1988.

Palmer, Kenneth T., A. Thomas Taylor, and Marcus A. Librizzi. *Maine Politics and Government.* Lincoln: University of Nebraska Press, 1992.

Pew Center on the States. *Beyond California: States in Fiscal Peril.* Washington, D.C.: Pew Center on the States, 2009.

Ransone, Coleman B., Jr. "The Governor, the Legislature, and Public Policy." *State Government* (Summer 1979): 117–20.

_____. *The American Governorship.* Westport, CT: Greenwood Press, 1982.

Reid, Jan. "The Case of Ann Richards: Women in the Gubernatorial Office." In Brooks, *A Legacy of Leadership,* 183–201.

Richardson, Bill. *Between Worlds: The Making of an American Life.* New York: Penguin Group, 2005.

Richardson, James. *Willie Brown: A Biography.* Berkeley: University of California Press, 1996.

Riley, Richard W. "Overcoming Restrictions on Gubernatorial Authority: The Unique Problem of Some Governors." In Behn, *Governors on Governing,* 31–36.

Roig-Franzia, Manuel. "The New (Same Old) Jerry Brown," *Washington Post,* July 19, 2010.

Romano, Andrew, and Michael Hirsh. "America, Inc." *Newsweek,* February 22, 2010, 36–39.

Rosenthal, Alan, ed. *The Governor and the Legislature: Eagleton's 1987 Symposium on the State of the States.* New Brunswick, NJ: Eagleton Institute of Politics, 1988.

_____. *Governors and Legislatures: Contending Powers.* Washington, D.C.: CQ Press, 1990.

_____. *Engines of Democracy.* Washington, D.C.: CQ Press, 2009.

Sabato, Larry. "Governors' Office Careers: A New Breed Emerges." *State Government* 52 (Summer 1979): 95–102.

_____. *Goodbye to Goodtime Charlie.* Washington, D.C.: CQ Press, 1983.

Salmore, Barbara G., and Stephen A. Salmore. *New Jersey Politics and Government,* 3rd ed. New Brunswick, NJ: Rivergate Books, 2008.

Schlesinger, Joseph A. "The Politics of the Executive." In *Politics in the American States*, ed. Herbert Jacob and Kenneth N. Vines. Boston: Little, Brown, 1965.

Senik, Troy. "Who Killed California?" *National Affairs* (Fall 2009): 53–68.

Shropshire, Mike, and Frank Schaefer. *The Thorny Rose of Texas: An Intimate Portrait of Governor Ann Richards.* New York: Carol Publishing Group, 1994.

Smith, C. Fraser. *William Donald Schaefer.* Baltimore: Johns Hopkins University Press, 1999.

Sribnick, Ethan G., ed. *A Legacy of Innovation: Governors and Public Policy.* Philadelphia: University of Pennsylvania Press, 2008.

Steinhauer, Jennifer. "It's Lonely Outside." *New York Times,* July 11, 2010.

Stoner, Andrew E. *Legacy of a Governor: The Life of Indiana's Frank O'Bannon.* Bloomington, IN: Rooftop Publishing, 2006.

Sununu, John H. "Reality and Perception in Gubernatorial Management." In Behn, *Governors on Governing,* 166–79.

Teaford, Jon C. "Governors and Economic Development." In Sribnick, *A Legacy of Innovation,* 107–23.

Thomas, Evan, et al. "Being Rod Blagojevich." *Newsweek,* December 22, 2008, 30–32.

Thomas, James D., and William H. Stewart. *Alabama Government and Politics.* Lincoln: University of Nebraska Press, 1988.

Thompson, James R. "Keynote Address on the Governor." In Rosenthal, *The Governor and the Legislature,* 5–16.

Thornburgh, Dick. *Where the Evidence Leads.* Pittsburgh: University of Pittsburgh Press, 2003.

Van Assendelft, Laura A. *Governors, Agenda Setting, and Divided Government.* Lanham, MD: University Press of America, 1997.

Vinovskis, Maris A. "Gubernatorial Leadership and American K-12 Education Reform." In Sribnick, *A Legacy of Innovation,* 185–203.

Ward, Robert B. *New York State Government.* Albany, NY: Rockefeller Institute Press, 2002.

Weissman, Art. *Christine Todd Whitman.* New York: Carol Publishing Group, 1996.

Whitney, Gleaves. *John Engler: The Man, the Leader & the Legacy.* Chelsea, MI: Sleeping Bear Press, 2002.

Wright, Ralph. *Inside the Statehouse.* Washington, D.C.: CQ Press, 2005.

Index

taxation, 162
See also specific governor
Karcher, Alan, 37, 125, 134, 143, 144
Kasdin, Stuart, 259
Kasich, John (R-OH), 243n25
Kean, Thomas H. (R-NJ), 50, 52, 84, 85, 118,
119, 189, 190, 259
economic/fiscal conditions, 46–47
gubernatorial power, 25–26
partisan division, 37
policy agenda, 98, 102, 103, 114
policy engagement strategies, 155, 156,
166, 172, 175–176, 178–179, 180
policy leadership, 74–76
policy success, 195
policy support, 125, 134, 143, 144
political legacy, 228, 230, 231
staff support, 69, 71
years in office, 248
Keating, Francis Anthony (R-OK):
crisis events, 49
legislative respect, 77
partisan division, 37
policy agenda, 107
policy engagement strategies, 156, 167,
170, 171, 173, 175, 181, 187
policy success, 197–198
political experience, 63
political legacy, 226–227, 235
years in office, 248
Kempthorne, Dirk (R-ID), 245
Kennedy, Ted, 177
Kenney, Charles, 53, 54, 83, 84, 86, 118, 259
Kentucky:
governors (1980–2010), 246
legislative power, 32
See also specific governor
Kernan, Joseph E. (D-IN), 245
Kerrey, Joseph Robert (Bob) (D-NE), 247
Keyserling, Harriet, 259
King, Angus S. (I-ME):
economic/fiscal conditions, 42
leadership criteria, 55
legislative power, 30, 33
party control, 33, 34
policy agenda, 87, 98
policy engagement strategies, 166,
174–175
policy leadership, 76
policy success, 201, 216, 217
policy support, 129, 134
political experience, 59

political legacy, 228
staff support, 69
years in office, 246
King, Bruce (D-NM), 23, 84, 148, 150, 188,
190, 191, 242, 259
policy engagement strategies, 156, 172, 183
policy leadership, 73
policy success, 18
policy support, 131
political legacy, 228
staff support, 67, 72
years in office, 248
King, Edward Joseph (D-MA), 246
Kitzhaber, John A. (D-OR):
second term, 1
years in office, 249
Knowles, Tony (D-AK), 244
Kopp, Donald, 139
Kousser, Thad, 16, 23, 90, 117, 203, 221, 222,
223, 259
Kramer, Daniel C., 85, 148, 224, 259
Krasniewicz, Louise, 85, 189, 259
Kulongoski, Ted (D-OR), 249
Kunin, Madeleine M. (D-VT), 105, 117, 118,
119, 224, 259
legislative respect, 77
policy agenda, 90, 101–102, 107
policy success, 194, 211, 219, 220
policy support, 136
years in office, 249
Kurtz, Karl T., 52, 223, 259

Lamm, Richard D. (D-CO), 244
Laney, James E. "Pete," 137
Lauth, Thomas P., 257
Leadership criteria:
adaptability skills, 79–82
business background, 57–60
legislative experience, 60–65
legislature orientation, 72–77
personality characteristics, 56–58
policy success impact, 209–213
political experience, 58–65
political friendships, 65–67
pragmatism, 78–79
staff support, 67–72
Leavitt, Michael Okerlund (R-UT):
adaptability skills, 81
policy agenda, 94–95
policy success, 212
policy support, 122
years in office, 249

policy legacy, 231
policy support, 122, 127–128, 138
staff support, 67–68
veto power, 184
Nation at Risk, A (1983), 99, 167
Natural disasters, 49
Nebraska:
  governors (1980–2010), 247
  See also specific governor
Negotiating skills, 171–174
Nelson, Ben, 22n16, 181
Nelson, E. Benjamin (D-NE):
  job satisfaction, 5
  policy agenda, 90, 101
  policy engagement strategies, 180–181
  policy success, 194
  policy support, 131
  years in office, 247
Neustadt, Richard E., 178
Nevada:
  governors (1980–2010), 247
  state constitution, 27
  See also specific governor
New Hampshire:
  governors (1980–2010), 247–248
  See also specific governor
New Jersey:
  environmental/energy policy, 195–196
  governors (1980–2010), 248
  Highlands Act, 195–196
  legislative power, 32
  state constitution, 25–26
  taxation, 161
  See also specific governor
New Mexico:
  economic development policy, 195
  governors (1980–2010), 248
  See also specific governor
New York:
  education policy, 235
  Financial Control Board, 234–235
  governors (1980–2010), 248
  legislative power, 31–32
  Municipal Assistance Corporation,
    234–235
  state constitution, 26
  See also specific governor
New York Times, 240
Niemi, Richard G., 52, 223, 259
Nigh, George Patterson (D-OK):
  adaptability skills, 81
  economic/fiscal conditions, 46, 97

job satisfaction, 8
political legacy, 228
years in office, 248
Nixon, Jeremiah W. (Jay) (D-MO), 247
North Carolina:
  governors (1980–2010), 248
  Smart Start, 226
  See also specific governor
North Dakota:
  governors (1980–2010), 248
  legislative power, 32
  See also specific governor
Northwest Airlines, 227
Nunn, Louis, 32
Nyhan, David, 261

O'Bannon, Frank (D-IN):
  economic/fiscal conditions, 42, 47
  personality characteristics, 56
  policy agenda, 102
  policy engagement strategies, 185
  policy support, 134
  years in office, 245
Ohio:
  education policy, 117553
  governors (1980–2010), 248
  gun control policy, 215
  legislative power, 31–32, 33
  See also specific governor
Oklahoma:
  education policy, 194–195
  governors (1980–2010), 248
  See also specific governor
Olson, Allen Ingvar (R-ND):
  partisan division, 35–36
  policy success, 208
  years in office, 248
O'Malley, Martin (D-MD):
  staff support, 68
  years in office, 246
O'Neill, William A. (D-CT), 244
Orechio, Carmen, 125
Oregon:
  endangered species, 24–25, 50
  governors (1980–2010), 248–249
  Measure 5 (1990), 24–25
  property tax, 24–25
  See also specific governor
Orr, Kay A. (R-NE), 247
Orr, Robert D. (R-IN):
  policy agenda, 105
  years in office, 245